D0501369

# A WRITER AT WAR

# A WRITER AT WAR:
## Arnold Bennett
## 1914-1918

### KINLEY E. ROBY

LOUISIANA STATE UNIVERSITY PRESS
Baton Rouge

For Mary

ISBN 0-8071-0243-1
Library of Congress Catalog Card Number 72-79335
Copyright © 1972 by Louisiana State University Press
All rights reserved
Manufactured in the United States of America
Printed by Vail-Ballou Press, Inc., Binghamton, N.Y.
Designed by Albert R. Crochet

# CONTENTS

# ACKNOWLEDGMENTS

I wish to express my deep-felt appreciation to Professor Stanley Weintraub for his unstinting help in bringing this study to completion.

I wish also to give my sincerest thanks to Dr. LaFayette Butler, who made available to me his fine private collection of Bennett papers and manuscripts, and to Charles T. Butler for his many kindnesses.

I am indebted to Dame Rebecca West and Frank Swinnerton for sharing with me their recollections of Arnold Bennett. I am further indebted to Mr. Swinnerton for his generous help in answering questions about Bennett and the people connected with him during the war years.

Richard Bennett, Mary Kennerley, and Olive Glendinning gave generously of their time in order to provide me with details of Bennett's personal life and of life at Comarques during the war.

The authorities of the library at University College London, at the New York Public Library, and at the British Museum kindly granted me permission to consult their Bennett manuscripts and documents. Lola Szladits, curator of the Berg Collection at the New York Public Library, and Janet Percival, assistant librarian at University College London, gave me invaluable help with the Berg and the Ogden materials.

Charles Mann, chief of rare books and special collections at Pattee Library, Pennsylvania State University, and Elizabeth Henning, State Services, library assistant there, helped me locate, over a long period of time, material not in the collections mentioned above.

To my wife Mary I express my deepest gratitude for having made this study possible.

# A WRITER AT WAR

# I
# THE BEST IS GOOD ENOUGH

"A material year. Largely occupied with intestinal failure and material success." Despite the reference to his illness, which he had been combatting with "Chetham Strode's direct treatment of massage and vibration," Arnold Bennett's journal entry for December 31, 1912, is stiff with satisfaction.[1]

He had reason to be pleased. Claiming to have done "practically nothing" between April and October, he had, nevertheless, in the remaining six months written 200,000 words. During the year, there had been 1,155 performances of his plays, and he had earned £16,000—as much as he had earned in all his previous working years combined.

The year 1913 brought him even greater success. His plays were performed 2,700 times. He published three books—*The Regent, Paris Nights, The Plain Man and His Wife*—and a play, *The Great Adventure*, adapted in 1910 from his novel *Buried Alive*. He also wrote most of *The Price of Love*, all of *The Author's Craft*, and completed two short stories, numerous articles, and one act of a new play, *Don Juan de Marana*. His income for the year was very close to £18,000. "All this," he said, "handsomely beats last year's record." He had a beautiful French wife; he was rich; he was famous; he was sought after; but like Old Man Kangaroo, he was to learn that being sought after was both more and less than he had expected.

For Bennett, who until the guns began to fire remained oblivious to the approaching calamity, 1914 appeared to hold even greater promise. He was forty-six years old, in moderately good health, and solidly astride a peak in his career. He was living sedately, even elegantly, at Comarques, his country home in Essex, working on *Don Juan de Marana* and on "From the Log

---

[1] Arnold Bennett, *The Journal of Arnold Bennett*, ed. Newman Flower (New York, 1933), 470.

of the Velsa" articles for *Century* magazine, and varying the Comarques routine with frequent trips to London to attend concerts and plays and rehearsals of *Helen with the High Hand*. Above all, he was waiting for the season to advance sufficiently to allow him to take out his yacht *Velsa*, which had become a consuming interest in his life.

Despite all this promise, some critics have seen 1914 as a terminal point in Bennett's career. They believe that by the outbreak of war his best work was already done. *Anna of the Five Towns*, *The Old Wives' Tale*, *Clayhanger*, and *Hilda Lessways* were written. He had published three short story collections— *The Grim Smile of the Five Towns*, *The Matador of the Five Towns*, and *The Loot of Cities*. The plays *Milestones* and *The Great Adventure* were on the boards, and he was not to have another stage success equal to them until *Mr. Prohack* in 1927.

"It is scarcely possible not to see Bennett as a war casualty," Walter Allen has said. "Bennett was a brilliant novelist; after 1914 he was generally no more than a brilliant journalist." [2] It is possible to look at Bennett's career that way. But to do so demands that one see all the work done after 1918 as an inferior imitation of what he had done before. It also forces one to assume that the war was a totally devastating experience for Bennett—which it was not, although it radically altered his life— and to accept as valid those condemnations of Bennett's technique in novel writing set forth by Virginia Woolf in "Mr. Bennett and Mrs. Brown." [3]

By adding Virginia Woolf's judgments to Walter Allen's, one is equipped with a set of literary cliches within which Bennett can be neatly folded in preparation for storage on a high and forgotten shelf among those other writers whose time has come and gone. Perhaps, however, it is possible to pass another sort of judgment on Bennett's career, one which takes more into account the actual events of his life during the crucial years 1914

[2] Walter Allen, *Arnold Bennett* (London, 1948), 35.
[3] Virginia Woolf, "Mr. Bennett and Mrs. Brown," *The Captain's Death Bed and Other Essays* (New York, 1950), 105–113.

through 1918. As a beginning it will be helpful to get as clear a picture as possible of him during those last months before the "Kaiser's War" shattered the routine of Bennett's life, a routine of apparent tranquility that was in fact hiding profound personal unhappiness and the agony of creative sterility.

There is a cartoon by Max Beerbohm, which appeared in *Observations* (Heinemann, 1927), showing a stout, white-haired, obviously affluent Bennett talking to a thinner, less imposing younger self. The caption reads: Old Self: "All gone according to plan, you SEE." Younger Self: "My plan, you know." That is the Bennett of the popular imagination. It is the Bennett whom Samuel Hynes finds in the character of Mr. Nixon in Ezra Pound's "Hugh Selwyn Mauberley." [4] It is an image of himself that Bennett deliberately placed before the public.

Lady Ottoline Morrell remarked on the flourish that was Bennett's public manner when she observed that Bertrand Russell was so irritated by it that he would not remain in the same room with Bennett, condemning him for being "vulgar." The judgment, Lady Ottoline insists, is not accurate: "He was superficially showy, but not vulgar, indeed he had a very great sense of delicacy in his life, and an exquisite love of his craftsmanship." [5]

He wished to be thought of—perhaps wished to think of himself—as a practical man of affairs who ran his writing business much as one would run any other business, with a maximum of efficiency for the greatest possible profit. In his pocket philosophies he consciously set himself forward as a man of common sense, and it is that quality above all others that shines through them. It was the true Midland wisdom breaking out in him. "Money'll do owt," the Five Towns say. "It will not," the skeptic replies. "Then it will do all that wants doing," Five Towns respond. Bennett was quite willing to allow people to think that it was a guinea that most stimulated his imagination.

[4] Arnold Bennett, *The Author's Craft and Other Critical Writings of Arnold Bennett*, ed. Samuel Hynes (Lincoln, Nebraska, 1968), ix.
[5] Ottoline Morrell, *Memoirs of Lady Ottoline Morrell: A Study in Friendship, 1873–1915*, ed. Robert Gathorne-Hardy (New York, 1964), 203–204.

His first serious attempt at writing, for example, was in competition for a cash prize, which he won.[6]

It is that picture of Bennett that has persisted. He is remembered as a kind of soulless writing machine—what his publisher Newman Flower called a "mechanized biscuit factory"—that clicked away very efficiently for a specified number of hours each day, turning out books, articles, and reviews.[7] Once the day's task was completed, the machine rose, donned an evening suit made by the King's tailor, and went out to dine with the nabobs of London's literary world. In company he was charming, if a bit overpowering; and his wit was spiced with a carefully cultivated stammer. The picture created is of the "card," and as amusing as it is, it has two weaknesses: It leaves out most of the man and all of his art. He is not to be disposed of so easily. There was nothing simple about Arnold Bennett; he abounded with contradictions.

"The best," he frequently said, "is good enough for me." [8] But it was not always certain what he meant by "best." He might mean the best silk shirt that London could provide, or he might mean the best dessert that a fashionable club dining room could provide for one shilling and sixpence. Newman Flower, Bennett's English publisher after 1915 and the editor of Bennett's *Journal*, was his guest on one occasion at a London club. Bennett suggested snipe pudding and then quickly changed his mind. "It's half-a-crown," he stammered. "We-we'd better have something else."

The two men were lunching together on a much later occasion when Flower mentioned the fact that Cassell would lose the £1,000 which the publishing company had paid Bennett's agent James B. Pinker [9] for the serial rights to *Riceyman Steps*, because the book would not sell as a serial. Bennett stared at him for a

---

[6] The magazine *Tit-Bits* ran a competition offering a prize of twenty guineas for the best parody of Grant Allen's thriller, *What's Bred in the Bone*.

[7] Newman Flower, *Just As It Happened* (London, 1951), 164.

[8] Marguerite Bennett, *My Arnold Bennett* (New York, 1932), 137.

[9] James B. Pinker was Bennett's agent from December, 1901, until his death on February 8, 1922. Following Pinker's death, his son Eric took over the business and Bennett remained with the firm.

moment, raised his right hand, and said that editors who did not want serial rights to the novel were fools and that Flower should tell them to go to hell. He would repay Cassell the thousand pounds. Then, without pausing, he lifted the menu and ordered kipper on toast. He carried two notebooks in his jacket pockets. In one he wrote down ideas that he might use in his writing. In the other he kept a careful record of every penny that he spent.[10]

He wrote rapidly, but he was serious about what he wrote, especially about his novels. "The novel," he said, "has no rival at the present day as a means for transmitting the impassioned vision of life." "The novelist," he said, "is he who, having seen life, and being so excited by it that he absolutely must transmit the vision to others, chooses narrative fiction as the liveliest vehicle for the relief of his feelings." The charge that Bennett wrote mechanically is denied by his views on the nature of fiction. "First class fiction," he insisted, "is and must be autobiographical." Not being able to invent a "psychology," the artist must depend on himself, on what he has seen and felt. "Good fiction is autobiography dressed in the colors of all mankind." [11]

On the other hand, writing was still a business. Bennett said that he had no respect for the artist who, having turned out a marketable piece of work, allowed it to be passed over because it was not properly placed before the buyers. He even deplored the fact that custom prevented his taking on such a well-paying task [12] as that offered Shaw, H. G. Wells, and himself simultaneously by Harrods' stores. Wells and Shaw took the "high line" in their refusal to write advertising copy, insisting that they were "priests and prophets" who could not be paid for their opinions. Bennett also declined but with great reluctance.

When Bennett was in New York in 1911, an editor chanced to meet him outside George Doran's offices and immediately asked for six short stories. Bennett took out a notebook and said that he would write the stories. What was the price? The

10 Flower, *Just As It Happened*, 100.
11 Arnold Bennett, *The Author's Craft* (New York, 1914), 40, 37, 63.
12 H. G. Wells, *Experiment in Autobiography* (New York, 1934), 535.

editor suggested one hundred and forty dollars for each story. Bennett put away the notebook. "I do not write stories for one hundred and forty dollars," he snapped. After some further bargaining they settled on two hundred and fifty dollars. Bennett's shrewd business sense included living up to the terms of his agreement. On this occasion, he took out his notebook again, consulted it, and asked when the stories were required. He was given a date. "I have to write a novel before I start your stories," he said. "I write one thousand words a day. . . ." According to Flower, Bennett delivered the stories "as dead on time as the grocer would have delivered the bacon." [13]

Bennett's wife Marguerite said that he was a man who did "not feel the need of a very intimate friendship," but Bennett did have many close friends. Frederick Marriott and his wife, who made a home for Bennett in the early years of his London adventure and who first encouraged him to write, to master spoken French, and to play the piano, were lifelong friends. It was through them that he met George Sturt, the novelist; H. G. Wells; Edwin Rickards, architect and amateur painter; and others.[14] He constantly added friends, often at the expense of his wife's companionship. Frank Swinnerton and Lord Beaverbrook were two that he added during the war years. On the other hand, his friendship with Sturt lessened as did his friendship with Wells. But the Marriotts and Rickards remained close friends with him throughout his life. A still deeper friendship existed between him and the novelist Pauline Smith, who all but owed her literary life to Bennett's constant encouragement, if not harassment, during their friendship of nearly thirty years.

Bennett was not a sentimentalist, though. Before his marriage,

---

[13] Flower, *Just As It Happened*, 160.

[14] George Sturt was a wheelwright who lived in Farnham and wrote under the name of George Bourne. He was one of Bennett's earliest literary acquaintances and influences.

Dudley Barker quotes Bennett as having said that "his view of life had been influenced more by Rickards than by any other man." Rickards was a very difficult man. In company he was sometimes gruff to the point of rudeness; and on one occasion at Comarques, his treatment of Bennett's other guests was so surly that Bennett was forced to remonstrate with him. See, Dudley Barker, *Writer By Trade: A Portrait of Arnold Bennett* (New York, 1966).

in an exchange of letters principally concerned with Bennett's novel *Sacred and Profane Love*, Wells charged Bennett with never having been in love as well as never having wept. Wells was right. Bennett replied that he had never been in love and that "tears start to my eyes, but they never fall. . . . I look down from a height on the show." But Bennett had only a year of grace remaining before Wells's assertion was no longer true. He fell in love and suffered a broken "engagement." [15] What wound there was healed quickly. Bennett married less than a year later (July 5, 1907) and proved again that he was not a sentimentalist. His wife recorded that they had no honeymoon, because he had been unwilling to break the schedule under which he was working at the time. It is best to begin a marriage as one plans to go on, she said, quoting he unromantic husband; but there is an almost audible sigh behind the words.

Very rarely in his journal or in his letters did Bennett open the door to that inner chamber where he kept his personal emotions locked away. He was, according to Mrs. Dorothy Cheston Bennett, "almost morbidly averse to self-advertisement in any form, particularly regarding private or intimate aspects of his life." [16] He maintained a distance between himself and the world. Some of that reserve may have been due to his background. As Ford Madox Ford observed in *The Good Soldier*, there are only two places in the world where it is possible for people to live together in absolute silence, Maine and the North of England. [17] Bennett was from the North, and he was capable of keeping his personal feelings private. Later, during the war, his guard sometimes slipped, and his journal entries record something of that hidden life.

[15] The letters quoted are dated 1905. In 1906 Bennett fell in love with Eleanor Green. Through a ludicrous misunderstanding he thought that he had become engaged to her and proceeded to make plans for the wedding. He wrote to her describing the progress of the wedding plans, but she did not read the letters. The absurdity lasted seven weeks; then Eleanor discovered what was afoot. Bennett's journal entry for Friday, August 3, 1906, reads: "At 11 A.M. on this day, at Caniel, my engagement to Eleanora [*sic*] was broken off."

[16] Dorothy Cheston Bennett, *Arnold Bennett: A Portrait Done at Home* (New York, 1935), 6.

[17] Ford Madox Ford, *The Good Soldier* (New York, 1955), 189.

Marguerite said that while her husband was usually open and generous, he was also capable of becoming suddenly suspicious. While in one of those moods, he trusted least those friends he loved most. Newman Flower thought him capable of great acts of personal generosity. He said that Bennett had "made" people who would not acknowledge the debt. He was free with money; yet Marguerite said that he could, at times, be "harsh, cruel, and pitiless." But to the world he kept raised a carefully nurtured facade. This *persona*, as Wells called it, was "a hard, definite china figurine," within which Bennett sheltered himself from a prying world.[18]

His character was complex and sometimes contradictory. So was his writing. It is not possible to discount any of it as being purely commercial—if by *commercial* one means containing nothing important of the man or of his art. On the other hand, it is not possible to say even of his best work that it was done with no concern for the market. Bennett put something of himself into everything that he wrote. Articles, pocket philosophies, fantasias, and the great novels all contain an essential part of the man.

Bennett was a professional writer. To him, such a writer "labors in the first place for food, shelter, tailors, a woman, European travel, horses, stalls at the opera, good cigars, ambrosial evenings in restaurants; and he gives glory the best chance he can." For some readers of his own time and for more later, this attitude put Bennett in the Philistine camp, aligned him with "the breed without the law." For Bennett it meant simply that his position in relation to art and to the world was clear. He was the enemy of the esthete: "The notion that art is first and the rest of the universe nowhere is bound to lead to preciosity and futility in art." [19]

In the early years of Bennett's career, George Sturt had tried to force him to distinguish between art and nonart and to put nonart away from him. Bennett refused. He was engaged in the business of writing for a living. He was much more responsive to the urgings of Eden Phillpotts, who persuaded him to write a serial. The result was *The Ghost*, which Bennett did not think very well of but which brought in some welcome money. For a period of seven years he edited a magazine called *Woman*. During that time, he wrote book reviews and articles on fashions, cooking, and domestic economy for the magazine under such names as Gwendolyn and Sal Volatile. He was doing what he could with what he had and doing it well, but his ambition was to be an independent writer. In 1900 he chucked the magazine; moved into the country with his mother, his sister, and his ailing father; and turned to full-time writing.

Between 1900 and 1914 Bennett published nineteen novels, three collections of short stories, six pocket philosophies, and had three of his plays produced. In addition he turned out a host of book reviews and articles, some of which he wrote for the *New Age* under the name of Jacob Tonson. The "Books and Persons" series was extremely influential in its time, although Bennett derived very little in the way of financial benefit from it. Dame Rebecca West has said that she and a great many other young writers and intellectuals looked forward to the appearance of the Jacob Tonson pieces with eager anticipation, finding in them a liveliness and freshness of viewpoint that was missing from the rest of contemporary criticism.

The extent of his influence is borne out by the rather backhanded compliment paid him by Arthur Quiller Couch's review of Compton MacKenzie's *Carnival*, which appeared in the *English Review* in 1911. "Q" praised *Carnival* for being indebted to "little or nothing in the works of Arnold Bennett, of Mr. Galsworthy, or of Mr. H. G. Wells—three eminent writers who appear to furnish the reviewer, between them, with all his touchstones of judgment and all his canons of taste." [20]

Those fourteen years both shaped Bennett's attitudes towards the art of writing and confirmed many of his convictions about it. First, the world was there to be lived in: As Bennett asserted in *The Author's Craft*, "The artist who is too sensitive for con-

[20] B. Compton MacKenzie, *My Life and Times, Octave Four 1907–1915* (London, 1965), 138.

tacts with the non-artistic world is thereby too sensitive for his vocation." He had come to terms with his conscience on two counts. Wells had accused him of having no "passion for justice." Bennett agreed. It was not an artist's business to champion causes. It was his business "to keep his balance amid warring points of view."

He also came to terms with the public's conservative tastes in literature. He said that an author should compromise. "The artist who will have the public only on his own terms "is either a god or a conceited and impractical fool." He saw the relationship between the author and his public as a bargain in which the artist had a responsibility as well as the public. "The sagacious artist," he said, "while respecting himself, will respect the idiosyncracies of his public." As to the danger that such compromising might turn the writer into a "popularity hunter," Bennett acknowledged the possibility, but thought that it would probably not occur if the writer had "anything to say worth saying." In any case, the writer who wished to gain a hearing could not ignore the realities of his profession. "The public," he said "is a great actuality, like war. . . . You can do something with it, but not much." [21]

Not every critic was able to accept Bennett's compromise. William Dean Howells, for example, found it very difficult to explain to his own satisfaction how Bennett could write so well at one time and so badly at another. He observed that Bennett "found a comfort or a relaxation or an indemnification in writing a bad book after writing a good one." [22] The "bad" books were *The Grand Babylon Hotel, Buried Alive, The Gates of Wrath, Hugo, The Glimpse,* and *The Ghost.* Howells set these novels apart from *A Man from the North, Anna of the Five Towns, The Old Wives' Tale,* and *Clayhanger* on the assumption that Bennett had written them less well than he was able to do.

His reason for believing anything so extraordinary can be traced to his profound admiration for Bennett's best work. His

[21] Bennett, *The Author's Craft,* 114.
[22] William Dean Howells, "The Editor's Easy Chair," *Harper's Magazine,* CXXII (March, 1911), 633.

admiration led him to conclude that "no man could have seen the truth about life so clearly as Mr. Bennett, with any after doubt of its unique value." But Howells is pained to note at the same time that "we have him [Bennett] from time to time indulging himself in the pleasure of painting it falsely." Howells concluded that, at times, Bennett deliberately subverted his art.[23] Wells once criticized Bennett in much the same terms. Referring to *Sacred and Profane Love*, he said, "There never was a woman like your woman [Carlotta], but no end of women journalists and minor actresses have imagined themselves like her." Bennett replied that "no character in any novel is more than a hint of the real thing. . . . All that I would claim for Carlotta is that now and then she does what a real woman would do." [24]

Howells' conclusion is wrong. That is not to say that Bennett never wrote a weak novel. He wrote many of them. But it is a mistake to pretend that Bennett's poor novels are of a different kind than the best ones. To do so is to assume that the "bad" novels can be ignored in an evaluation of Bennett's writing, that they are without value, and that Bennett wrote seriously only on occasion and possessed in reference to his craft, as F. L. Lucas said so maliciously of Browning, "the conscience of a pavement artist." [25]

It is probably closer to the truth to say that Bennett's novels are uneven in conception and in execution but that they are all products of a single imaginative process. Furthermore, it is clear that Bennett was sometimes wrong about the quality of his books. *The Glimpse*, for example, is a very weak novel; but Bennett thought it "much too good" and "much too spiritual" for the *Black and White* magazine, in which it was serialized in 1908. When it came out in book form, he was puzzled that so few people wrote to him praising the novel. Bennett actually thought that some of *The Glimpse* was as good as the best he could do. He was also satisfied with *The Pretty Lady*. Few read-

[23] *Ibid.*, 623, 633.
[24] Arnold Bennett and H. G. Wells, *Arnold Bennett and H. G. Wells*, ed. Harris Wilson (Urbana, Illinois, 1960), 122–23.
[25] F. L. Lucas, "Browning," in John L. Stewart (ed.), *The Essay, A Critical Anthology* (New York, 1954), 201.

ers have found it good. Walter Allen has called it "a triumph in vulgarity." [26] Of this aspect of Bennett's talent, Rebecca West has said that there was a certain similarity between Bennett and Wordsworth in their inability to be objective about the quality of their own work. Bennett, she said, "was utterly without the power of self-criticism, and he would issue his worst in confident illusion that it was simply different in kind from his best." [27]

Those who were writing about Bennett's art in the closing years of the Edwardian era were more interested in what Bennett was doing with the novel form and with the technique of the novel than in making excuses for his failures. It was generally conceded that he was a leader among the writers of the new novel. He shared the position, in Henry James's view, with Joseph Conrad, Maurice Hewlett, John Galsworthy, and H. G. Wells. In "The New Novel, 1914," James placed Wells and Bennett in the vanguard of the innovators and suggested that they were the literary parents of that younger group of writers —Hugh Walpole, Gilbert Cannan, Compton MacKenzie, and D. H. Lawrence—whom Virginia Woolf would later call the Georgians.[28]

Writers other than James were willing to agree that Bennett was altering the shape of the novel. There is almost nothing in the criticism of the period to suggest, as Virginia Woolf did nine years later, that Bennett was working in a moribund tradition. If Virginia Woolf was right and the character of the English people did indeed change in or about December of 1910, the effects of the change had not by 1914 made themselves sufficiently felt to persuade either the critics or the reading public that the novel as Bennett was writing it was failing to meet the needs of the new Englishman.

Critics varied widely in what they discovered in Bennett's novels. For James the problem was largely one of technique. The name which he gave to that technique was "saturation." What James meant by the term was the presence in the writing of an

[26] Allen, *Arnold Bennett*, 91.
[27] Rebecca West, *Arnold Bennett Himself* (New York, 1931), 17.
[28] Henry James, "The New Novel, 1914," *Notes on Novelists with Some Other Notes* (New York, 1914), 318.

astonishing degree of documentation. More particularly, he said of Bennett's work that the documentation was not only "copious" but also "special, exclusive, and artfully economic." It was, in James's opinion, the single most important element in Bennett's style and was the quality that produced emulation in other writers.[29]

James felt that the essential interest which Bennett's writing held was the degree to which Bennett was in possession of his material. The meaning and the drama in the writing sprang from this sense of possession. The details present in the writing in such quantity were justified by the fact that Bennett had them at his command, that they were interesting in themselves, and that they were their own meaning.[30]

The American critic Wilbur Cross, writing as late as 1930, saw Bennett's efforts as a reaction against that view of literature embodied in the theories and practices of Thackeray and Stevenson. He quoted Thackeray as having said that it is not the novelist's function to "depict men *in* the actual business of life." Instead, men should be shown "in their passions, loves, laughters, amusements, hatreds, and what not." Cross went on to point out that whereas Thackeray saw little hope of working "linendrapery" into a novel, Bennett was clearly engaged in bringing fiction into "the business of life." [31] His best novels from *Anna of the Five Towns* to *Riceyman Steps* demonstrate his determination to render life fully and truly.

Bennett's conflict with Stevenson and the tradition within which that author had worked had its basis in the fact that Stevenson established a clear distinction between art and life. Life, Stevenson said, was "monstrous, infinite, illogical." Art, on the other hand, was "neat, finite, self-contained, rational." [32] The implication is clear: a work of art should not attempt to reproduce life—cannot, in fact, reproduce it. Bennett thought otherwise.

There were those who had doubts about what Bennett was doing. H. G. Wells wrote to Bennett in 1905 to protest that

[29] James, "The New Novel," 319.
[30] *Ibid.*, 324.
[31] Wilbur Cross, *Four Contemporary Novelists* (New York, 1930), 89.
[32] *Ibid.*, 90.

Bennett was "always taking surface values. . . . For some un-fathomable reason," he said, "you don't penetrate." Bennett de-fended himself by saying "You will never see it, but in rejecting surface values you are wrong. As a fact they are just as im-portant as other values." In another place he said, "I have never yet been able to comprehend how . . . spirit can be conceived apart from matter." [33]

Henry James followed his praise of Bennett's work in "The New Novel, 1914" with a biting attack on the "saturation" tech-nique. Is documentation its own justification? he asks. Does a significant meaning actually emerge from the mass and the ar-rangement of the material itself? His answer is that it does not. Referring to *Clayhanger*, he said that bringing together such impressive quantities of facts about life in the Five Towns may satisfy the reader for a time but will not permanently satisfy him. Eventually he will ask, "But is this all? These are the circum-stances of the interest—we see; we see; but where is the interest itself, where and what is its center, and how are we to measure it in relation to *that?*"

He concluded that the reader who expected more from Ben-nett's novels than a view of "the stones and bricks and rubble and cement and promiscuous constituents of every sort" that had been heaped there would be disappointed. The reader was cer-tainly not to expect a "pursued and captured meaning." [34] James appears to have overlooked the judgment implicit in all of Ben-nett's major novels that life is meaningless. The "captured mean-ing" James sought and did not find is simply that life is without meaning. In taking such a view of the human experience, Ben-nett anticipated a major theme in English and American litera-ture that came to maturity in the post–World War I years and has persisted into the present.

Naturally, Bennett did not see his method as a "promiscuous" heaping of rubble. For him details were the building stones of the novel and were the products of a precise and highly disciplined process of observation. "Good observation," he said, "consists

[33] Bennett and Wells, *Arnold Bennett and H. G. Wells*, 122, 125.
[34] James, "The New Novel," 326.

not in multiplicity of detail, but in the coordination of detail according to a true perspective of relative importance, so that a finally just general impression may be reached in the shortest possible time." [35]

His justification for making the detailed observations and recording them lay in his conviction that "all physical phenomena are interrelated, that there is nothing which does not bear on everything else." You may profess not to be interested in meteorology, he said, but you are. "For an east wind may upset your liver and cause you to insult your wife." In a more serious tone he added, "No human phenomenon is adequately seen until the imagination has placed it back in its past and forward into its future." [36]

There is no doubt that Bennett was a master of detail. At his best the minutiae, which is both a texture and a context in the novels, takes on a vividness and an intensity generally found only in poetry. In *The Old Wives' Tale* Bennett describes the death of an elephant. The animal is dragged away from the Wakes' ground, where it met its death, and is ultimately hacked to pieces for souvenirs. The elephant is generally taken to be a symbol of Victorian England. It is also a curiosity with such a power to attract that Mrs. Baines, Constance, and Mr. Povey leave the ship together—an unprecedented event—in order to look at it. But it is first and finally, vividly and intensely, an elephant. What locks the incidents surrounding its demise into life is not the death of Mr. Baines but the detail of the string of boys who appear the following day at Mr. Critchlow's chemist shop and who say to that fierce old man, "Please a pennoth o' alum to tak' smell out o' a bit o' elephant." [37]

Wells and James were wrong about Bennett's technique. It is not an acceptance of surface values in place of more important values. Nor is it a mechanical piling up of "rubble." Bennett was carrying out a large design with considerable fullness of treatment. James seems to have failed to grasp this fact. As a conse-

[35] Bennett, *The Author's Craft*, 14.
[36] *Ibid.*, 19, 20, 32.
[37] Arnold Bennett, *The Old Wives' Tale* (New York, 1950), 89.

quence he also failed to see the details in relation to the design.[38] Detail in Bennett's novels reproduces the facade which life throws up in the form of fancy waistcoats and glittering restaurants, as well as the grime of the Potteries. Detail creates the context within which the human drama takes place.

It is a context which largely defines the nature and the direction of the dramatic action. In addition, detail has emotional and psychological significance. It is possible to say that the emotional lives of Bennett's characters draw their force from the heavily "documented" context and are a product of the amassing of detail. The past of every life described has so powerful a force, gained from the sheer totality of its rendering, that the future seems to be foreordained by it. The context or facade is for Bennett the reality of life. There is nothing behind it, no guiding principle, no cosmic purpose. It is in this sense that life in Bennett's novels is meaningless.

The sense of inevitability created by Bennett in the lives of his characters gives to his writing a distinct emotional tone. The tone is one of melancholy, perhaps even disillusionment. There is an interesting example of how it manifests itself even in his journalism. In "Life in London: One of the Crowd," another in *The New Age* series, Bennett describes a clerk's departure from his London office at the end of the day, his ride home on the train, his evening at home, and his return to work the next morning.

Bennett sums up the man in the following way: "His case is not peculiar. He is just an indistinguishable man on the footpaths, and all the men on the footpaths, like him, are secretly obsessed by the vision of a train just moving out of a station." [39] The man's life is a routine of work, interrupted by emotionally neutral hours spent at home. At the center of life lies the anxiety that he will miss his train. His life is devoid of passion. He is almost without vitality.

This absence of passion in his characters is evidence of Ben-

[38] Frank Swinnerton, *The Georgian Scene* (New York, 1934), 192.
[39] Arnold Bennett, "Life in London: One of the Crowd," *The Living Age*, CCLXX (August 26, 1911), 558.

nett's own profound distrust or fear of that emotion and accounts, at least in part, for the melancholy quality of his writing. In the last analysis there is nothing in his novels to relieve the tedium of existence. It is possible that he wrote too close to life and, as Northrop Frye has suggested, the reality achieved became a "self-defeating process," bringing into action "some mysterious law of diminishing returns." [40]

Passion in the Five Towns, as in E. A. Robinson's New England, appears to have been "a soilure of the wits." Even in *Don Juan de Marana* Bennett was unable to create the illusion of true passion. He thrust it away like a contamination, and the play becomes an oddly academic discussion of the possibility of defending the indulgence of passion as the pursuit of an ideal. Passion remains off-stage and, of course, loses the argument.

Personal courage, shrewd good sense, the capacity for folly, the ability to endure are all found in Bennett's characters in varying degrees. But a *passionate* attachment to anything in life —with the exception of money in the cases of the two misers Ephriam Tellwright and Henry Earlforward—is not to be found in his writing.

G. F. Bettany, one of Bennett's early champions, concluded that "disillusionment is the key-note of his novels" and that "there is an element of hardness about his attitude toward life." [41] Indeed there is. It appears in his writing at those moments when he suddenly reduces to one the number of life options open to his characters. An example is the fate which overtakes Mrs. Baines following the death of her husband. Mrs. Baines, still a vigorous and attractive woman, might have determined to forge a new and vital life for herself. Instead, however, she puts on the black mourning prescribed by custom and surrenders herself by way of Aunt Harriet's embrace "into the august army of relicts."

The reader is chilled by the grim finality of that reception as

[40] Northrop Frye, *The Educated Imagination* (Bloomington, Indiana, 1968), 90.
[41] F. G. Bettany, "Arnold Bennett: An Appreciation," *The Living Age*, CCLXIX (April 15, 1911), 135-37.

well as by Bennett's refusal to allow Mrs. Baines, in terms of the life he has created for her, any alternative to the Midland version of *suttee*. Bennett's characters, at crisis points in their lives, tend to deny something to themselves or to be deprived of something. Their greatest achievements appear to be their renunciations. Sophia Baines's refusal to become Chirac's mistress is a case in point. Anna Tellwright's submission to her father is another. The monk Sanchez in *Don Juan de Marana* says that "wisdom is to find the next duty and to do it." That duty is, very likely, going to be unpleasant. Bennett's characters do not, as a rule, have a great talent for catching hold of what he referred to as "that gewgaw known as happiness."

There is a darkness in his writing which suggests a corresponding darkness in his own outlook. But he kept that lurking despair well hidden. And if his life was apparently devoid of passion, it was not without enthusiasms. His trip to America in 1911 filled him with excitement. America appeared to him to possess an enormous wealth of literary subject matter. He said that the country was brimming with the stuff of which literary romance is made and that Balzac would have revelled in it. He could, he said, imagine Balzac's excited cry, "Give me a pen, quick, for heaven's sake!" [42] Marguerite reported that the strain on his nerves caused by American hospitality forced him to take two baths a day to offset it. [43]

It was the great, sprawling American factories and towering office buildings that excited Bennett's imagination. The management of mills, the operation of a hotel or a department store were complex processes which fascinated him. He wrote two novels about hotels, *The Grand Babylon Hotel* and *Imperial Palace*; one about a department store, *Hugo*; and one that concerns itself with the operations of a branch of government in wartime, *Lord Raingo*. In fact in nearly all of his major novels he concerns himself with some technical process or some problem in organization and management.

His interests at Comarques were more modest. He walked;

---

[42] Arnold Bennett, "The Future of the American Novel," *North American Review*, CVC (January, 1912), 82.
[43] M. Bennett, *My Arnold Bennett*, 68.

played tennis at home and at the Frinton tennis club, which he had joined shortly after moving to Thorpe-le-Soken; and, as Marguerite said, "wound the clocks." But his interest in how the household was being managed was intense and also disruptive. He found it impossible to leave domestic management in Marguerite's hands. It may have been that her difficulty with the language and her carefully nurtured "foreignness" prevented her from running the house successfully. But, in any case, she was never given a chance to test her capabilities. Bennett interfered in everything from the arrangement of the furniture to the poultry bill. At the same time he was intensely bored with life at Comarques, and no amount of fidgeting over the cost of groceries relieved that tedium.

He was very much interested in painting and yachting, and he enjoyed dining out and going to the theater. But his paramount interest was in writing and in the business side of the writing. If Bennett ever came close to demonstrating a passion, aside from the fixation about punctuality which grew on him during the war years, it was for managing his business. Even Pinker had to defer to his decisions about what was to be done with a piece of writing. On occasion, the agent found himself little more than a courier between Bennett and some editor or publisher.

The principal "business" occupying Bennett and Pinker in the opening months of 1914 was the disposition of Bennett's plays and the process of getting the newer ones produced. *Milestones*, written in collaboration with Edward Knoblock; *The Great Adventure*, a stage version of Bennett's novel *Buried Alive*; *What the Public Wants*, which became a war casualty and was an adaptation of *Helen with the High Hand*, an early novel; an adaptation of *The Grand Babylon Hotel*, written for the stage by Sewell Collins; *Rivals for Rosamond*, a renovation of Bennett's play *A Good Woman*; and a production of *Don Juan*, scheduled for the fall of 1914, were the plays with which Bennett was concerned.[44]

---

44 This information was drawn from the unpublished letters of James B. Pinker and Arnold Bennett in the private collection of Dr. LaFayette Butler, Hazelton, Pennsylvania. Quotations from this source will henceforth be cited Butler Collection with the date of the correspondence.

In March, Pinker went to New York. While he was there, he met Charles Frohman, New York theatrical manager *par excellence*, who had become interested in Bennett's plays, particularly *The Great Adventure*. He told Pinker that he would like to see any new plays Bennett wrote. In May, Frohman was in London and turned down *The Honeymoon*, which had opened at the Royalty Theatre in 1911, saying that "it missed the commerical chance." He still wanted *The Great Adventure*, but Pinker was either unable or unwilling to let him have it.

By 1914 Bennett had written some twenty plays and was in the midst of another one, *Don Juan de Marana*. Only a few of the twenty plays had been produced; but Bennett had reason to be satisfied with the success of *Milestones*, which opened March 5, 1912, at the Royalty Theatre, and *The Great Adventure*, which opened in London on March 25, 1913, at the Kingsway Theatre.[45] Both were enormously successful plays commercially as well as critically. Bennett appeared to be well on his way to a successful second career as a dramatist.

Because he was not really sure of himself as a playwright and because he was likely to be most positive when he was least certain of his ground, he hedged his bets in *The Author's Craft*, written that year and published in 1914, by making a comparison between the relative difficulty of writing a play and writing a novel, laurels going to the novel. His remarks on the subject offended nearly everyone but especially Bernard Shaw, who retaliated with a brilliant parody purporting to be Macbeth's encounter with Macduff before Dunsinane as described by Bennett in a novel.[46] Perhaps no other piece by Bennett has created such controversy or has been so consistently misrepresented as the section of *The Author's Craft* dealing with the drama. Because of that section, it is generally held that Bennett considered the writing of plays a second-rate art.

[45] It had opened in 1911 in Glasgow. Bennett was present, and after the final curtain there were "shouts for the author." Bennett hid himself in the corner of the box. He refused to come out until everyone had left the theater. Reginald Pound, *Arnold Bennett, A Biography* (London, 1952), 225.

[46] George Bernard Shaw, "Arnold Bennett Thinks Play Writing Easier Than Novel Writing," *Pen Portraits and Reviews* (London, 1949), 43–52.

"It is easier to write a play than a novel," he said. "An enormous amount of reverential nonsense is talked about the technique of the stage. . . . It takes six plays to make the matter of a novel." [47] Taken out of context, as they usually are, these statements seem to prove conclusively that Bennett did, indeed, think that plays were artistically inferior to novels. In context, however, the meaning is slightly different.

Bennett meant, in part, that it was easier to write a short work than to write a long one. "There may be few perfect sonnets," he said. "There are fewer perfect epics." He was not, of course, speaking wholly quantitatively. "The dramatist," he said, "may have to imagine a landscape, a room, or a gesture; but he has not got to write it—and it is the writing which hastens death." It was to the problem of composition that he was addressing himself: "The emotional strain of writing a play is not merely less prolonged than that of writing a novel, it is less severe even while it lasts, lower in degree and of a less purely creative character.[48]

The "reverential nonsense" which he spoke of was not a denigration of plays or playwrights but an attack on the kind of advice producers tend to give budding dramatists. He resented having been told by a respected actor-manager that "a dramatist who wished to learn his business must live behind the scenes—and study the works of Dion Boucicault!" [49] Bennett's impatience is understandable. The journeyman in him reacted sharply. The place to learn the technique of the stage, he said, is "not behind the scenes but in the pit." [50]

A play, he pointed out, is something quite different from a novel in that it is spoken and acted. He saw it not as the effort of a single shaping intelligence but as a collaboration among writer, producer, director, actors, and audience. The dramatist, he said, is obliged to leave undone many things that the novelist must do. The dramatist may visualize a scene, but he must not

---

[47] Bennett, *The Author's Craft*, 76.
[48] *Ibid.*, 76, 79, 89.
[49] Dion Boucicault was an actor-manager who, with Marie Tempest, Manager of the Royalty Theatre, produced and took the lead roles in Bennett's *The Honeymoon*, which opened at the Royalty on October 6, 1911.
[50] Bennett, *The Author's Craft*, 71.

"visualize it completely." The director and the actors must be left free to interpret. A play was one thing; a novel, another. The comparison between them could only be a comparison of the "writing with writing."

In an interview with the *Daily News and Leader*, published on July 30, 1914, he was asked what he thought of the stage as a medium. He replied that he found it narrow and unsatisfactory. On being asked if the censorship imposed on the stage were at fault for the narrowness, he said that the public was much more to blame for the state of the theater than was the censor. As to what was wrong with the public, he declined to comment, saying only that he would not dream of writing a play on the same intellectual and emotional plane as he would write a novel. "On certain subjects," he observed, "the public insists upon a sort of ecclesiastical atmosphere in the theater. Why? The English theatrical public is still enormously behind the times." But he confessed that he liked writing plays and would go on writing them, although he did "not much care for casting, rehearsals, cutting, firstnights, and all the rigmarole of play-production." In this regard he differed markedly from Shaw, who delighted in the "rigmarole" of the theater.[51]

The somewhat brash character who comes through the *Daily News* interview is the public Bennett of the prewar period. To a certain extent he was, as Dame Rebecca West has suggested, his best character. He may have enjoyed being thought something of a "card." He certainly enjoyed expensive clothes, good food, and the company of beautiful women. It was one of his principal delights to arrive at the theater or enter a restaurant with a strikingly handsome woman on his arm, and he had a certain flair for the dramatic which comes out in his interviews and in some of his letters. As for being a business man of letters, it was in part a role which he cultivated out of the conviction that writing was a business; but it was also a kind of shield. He had come from humble circumstances, and he had come from

[51] Arnold Bennett, "On the Call of the Stage," *The Daily News and Leader*, July 30, 1914, p. 10.

the North. His hostility toward inherited social rank reveals a defensiveness about his own origins; and the brusqueness with which he treated those who were not his intimates suggests a lingering sense of inadequacy which even his London successes had not entirely dispelled.

In 1914, Bennett was approaching a watershed in his career. While it will never be possible to do more than guess at how his writing might have developed had the war not ploughed up his life in that year, it can be asserted that he was moving toward a crisis in his creative powers, the onset of which was hastened and intensified by the outbreak of war. What must be reaffirmed, however, in the midst of these suggestions of approaching trouble, is that between the publication in 1898 of his first novel, *A Man From the North*, and the summer of 1914, Bennett had established himself as one of the major writers of his time.

Of the twenty-odd novels, counting *These Twain*, which Bennett wrote before the war, at least five are major works. The rest are lesser efforts, although some, like *The Card* and *Buried Alive*, are delightful examples of their kind, even if they are not up to the excellence of his best fiction. *Anna of the Five Towns*, published in 1902, is Bennett's first important novel. It is a novel of great emotional power, built from materials which no contemporary of Bennett's, with the possible exception of George Moore, could have handled with comparable skill and conviction.

Anna Tellwright is a moving and sympathetic character, whose fate is deeply distressing and yet wholly convincing. D. H. Lawrence, who read *Anna* eleven years after its publication, was so profoundly moved by the novel and so pained by Anna's suffering that he wrote *The Lost Girl* as a protest against Bennett's uncompromising rendering of Anna's life. Compared with *Anna*, however, *The Lost Girl* is merely silly; and Lawrence's Natcha-Kee-Tawaras with their silent Cicio, who takes Alvina away from Woodhouse and delivers her from Anna's fate, are utterly implausible. Despite the difficulties which beset the writing of *The Lost Girl*, the limitations of its conception and its execution emphasize the nature of Bennett's success with

*Anna* and offer convincing proof that Bennett's mastery of his material, even as early as 1902, deserved the most serious critical acclaim.

His next great achievement was *The Old Wives' Tale*, published in 1908. The best known of Bennett's novels and in some ways his greatest, it is generally praised for being a realistic treatment in the French manner of English middle-class life as it was lived in the Pottery district of England through the fading years of the Victorian era. The portraits of Constance and Sophia, the deathbed scenes, the episode of the public execution are also regularly praised as is Bennett's painstaking representation of the inexorable march of time.

What is less frequently noted is that Bennett makes a statement in *The Old Wives' Tales* that anticipates a major theme in twentieth century British and American literature. His judgment that life is meaningless makes *The Old Wives' Tale* a thoroughly modern novel. His refusal to find meaning behind the facade of events cannot be accounted for by his early admiration for the French Naturalists. He is not merely being objective in the handling of his material. When Sophia gazes on the corpse of Gerald Scales, she can only ask of life, "What is the meaning if it?" The silence which follows her question is a negation of meaning, and in that negation Sophia has her answer.

Bennett followed his success with *The Old Wives' Tale* with an even more ambitious work. In 1910 he published *Clayhanger*, the first novel of a trilogy that was completed with *Hilda Lessways* in 1911 and *These Twain* in 1915. The setting is still the Potteries, and the first two volumes are powerful presentations of the early life and young manhood of Edwin Clayhanger and of the life of the Five Towns, drawn with great realism and sometimes with stinging satire. The third volume is not properly a part of the trilogy. In *These Twain* Bennett set out to be more autobiographical and to explore the mysteries and the agonies of his foundering marriage.

Although a crisis of serious proportions was building for him, Bennett came to the war a great novelist with his talents still strong. But he was rapidly exhausting two important sources of his inspiration. One was connected directly with his art; the other with his personal life. Of most immediate concern was the fact that he was coming to the end of his Five Towns material. In *These Twain* he mined all but the very last of that rich ore, which had been the heart of his serious writing for fifteen years. At the same time he was coming to see that he could hope for no improvement in his relationship with Marguerite and that there was a real possibility that their marriage would continue to disintegrate under the pressure of their contending personalities. He was, in short, being deprived to a greater and greater degree of that emotional fulfillment which had contributed so markedly to his successful handling of *The Old Wives' Tale*.

What effects these two conditions, added to the third and nearly fatal fact of the war, had on Bennett's art is the subject of much of what follows. He entered the war essentially a private citizen and emerged from it a public figure. In the course of the war years he passed beyond his preoccupation with the Five Towns. He changed his views on some aspects of what the artist's responsibilities were toward himself and toward his public and became more fixed in others. And he suffered the almost unutterable anguish of seeing his artistic powers wane and all but perish under the terrible pressures generated by the war and by the realization of his worst fears about his marriage.

But the tale is not altogether tragic. Bennett survived the war and so did his talent. He won through to an emotional stability and to a creative awakening such as he had not known for twenty years, and with the publication of *Lord Raingo* in 1926 he saw his full power as a novelist reborn out of the ashes of a life that had been all but consumed in the fires of a personal as well as a world war.

# II

# THE FLOWER FADETH

Comarques
4th August, 1914

Dear Pinker:

    I was at Calais harbor on Sunday, and saw the first day of mobilization. I enclose an article (in duplicate) on my experiences —about 1600 words. It ought to be either in a daily, or in one of the big weeklies *this next Saturday*, if it is to retain whatever interest it has.

    The *Nation* of course would be delighted to have it; but I thought you might find something of wider circulation.

Yours sincerely, Arnold Bennett [1]

    For Bennett the war had suddenly become a reality, something to be reported on. "In Calais Harbor" was published in the *Nation* on Saturday, August 8. American rights went to *Harper's Weekly*, which brought out the piece on September 5. With that knack given to good journalists, Bennett had managed to be at the right place at the right time and had then capitalized on his advantage.

    The circumstances attendant on his being in Calais are interesting in that they are indicative of the degree to which he resisted believing in the possibility of war. They also show that he was unwilling to be merely a passive witness to events. He had set out from Comarques on Friday, July 30, for a yachting excursion to the Isle of Wight and the Cowes Regatta, but winds had held him at Dover all of Saturday. He found the harbor "full of men-of-war" and the day gloomy "in spite of the sunshine and in spite of the bright crowds and the band on the Esplanade."

    The Saturday afternoon papers, brought aboard the *Velsa*,

---

[1] Arnold Bennett, *Letters of Arnold Bennett*, ed. James Hepburn (London, 1966), I, 212.

were full of rumors of war. "It seemed to me monstrous, then," he said, "that the glory of the Cowes Regatta should be even impaired by fears of war. (That the Regatta might be wiped entirely off the Calendar did not occur to me, because it was unthinkable.)" The sight of sailors and their officers moving the huge iron booms used to close the harbor excited and oppressed him. And when another group of naval officers boarded a tug and began to cruise back and forth across the harbor, the mystery became insupportable to Bennett. He got into the *Velsa's* dingy and rowed after them, but he did not solve the mystery of the tug.

After he had returned to the yacht, a royal train drew onto the pier. Bennett guessed correctly that the Empress Dowager of Russia was on it. But "one was," he said, "more inclined to believe in the dispatch of another special peace envoy. One instinctively related every phenomenon observed to the theory of the chances of war." He recorded his own growing tension by confessing, somewhat obliquely, that "absurd irrationality colored the whole of one's secret life. A harbor clock striking at eight had the very ring of destiny, and as for a tramp steamer suddenly blowing off steam—its effect on the nerves was appalling." He found being bottled up in Dover harbor intolerable. By midnight on Saturday he had made up his mind that "wherever I spent Sunday I would not spend it in Dover harbor." By an act of will he had also convinced himself that "there would be no general European war." [2]

On Sunday morning, after telling the harbor official that he did not have a fixed destination, he then sailed toward France, intending, in fact, to make for Dungeness or Boulogne or Calais. Bennett's Dutch captain had doubts about entering foreign waters, but Bennett "reassured him." A gale developed, forcing the *Velsa* into Calais harbor where there was a safe anchorage once the yacht had gotten past the piers. A shore loafer caught the mooring rope and said that general mobilization had begun. "That is going badly, the war," he added. Bennett, having recorded a loss of calm in Dover harbor, was not going to allow

[2] *Ibid.*

himself any emotional excesses in a foreign port. He replied to the loafer that he "hoped *that* that would arrange itself."

The French health officials were mildly pessimistic and "amiably took a half crown instead of three francs for dues." Having been told by one of the French officers that "all foreign currency had ceased to circulate except English," he went ashore. The wind was still high. Dust was blowing, and from the town "fragments of the Marseillaise came down on the wind." He found a mobilization order posted and read it, calling it "fairly comprehensive." Other announcements were posted on the walls, including one which ordered all foreigners to report at once to the Mayor in order to obtain permission to "clear out or remain." "Personally," Bennett said, "I ignored this, relying on my blue ensign." The ensign was the British Naval Reserve ensign which he was flying from the *Velsa's* mast. He flew the ensign all that night, "monstrously contrary to the etiquette of yachts," and felt quite secure.

He wandered along the quay and a sentry warned him away from two moored submarines. Making his way to the train station, he discovered that no Paris trains were running and no newspapers were available. Two women in a bookstall told him that "newspapers existed not for the present in Calais." From the station he went to the beach and found it deserted, except for a priest in charge of some boys. Bennett said they presented a "very curious spectacle." "They took off their shoes and stockings, and against each shoe the wind immediately raised a hillock of sand. The priest took off his shoes and stockings and tucked up his skirts. As he entered the water he carefully washed his feet; it was a wise action." [3] In Bennett, the novelist and the journalist are nearly always in evidence; he generally kept the prophet more carefully hidden.

Leaving the harbor, he worked his way through dusty streets clogged with baggage wagons and motor cars. He found the town "dominated by the jangle of car bells." The people were talkative, but they appeared to Bennett to be neither depressed

[3] Arnold Bennett, "In Calais Harbor," *Harper's Weekly*, LIX (September 5, 1914), 223.

nor exhilarated. The cafés were only half filled. He saw two women whose expressions, he said, were ones of "positive sorrow." He noted that the café *chantants* were functioning, but that two operatic performances scheduled for the Casino had been cancelled.

The following morning Bennett took the *Velsa* out of Calais in the rain. Two French submarines at the harbor mouth returned his salute. Ten hours later, after a "magnificent passage," he was in Brightlingsea, where he found the beaches crowded with people enjoying the summer's unusually fine weather and giving themselves wholeheartedly to the holiday spirit. Bennett noted that gasoline was hard to come by; but as the *Velsa* had a reserve supply of sixty gallons, he felt secure, at least for the immediate future.

Any plans for extending the cruise were cut short, however, by the fact that the cook was in the Naval Reserve and subject to immediate call. Before the *Velsa* was properly moored, word was sent onto the boat that the cook was "wanted." He was given twenty-four hours to make his arrangements and report for duty or be subject to immediate arrest. Bennett was angry with the authorities for not giving the man time to settle his financial affairs before being forced to vanish "from his family like a phantom," concluding that as an employer the War Office had something to learn. And the treatment of his cook served to arouse his interest in the problem of servicemen's pay and the care of their dependents, which became one of his chief journalistic preoccupations and received its first treatment in *The Daily News and Leader* article "Patriotism and Pay," published on September 1.

Bennett landed at Brightlingsea on Monday, August 3. The next day England declared war on Germany. Bennett made only one reference in his journal to the event itself. Writing two days later, he noted that "on the day after the war" the boys wanted a tent. Cedric George Beardmore and Richard Bennett, two nephews, were probably at Comarques at that time, but there were also two young French visitors, sons of one of Marguerite's friends. The war left the French youngsters stranded, and Bennett found it necessary to place them in an English school for a while since return to France was impossible.

On August 5, he and Marguerite were in Clacton, a nearby town, where he recorded seeing "a great crowd of holiday makers." His wife said to a man selling fish that he must be making a great deal of money. The man replied that he would not do so for long because he did not expect to get any more fish after that day. Bennett records the remark without comment, perhaps having judged that none was needed. But at the outbreak of the war he was unprepared to accept the possibility of England's being involved in armed conflict; he was, in fact, staggered by what had happened.

The tone of "In Calais Harbor," however, reflects a liveliness and an enthusiasm that is also present in the journal entries after August 4. The experience in the French port brought him alive to his surroundings in a way that he had not been for months. In the previous spring he had struggled to hammer out an article on a barber; but with the Calais article his immediate experiences quite suddenly became significant—personally and journalistically significant. The coming of war and the accompanying emotional upheaval broke the creative log jam which had been frustrating Bennett since January. He could write articles again. He had something to say.

The way in which he exploited his experiences and his opinions and converted them into saleable copy is demonstrated by "In Calais Harbor" and by "Let Us Realize," which was published in *Harper's Weekly* on September 29. The main point of "Let Us Realize" is that the war being fought in Europe was the last or nearly the last struggle between an old ideal which found war noble and a new ideal of democratic, social action which repudiated war and denied its nobility. In July, Bennett had told his wife, who was planning to return to France for an operation, that war is an anachronism. In "Let Us Realize" he put the same idea into a new form, making it into a generalization around which all democratic peoples could rally.

In "Let Us Realize" he also drew from the impressions and

observations recorded in his journal during August and early September. Two of his neighbors took down all their pictures and sent their silver to the bank. They were not clear about why they had done it. In his article Bennett classified their behavior as "wild fancy," saying that the women belonged to a very large group of people who were not keeping their imaginations in check. A local merchant named Johnson called on Bennett. After saying that he was a great patriot, the man announced that he was prepared to give all his money in support of a wild scheme which he had hatched for taking over small mills in the district as an act of national defense. In the article Johnson appears, nameless, of course, as another example of those who were allowing themselves to be thrown off balance by the war.

But in general Bennett was proud of Thorpe-le-Soken's response to the war. He had the greatest admiration for the village's recruiting record, and in "The English Village in War," published by the *Daily News* in October, he reported that seventy-three men had entered the various branches of the service since the outbreak of war. They varied in rank from cavalry commander to rawest recruit and were spread among the Field Artillery, Hussars, East Surreys, Essexes, Public School and University Corps, Electrical Engineers, West Yorks, Rifle Brigade, Royal Garrison Artillery, Royal Horse Artillery, Suffolks, King's Royal Rifles, Field Ambulance, Cyclist Territorials, National Reserve, and the Navy.[4] He added that if all of the United Kingdom had proved itself to be as "martial" as his village, there would be nearly 3,000,000 men under the colors.

In "Let Us Realize" Bennett classified himself as one who belonged to a group with a "stolid attitude" toward the war. He was not praising himself. He said that he was unable to accept the possibility of general war: "War? . . . War was grotesque, a monstrous absurdity. It was unthinkable." In September, when the billeting of army officers in his house began, he found their presence a great inconvenience. In all this, he said, he was really

[4] Arnold Bennett, "The English Village in War," *The Daily News and Leader*, October 29, 1914, p. 4.

still objecting to the war. But the objections wore out as he gradually came to realize that to object to the war was as futile as "to object in my heart to the eclipse."

To understand how extensive Bennett's accommodation was and what a reversal of attitude it represented regarding England's entry into the war, one need only read the long journal entry for August 6, set down roughly two months before the appearance of "Let Us Realize." "The war is a mistake on our part," he said, "but other things leading to it were a mistake, and, these things approved or condoned, the war must be admitted to be inevitable." He judged that Sir Edward Grey, Foreign Secretary, "a man of high common sense," had acted justly.

In his original concern with England's decision to fight, he faced his doubts briefly, then thrust them away. "You cannot," he said with what seems to be a troubled surrender to a logic not wholly convincing, "properly or fairly try to govern a country on a plane of common sense *too* high above its own general plane." With that statement Bennett accepted the government's decision to involve the country in the European conflict. He was not so much making a virtue of a necessity as making a necessity of what he knew to be policy.

As the weeks advanced, he became increasingly alert to the reactions of those around him and to the small events which chronicled the changes in the fabric of everyday life. An officer called at Comarques to complain that a fox terrier was rushing into the road at dispatch riders on motor bicycles. He was not certain that it was one of the Bennett dogs, but he told them it was going to be shot if found loose. Bennett, undisturbed by the officer's threat, said that the dispatch riders were "the most picturesque feature of the war" in Thorpe-le-Soken. The villagers estimated the riders' speed in passing through the village at fifty miles an hour. Bennett was "willing to concede forty."

Edith Johnston, daughter of a neighboring farmer, told Bennett that her father was "laying in ammunition against the time when the populace" would "raid the countryside demanding provisions." He intended to give out food according to a system and not "to the strongest." Bennett reported that Johnston brought his men together every morning in order to tell them what was really going on in the war and to root out any rumors which might be misleading them. Edith told Bennett that she thought the war "necessary and advisable" because the population was "too thick," a view which he recorded without comment.[5]

Another neighbor, a Miss Osborne, came to collect linen and subscriptions for the local branch of the Red Cross. Baroness Marie Byng, an author and the wife of General Julian Byng, offered her home, Thorpe Hall, for a hospital. It was Bennett's opinion that she did it in order to be able to fly the Red Cross flag over Thorpe Hall and by that means protect it from bombing.[6] His judgment on Baroness Byng's motives is an appealing, if somewhat puzzling, combination of malice and naiveté.

Many young women from the area offered their services to the hospital, and Bennett was pleased by these evidences of patriotism. "This instinct to do something on the part of idle young women, or half idle," he said, "is satisfactory to behold." In "Let Us Realize," however, he expressed doubt that "the intense yearning to nurse wounded men on the part of young girls who had never seen a wound" was altogether praiseworthy.[7]

He was even less satified with the behavior of a Clacton bakery which was making, according to report, an extra fifty pounds a week out of bread "through increased charges for which there is no justification." He went on to add that farmers in the neighborhood had raised the price of butter 3d. a pound. Although Bennett was able to turn some of his local observations into publishable material—a surprising quantity, in fact—there is still something slightly disturbing about the amount of trivial observation recorded in his journal in this period. Bennett was clearly frustrated by his sense of isolation from important events; and, unfortunately, he could not sail out to sea as he had done

---

[5] *Journal*, 515.

[6] Arnold Bennett, the Unpublished Journal, Wednesday, August 12, 1914. The "War Journals 1914–1918" are in a single volume in the Berg Collection, the New York Public Library. Quotations from the unpublished portions of the journals are cited with the date of the entry because pagination in the journal is inaccurate.

[7] Arnold Bennett, "Let Us Realize," *Harper's Weekly*, LIX (September 29, 1914), 297.

under similar emotional circumstances that day in Dover harbor. Comarques was firmly anchored in Thorpe-le-Soken.

His forced inactivity, however, gave him leisure to reflect on the political situation in Europe, and he found cause for concern in the fact that no one in the English government, certainly not Sir Edward Grey, "had grasped the movement of social evolution." And he added, "but then very few people have." Later he expressed concern that no one seemed to consider the possibility of a general upheaval following the war. He felt such an upheaval was a real likelihood. The fact, he said, that Midlanders had remained indifferent toward the war, and that a minority of them would continue to be indifferent, was an indication that "the governmental social policy of this kingdom had been a failure, because it is proof that they [Midlanders] believe that they have nothing to lose." [8]

He thought the Germans had been mastered by their own "arrogant military tradition." He saw a German defeat as a direct threat to the German Emperor. A Russian failure to smash Germany, he also realized, would probably topple the Czar as well. He turned out to be right both ways.

Aside from the immediate concern which Marguerite felt for her French relatives, a concern which left her nervous and, according to Frank Swinnerton, "tragically agitated," the peace of Comarques was further threatened by the probability that Lockyer and Cook, head and second gardeners, would be called up, and that Read, the chauffeur, might also be called. Lockyer, whom Bennett described as "a grim and very serious patriot and the chief pillar of the Rifle Club," was already a member of the National Reserve. Bennett was "startled" to realize that if Lockyer went Comarques would be without electricity since only the head gardener could run the generator properly. "This," he said, "seemed dreadful at first, but by the afternoon I was reconciled to the idea of no electricity and also to the idea of the garden being neglected."

He went at once to Read to ask him if, as an ex-Territorial,

[8] *Journal,* 514.

he thought of enlisting. Read said that he had no thought of going "unless it was compulsory." Bennett had to be satisfied with
that answer, however lacking it was in patriotic fervor.[9] But he
was beginning to ask himself, when he saw young men out of
uniform, why they were not in the army. "How quickly one
becomes militaristic," he said of his attitude.

As cut off as Comarques was from events of national importance, Bennett soon found himself affected by an event which
seemed to threaten his very livelihood. In August, London was
suddenly swept by a publishers' panic. On the 4th, Pinker sent a
letter to Bennett which he had received from Algernon Methuen,
Bennett's publisher. "Owing to the serious international situation," Methuen wrote, "with its accompanying financial troubles,
[we] may be obligated to postpone publishing *Price of Love*." [10]
The planned date for issuing the book was September 2. Contributing to the panic was a supposed paper shortage which,
however exaggerated in the publishers' minds, brought an end
to the serialization of *The Price of Love* in the *Daily News*.

Frank Swinnerton in *Background with Chorus* recalled that it
was generally held that the war would be short and that everything must be stopped for its duration. Methuen advised "all his
younger authors to abandon novel-writing." According to Swinnerton, Methuen went so far as to ask Wells and Bennett either
to stop writing altogether or to accept reduced wartime payments. On September 18, Pinker wrote to Bennett in possible
reference to such a request: "I enclose a letter I have just received from Methuen. What shall I say in reply? What can one
say!" [11] What Bennett did not say was that he would stop writing or that he would accept reduced rates for his work.

Although he had cash reserves on which to draw, in August he

---

[9] Read had a mind of his own. On the return trip from Rome in the previous
spring, Read had on one occasion refused to stop in order to allow Bennett
and his wife an opportunity to look at a town through a narrow opening in
the hills. Bennett cheered himself up on that occasion by saying that in the
long run a glimpse was probably more satisfying.
[10] Butler Collection, August 4, 1914.
[11] *Ibid.*, September 18, 1914.

had no way of knowing how long the panic would continue; and in spite of the reserves, he found it necessary during September to borrow £2,500 from Pinker to meet his expenses. His eagerness to locate markets for his articles becomes increasingly understandable as the panic deepened, and on August 8 he told Pinker that he was "exercising every economy which can be exercised without dismissing labor." Many writers were much harder hit than Bennett. "Just at that moment," Pinker wrote on August 7, "the trade have cancelled all their orders for books. . . . Here my business is practically at a standstill. . . . I am engaged all day in . . . struggles to meet convenience of clients some of whom are in extreme difficulty." [12]

Bennett responded with an offer of one hundred pounds and told Pinker to lend it to those writers who were most in need. Bennett said that he would not have to know who received the money. Pinker thanked Bennett for the offer but declined it. As a business note included in the letter, Pinker said that he was sorry to hear that W. H. Smith's [13] "have refused to pay your accounts which are due."

Fortunately, Bennett was able to offset his anticipated losses by finding markets in England and America for his journalism. There was, in fact, a tremendous demand for "war" material. Pinker wrote to Bennett on August 10 to say that Conrad was in Russian Poland and that if he "could only get some stuff from him now," he could "turn that paper into gold." Newsprint had not given out; the presses went on rolling for a public ravenous for news and commentary, but the book publishers continued to be timorous.

The *Daily News* published "What the German Conscript Thinks" on August 24. Nearly a week earlier Bennett wrote to Pinker to tell him that "*The Daily News and Leader* had made a rather urgent request" for a war article. But he felt unable to produce the sort of article they wanted. "I suppose," he continued, "the idea is to balance the Wells articles in the *Chronicle*.

[12] *Ibid.*, August 7, 1914.
[13] W. H. Smith's was the name of a chain of lending libraries and bookstalls. The terms of Bennett's contract with the company are not known.

Of course I have neither the ability nor the wish to compete with Wells at this game." [14] *Everybody's Magazine* asked him to write a forecast about the war, to be published six weeks later. Naturally, he refused, but in telling Pinker about the offer, he suggested that *Everybody's* might be persuaded to take a later article if he could first work out something with the *Daily News*.

*Harper's Weekly* published "Let Us Realize" and "In Calais Harbor" in September. On the same day that the *Daily News* article appeared, Pinker wrote to Bennett to say that the *Daily News* wanted weekly articles and was willing to pay twenty guineas each for them. Bennett, pressed for money, accepted with alacrity. From that week forward the paper ran one of his articles nearly every week until May, 1916. The price paid for the articles was low—for Bennett, very low. It has been suggested that he accepted the amount out of patriotic motives, but he could also see the possibility of being in serious financial difficulty if the book market continued to slump. A third reason for accepting was that the *Daily News* provided Bennett with a truly national audience and gave him the gratifying feeling that he was actually taking part in the great events of the hour.

By the last week of September, Bennett had reason to feel that he had sufficiently shored up his financial affairs with journalism and loans from Pinker to afford to refuse a *Daily News* request for a serial. "It would be quite impossible for me to produce such a novel," he wrote, "unless I was in need of money." He suggested that the offer be made to Mrs. Belloc Lowndes, who, he thought, "would not do it worse than anybody else." Part of the reason for his refusing to do the story may have been connected with his troubles with Warren, an editor on the *Daily News*. Late in September, Bennett wrote an article titled "The German Army on Its Way to Berlin," and Warren changed *Berlin* to *Paris*. "The ass," Bennett wrote to Pinker, "meant well, but so does Van Kluck." [15]

[14] The letter from which this quotation was taken is part of the Arnold Bennett/James B. Pinker correspondence in the Ogden Manuscripts collection, University College London Library. Quotations from this source will be cited Ogden Collection with the date of the correspondence.
[15] Ogden Collection, October 1, 1914.

Bennett's sense of well-being ended abruptly. On September 25, Pinker notified Bennett that the American article market had collapsed. A firm offer from an American publisher to buy six to ten of the *Daily News* articles at a price of five hundred dollars each had been suddenly withdrawn. Pinker found himself unable to place any of Bennett's articles. "The fact is," he said, "our friends have just ruined the market. I hear that most, if not all, of Wells's articles have been given away in America, and other authors are doing the same thing." [16]

James Barrie, John Galsworthy, novelist A. E. W. Mason, and H. G. Wells were, in fact, giving their stuff away. Pinker, of course, was outraged by what he considered their bad judgment and misguided patriotism. "If those official people," he said, "had taken your advice, we should not only have had an effective campaign in the American press, but we should have made money out of it." He went on to say that Bennett had lost about one thousand pounds up to that point "with no compensating comfort for you in the reflection that the money or sacrifice was for a good purpose." [17]

In America the situation became so bad that even *The New York Times* openly pirated Bennett's article "When the Truce Comes," taking it straight from the *Daily News*. Bennett made representations to the Author's League but declined to take the matter to court. On October 26, Pinker reported that articles were being lifted before copyright could be posted. In an attempt to protect himself from further piracy, Bennett had a copyright notice printed with each of the *Daily News* articles. The following note appeared in the same insert with the notice of copyright: "The above notice is printed solely in order to comply with the American Copyright Law. Neither *The Daily News* nor the writer of the article has any desire to prevent full quotation from the article in Great Britain."

Writing in November to his American friend Elsie Herzog,

[16] Butler Collection, September 25, 1914.
[17] Butler Collection, September 28, 1914. The "official people" probably refers to the Ministry of Information officials at Wellington House, particularly G. H. Mair and Masterman, who had called the "eminent authors" meeting.

Bennett complained that he couldn't get his articles published in the United States and that there had been pirating of his material to such an extent that he couldn't "guarantee to deliver the goods to an American buyer." [18] But two of his pieces, "Democracy Justified" and "The Public and the Censor," did appear in *Harper's Weekly* in November.

His loss of the American article market and his loss of royalty payments, brought on by Methuen's failure to publish *The Price of Love* and its cancellation in the *Daily News*, were not the only financial losses he suffered in August and September. On August 12, Pinker wrote to Bennett to say that because of the war Frank Vernon, who was preparing a production of Bennett's *Don Juan* (the play was scheduled for a Fall premiere), had canceled all plans for the play. Pinker added somewhat wryly that "that was to be expected." Vernon had not had his heart in the production from the beginning.

Vernon's note to Pinker was a harbinger of more serious news. J. E. Vedrenne told Bennett that the autumn tours of *Milestones* would be a heavy loss even in the event that the railways allowed them to go on the road. Vedrenne also asked Bennett to forego his fees if the tour did get under way. Knoblock, he said, had agreed. Bennett declined. Receipts from *The Great Adventure*, playing at the Kingsway Theatre and starring Lillah McCarthy and Granville Barker, fell by five hundred pounds between the first and second weeks of August. It was a severe financial blow to Bennett. His returns from his plays, especially from *Milestones* and *The Great Adventure*, had made up a considerable part of his income, an amount which gradually faded to nothing as the fall advanced. Other plays were equally hard hit. Among those to suffer were William Somerset Maugham's *The Land of Promise*; *The Belle of New York* at the Lyceum; Knoblock's *Kismet* at the Globe; and *The Passing Show* at the Palace Theatre, in which Basil Hallam sang "I'm Gilbert the Filbert, the Nut with a K. . . ." [19]

In an effort to have reliable information about the progress of

[18] *Letters*, II, 359.
[19] Lillah McCarthy, *Myself and My Friends* (London, 1933), 247.

the war, Bennett subscribed to the Central News Service, whose releases reached him by way of telegrams sent to the local post office and delivered by the postmaster to Comarques. After reading his first telegram, Bennett asked the postmaster if he would like to have the message in order to display it. The postmaster said that he would. The next morning Miss Nerney, returning from the village, said that as she passed the post office two men were reading the telegram. One of them asked who Arnold Bennett was; and the other said, "He's the War Minister." Then he corrected himself. "Oh, no, he isn't," he said. "He's the actor chap that lives down the road." A few days later Bennett passed the post office and saw one of his telegrams tacked on the wall. It read: "British Gold Coast Forces Take German Togoland. No Resistance by permission of Arnold Bennett." [20]

On September 2 he received an invitation from C. F. G. Masterman to attend a conference of "eminent authors" at Wellington House in London. Charles Masterman, Chancellor of the Duchy of Lancaster and a Liberal Cabinet Minister, was in charge of Wellington House, one of the government's propaganda agencies. Masterman was an impressive and, at the same time, rather pathetic man. Too brilliant for his job, his unendurable superiority alienated a sufficient number of people in power to bring about his dismissal. Frank Swinnerton described him as a sick and embittered man, but one who had a swiftness of intellect that could not be disguised and that flashed out with the rapidity of lightning. Masterman had been given the task of attempting to harness the powers of the country's writers and placing them in the service of the government.[21]

Bennett attended the conference at Buckingham Gate on September 3. Among those present were Sir Henry Newbolt, J. W. Mackail, Arthur and R. H. Benson, John Galsworthy, Sir Owen Seaman, G. M. Trevelyan, H. G. Wells, John Masefield, Robert Bridges, Anthony Hope Hawkins, G. K. Chesterton,

[20] *Journal*, 518.
[21] Bennett and Masterman became good friends. Masterman once told his wife that if she were ever "really in a hole" to "go to A. B. He's the one." When Masterman died in 1927, Bennett collected some £4,000 for the education of Masterman's children.

Gilbert Murray, James Barrie, Thomas Hardy, Hall Caine, and Israel Zangwill. It was a fair sampling of the great and the near-great of England's post-Edwardian literary world. Bennett took a most prosaic attitude toward the meeting. He talked with James Barrie and liked him, thought Zangwill had too much to say, and approved of Wells's and Chesterton's remarks. After the meeting he went to Wells's flat where he met a young man who had an interesting recruiting story, which Bennett determined to turn into an article; but he had come from the conference at Wellington House with such a "fearful" headache that after leaving Wells's flat he decided to dine alone at the Reform Club. Hardy, recalling the conference, saw it as an altogether more dramatic event than Bennett had hinted at. He wrote that the September sun shining in from the dusty street cast a tragic light over the group "sitting around the large blue table, full of misgivings, yet unforeseeing in all their completeness the tremendous events that were to follow." [22]

The question of what the writer's role was to be in the war was not a simple one. Bennett clashed very early with the *New Statesman* over the nature of that role. On August 29, the *NS* reviewed the war literature and observed with acid tone that "almost without exception during the last fortnight our eminent novelists have rushed into print as authorities on all matters of foreign policy and military strategy."

Bennett replied in a letter addressed to the editor of the paper: "As war is preeminently an affair of human nature, a triumph of instinct over reason, it seems to me not improper that serious novelists (who are supposed to know a little about human nature and to be able to observe accurately and to write) should be permitted to express themselves concerning the phenomena of a nation at war without being insulted." Clifford Sharp sent Bennett an apology, but nothing was really settled. [23]

Where did the writer's responsibility lie? There is no doubt that Bennett felt he had a part to play in the general war effort.

[22] Florence Hardy, *The Life of Thomas Hardy 1840–1928* (New York, 1962), 366.
[23] *Letters*, II, 349.

His response to the war was emotional. Writing to George Doran in early September, he said, "I would give every cent and [? acre] I possess, and start again with nothing, in order to secure the overthrow of a handful of men at Berlin." He was not often so personally open; his frankness is a measure of the intensity of his feelings. He had, furthermore, committed himself in a more objective way to the nation's cause. He had put all of his pacifism behind him. "I have only one fear as to the war," he wrote, "and that is the pacifist and financial influences . . . may force a peace too soon." He felt that, given time, the allies could "finish up Germany's activities in the war department for at least fifty years." [24]

Frank Swinnerton believes that from a very early period in the war—probably from the time the *Daily News* articles began—Bennett saw his task to be that of maintaining "civilian morale" at a high level. Feeling as he did, it is understandable that he should be willing to place his talents at his country's disposal. In practical terms that service was first rendered in a piece called *Liberty. A Statement of the British Case*, written in the first week of September for the *Daily News* and the *Saturday Evening Post*. By the end of the month Hodder and Stoughton had bought it for English book publication; and in October George Doran bought it for the American book market, eventually issuing it as a pamphlet.

*Liberty* opens with a rather superficial and slightly ironic summary of the events leading up to the outbreak of hostilities. The summary is followed by a section in which Bennett pillories the German military caste, laying at its feet the responsibility for the war. Its arrogance, he said, yoked with German fears of the swiftly growing Russian and French armies, had brought on the calamity. He characterized the mentality of Europe's diplomats as "ignoble, infantile, cynical, and altogether rascally. . . ." In the face of Germany's intentions he insisted that "all diplomacy was futile, and most of it was odiously hypocritical." [25] Only Sir

---

[24] *Ibid.,* 351.
[25] Arnold Bennett, *Liberty: A Statement of the British Case* (London, 1914), 19–36.

Edward Grey escapes abuse; and even he, cast in the role of St. George and sent out to slay the German diplomatic dragon, had found the beast too tricky for his honest English sword.

With his American audience in mind, Bennett devoted a few lines in the second section of *Liberty* to German threats against the security of the United States, neatly giving as official German policy some of General von Edelsheim's theories, printed in a military memorandum, "Operations Upon the Sea," on how to carry out successfully an invasion of the United States.

In the third and last section Bennett makes it clear that England is fighting a war to bring to an end the kind of terrorism and barbarism of which Germany is guilty. The English ideal of liberty is set against the German ideal of enslavement of its own as well as other people. "We have," Bennett said, "a silly, sentimental, illogical objection to being enslaved. . . . It is for liberty that we are fighting. We have lived in alarm, and liberty has been jeopardized too long." [26] A month earlier he had found it impossible to imagine that anything could be of sufficient importance to cause the cancellation of the Cowes Regatta.

It is not necessary to insist that Bennett believed that *Liberty* was a complete and wholly unbiased statement of the English position. Neither is it necessary to say that he was wholly disingenuous, or that his only motives in writing the piece, aside from making money, were to stiffen the resolution of the English people and to win the support of the Americans. Bennett obviously felt that *Liberty* would help the English government to rally support for its policies, but he had not had to agonize over his fiddling with the "truth" in *Liberty*. Other writers were engaged in the same work. G. K. Chesterton in his autobiography recorded with some degree of satisfaction that he once wrote a very bellicose article titled "The Barbarism of Berlin" and saw it printed, with Masterman's connivance, as a "quiet philosophical study in Spanish." [27] What that meant was that people read the article as a piece of scholarly research when it was in fact de-

---

[26] *Ibid.*, 58.
[27] G. K. Chesterton, *The Autobiography of G. K. Chesterton* (New York, 1936), 258.

liberate propaganda. Chesterton was not troubled in the least by such fakery.

With the exception of "What the German Conscript Thinks," Bennett's articles in the early weeks of the war had grown out of attitudes and events recorded in the journal. But the early doubts about England's entry into the fighting so clearly recorded there had been silenced. He became thoroughly militarist. If *Liberty* is propaganda, it is also a reasonably close reflection of Bennett's new convictions regarding the war and not a cynical invention for the occasion. The piece is close to some of the ideas expressed in "Let Us Realize," but there is still that degree of distortion in it which gives pause. For many years Bennett had made it his aim to render life in his writing as truthfully as possible. *Liberty* is a deliberate departure from that principle.

Bennett did not become a government hack, however. He kept himself sufficiently free to attack those policies to which he objected. Conscription was one of his targets. Late in August he wrote an article about recruiting in which he told "some incontrovertible truths about this recruiting question." The article was called "The Rat-Trap and What the Conscription Bill Amounts To." It was too strong a statement of his views for any paper or periodical to touch, and it was never published. Its attack on the Bill was harsh: "In the profoundest and most dangerous sense it is a pro-German movement," he said and called the Bill "disingenuous." He protested that every male affected by it ran the "risk of being treated as a deserter." The proposed bill would have required that every man of military age not in uniform be held responsible for proving that he should not be in uniform. His failure to do so to the examining committee's satisfaction would expose him to criminal prosecution.[28] Bennett's counter proposal was that, given proper inducements and adequate support for dependents, young men would volunteer in greater

---

[28] Arnold Bennett, "The Rat Trap and What the Conscription Bill Amounts To." Never published. The manuscript of the article is in the Berg Collection, The New York Public Library.

numbers than the services could use. Conscription would be needless.

During the fall of 1914 he wrote four articles dealing either directly or indirectly with recruiting and with pay for servicemen: "Patriotism and Pay" (*Daily News*, September 1, 1914), "I Told You So" (*Daily News*, September 11, 1914), "The Fund and the State" (*Daily News*, September 16, 1914), and "Recruiting" (*Daily News*, November 4, 1914). "Patriotism and Pay" is a straightforward appeal for higher pay for servicemen. "The Fund and the State" is a complaint about the low pay for soldiers which points out that a fair level of pay for them is fully as important as the proper organization of civilian charity for their dependents. "I Told You So" attacks conscription and Lord Roberts, who, before his death, expressed doubt that Englishmen would volunteer for service in very great numbers. "Recruiting" analyzes political and military conditions affecting the rate of recruiting.

In "I Told You So" Bennett drew on the experiences of two of his employees to show how the War Department was mishandling its volunteers. Lockyer, Bennett's head gardener at Comarques, had offered himself for induction; but he had been so shockingly ill-treated in his attempts to enlist that he finally returned home. Among other indignities suffered he had been left to sleep on the floor of an unheated barracks with only a flea-infested blanket for warmth, given almost no food, and totally ignored. After several days of neglect, during which time he began to grow ill, he walked back to Thorpe-le-Soken without ever having been given the opportunity of signing induction papers. Bennett's cook, who had been forced to leave his family before having made proper financial arrangements for them, was his second example. If Bennett had not continued to pay a portion of the man's salary to his wife, the family would have been in real want.

Bennett reemphasized his point that adequate facilities for handling enlistments coupled with an enlightened policy of support for dependents would make conscription unnecessary. He pur-

sued his argument in "Recruiting," turning away from examples
of mismanagement on the part of the War Department to examine other factors that were slowing down the recruiting drive.
While Allied victories [29] tended to slow the rate of volunteering,
he wrote, of greater influence was the general knowledge that
army contractors were blatantly corrupt, that army canteens
were being operated by profiteers at the expense of the enlisted
men, and that the sensational press (Bennett meant Northcliffe's
papers, among others) [30] had disheartened many with their attacks on government officials. In closing, he came back again to
the treatment of dependents and wrote angrily: "As it was in
Cobbett's time so proportionately to the general advance of
well-being is it now. "Women and children last," if they are the
women and children of our defenders! A damnable conservatism
alone stops us from behaving with common honesty." He concluded by saying that if such wrongs were not righted, the "democratic element" would never forgive the government. It was
a strong statement of his political liberalism and one that he
was to repeat in various forms throughout the war.

His willingness to criticize the War Office brought him into
conflict with those who thought that in a time of national crisis
all disagreement with official views should be suppressed. Late
in October John Galsworthy called on Pinker and expressed his
doubts about the propriety of Bennett's public statements. He
objected especially to "When the Truce Comes," calling its
timeliness into question. Through the letters column of the *Daily
News*, which supported conscription, Bennett had a sharp ex-

[29] The victories to which Bennett referred were in reality only propaganda
victories. Mons (August 23, 1914) and the Marne (September 5–9, 1914) could
not be claimed as victories for the British Expeditionary Force since the B.E.F.
retreated from Mons and did not encounter the German army at the Marne. In
the first battle of Ypres (October 12–November 11, 1914), the B.E.F. held the
German drive but destroyed itself in the process.

[30] Throughout the war, Bennett attacked the Northcliffe press for its reactionary philosophy and its yellow journalism. In 1909, Bennett's play *What the
Public Wants* took Alfred Harmsworth (later Lord Northcliffe) for its hero
and the press and the theater for its subjects. Bennett's attitude toward
Northcliffe was a puzzling mixture of grudging admiration and bristling
hostility.

change with Eden Phillpotts [31] over a reference to Lord Roberts made in one of Bennett's conscription articles. Phillpotts said that Bennett had insulted the memory of a great soldier. Bennett hotly denied the charge, pointing out that when he had written the article in question, Roberts had been in good health. He went on to say that Lord Robert's prophecy that fewer than half a million volunteers would come forward did indeed show a lack of faith in his country. Bennett went on from there to say that "conscription is a matter to be decided by the citizens of this country, not by its professional soldiers." [32] In actuality the idea of conscription was not new. As early as 1906 the Government, with King Edward's hearty support, was toying with the idea of a conscripted peacetime army as a part of its services' reform plans.

Bennett held strong feelings about the right of the English citizenry to make decisions for itself in such matters as conscription, and he felt equally strongly that information which would help them to decide intelligently should not be held back by a fainthearted government. On September 24, the *Daily News* published his article "Official Journalism." It was a free-swinging attack on the ineptitude of official censorship and the poor writing coming from the Press Bureau, the official government news distributing agency.

"An amazing naiveté is the chief characteristic of all censorships," he wrote and went on to express concern that censorship as it was being practiced favored paternalism and exclusiveness —two antidemocratic influences he attacked repeatedly in the newspaper series. Rounding out his argument, he wrote, "Not only responsible journalists of all shades, but serious citizens everywhere feel a quiet and profound resentment against the existing policy of the authorities in regard to war news—withholding it themselves while stopping its collection and dissemi-

---

[31] An English writer who had urged Bennett to write serials and with whom he collaborated in 1900 on the play *Children of the Mist*. The play was never produced.
[32] *Letters*, II, 360.

nation by others. It is a policy as insulting as it is dangerous. And let there be no mistake."

In the eleven *Daily News* articles published between August 24, the first in the series, and December 10, the last piece to appear in 1914, Bennett introduced the themes which were to preoccupy him throughout the war. Conscription, compensation for soldiers, support for their families, and the folly of censorship have already been mentioned. Another very important theme was his militant, almost belligerent, support of democracy. Bennett seems to have defined the term *democracy* as not only a political arrangement by which everyone was enfranchised but also a social pattern within which caste and privilege were eradicated. This powerful social sense is not expressed elsewhere in his writing with anything like the force given it in the articles.[33]

The first piece in the series to reveal his discontent with the structure of society and with the conservative powers within it fighting to prevent change is "The Ant Hill" (*Daily News*, October 24, 1914) in which he said that Europe was at war because civilization had failed. It had failed because it had adhered to the principles of anarchy and competition, "according to which war is biologically justified." The war, he insisted, threatened democracy with a "triumphant militarism," whose purpose was to defeat the democratic processes, restore the House of Lords to power, reestablish privilege, and impose taxes on consumption rather than on income and possessions.

Bennett saw the true issue of the war not as the struggle for territory but as the struggle for ideals—the ideals of democracy, social justice, and peace. His objection to conscription was part of a general objection to what he called the pro-German element in English society, meaning those who espoused the same social

---

[33] Throughout Bennett's novels and short stories, particularly those dealing with the Five Towns, there are more or less direct references to the hardships of the poor and the drudgery of the laboring class. There is even the stirring of a social conscience in Edwin Clayhanger in *These Twain*, but the impulse comes to nothing. In his fiction Bennett accepts poverty and inequality as an ineradicable part of life. In his articles he demonstrates a strong support for measures to correct the social and economic imbalances plaguing England.

philosophy as the Prussian aristocracy. And Bennett insisted that it was Prussianism, both in and out of Germany, that had to be smashed before the world would be made safe for democracy. It is, perhaps, in "The Ant Hill" that Bennett comes closest to making a clear statement of his concept of what society should be; and while it would be futile to attempt to establish him as a social philosopher, it is clear that he was no longer willing, as he had professed to Wells in 1905, to merely "look down on the show."

Another article in the series was "Military Efficiency" (November 26), a forerunner of articles in which he defended miners and mill workers in their struggles with the government and with mine and mill owners. "Military Efficiency" opened with a rather low-keyed criticism of those writers of "Letters-to-the-Editor" who had been insisting that management of the war should be left to "experts." As Bennett pointed out, the so-called "experts" were really those who were in power. "Nothing is more dangerous than an expert," he wrote, "and nothing is more valuable—except general common sense." [34]

He came to the defense of the Midlands in early December with the article "Football." The London papers had been carrying letters which charged the Midlanders with being slack and not having volunteered in sufficient numbers. It had been asserted further that they spent all their time watching football and that football ought to be discontinued until after the war. There were strong overtones of class hostility in the letters, but Bennett did not reply in kind. Pointing out that the Midlands had a recruiting rate higher than that of any other section of England, he agreed nevertheless that it was a good time to curtail amusements and suggested that London should set the example by stopping football there, closing movie theatres and music halls, and discontinuing all other amusements, including fox hunting, horse racing, and golfing.

[34] During this period, *common sense* was a term as common and a quality as widely claimed as wit in the eighteenth century. Wells, Shaw, Bennett, and others all claimed to possess it in abundance and denied that their opponents were capable of recognizing it.

He clashed with Shaw over "Common Sense About the War," a pamphlet which Shaw wrote for the *NS* and which the *NS* published on November 14 as a special supplement. It was a very long article dealing with conscription, support for soldiers' dependents, and related matters; but its main concern was with the diplomatic history leading up to the war. It was Shaw's contention that England's militarism had at least equalled Germany's and that whereas Germany had seized on the assassination of Archduke Ferdinand as an excuse for war, England had seized on the invasion of Belgium for a similar purpose. Shaw claimed that as an Irishman he was under no compulsion to flatter the government of England, and that a little truth would do everyone good.[35]

On November 15, Bennett wrote to Pinker to say that he would send an article "dealing drastically with the bad parts of Shaw's manifesto of the war. . . . About two-thirds of Shaw's statement is strictly first-class, and indeed quite unequalled. Most of the rest is absurd and may do some harm." [36]

Bennett's response was printed in the *Daily News* and *The New York Times* on December 18 under the title "The Nonsense About Belgium," the phrase having been taken from Shaw's article. Bennett began with very high praise for Shaw's effort: "One of its greatest values is its courage, for in it Shaw says many things no one else would have dared to say. . . . On such subjects as recruiting, treatment of soldiers' and sailors' dependents, secret diplomacy, militarism, Junkerism, churches, Russia, peace terms and disarmament . . . it contains the most magnificent, brilliant, and convincing common sense that could possibly be uttered.[37] His objections, however, were expressed with equal force. Having attacked Shaw's entire handling of the Belgian question—especially his efforts to throw the validity of

[35] Stanley Weintraub presents a detailed and diverting account of the extraordinary uproar created by "Common Sense" in *Journey to Heartbreak: The Crucible Years of Bernard Shaw, 1914–1918* (New York: Weybright and Talley, 1971).

[36] *Letters*, I, 215.

[37] Arnold Bennett, "Arnold Bennett Answers Shaw," *The New York Times*, November 18, 1914, p. 3.

England's treaty obligations to Belgium into doubt—Bennett concluded by repeating his praise and then making a general criticism of the article. He found many of Shaw's judgments to be flippant and perverse. He went on to say that its inexactitude amounted to a scandal. "Mr. Shaw has failed to realize either his own importance or the importance and very grave solemnity of the occasion. The present is no hour for that disingenuous, dialectical bravura which might easily relieve a domestic altercation." Bennett closed by urging Shaw to reconsider and rewrite.

Shaw, of course, responded. His letter to the *Daily News* and to *The New York Times* dealt with Bennett's main charges by renewing his attack on the English Junkers who had promulgated the diplomacy which led to war. With wicked satire he excused Sir Edward Grey from responsibility in the matter by saying that "Sir Edward never completely grasped the situation or found out what he really was doing and even had a democratic horror of war." As for Bennett's assertion that Shaw had not assumed his responsibilities but had been frivolous, Shaw answered that charge by saying, "We who are mouthpieces of many inarticulate citizens, who are fighting at home against the general tumult of scare and rancor and silly cinematograph heroics for a sane facing of facts and a stable settlement, are very few. We have to bring the whole continent of war-struck lunatics to reason if we can." He then invited Bennett to pay him some more nice compliments and to "reserve his fine old Staffordshire loathing for my intellectual nimbleness until the war is over." [38]

It was a draw, and each man stepped out of the ring under his own power. Pinker wrote to Bennett to mention a visit he had had from Henry James, during which he asked James if he had read Shaw's manifesto. James replied, "I have it here, and have made several attempts, but his horrible flippancy revolts me. To think of a man deliberately descending into the arena at the present crisis and playing the clown!" [39] Two days later

[38] George Bernard Shaw, "Shaw in Rebuttal to Arnold Bennett," *The New York Times*, November 19, 1914, p. 3.
[39] *Letters*, I, 217.

Bennett recorded in his journal that Mark Judge, Chairman of the Committee on War Damage, had suggested, with Shaw's approval, that Bennett edit Shaw's "Manifesto" for volume publication. It was never published in book form, although reprinted as a pamphlet by the *NS* in 1915.

That Bennett was highly stimulated by his engagement with current issues is beyond doubt. Writing to Elsie Herzog in the early fall, he said, "I haven't been so interested in life since I was born as I am now. England is full of drilling soldiers, but it is also full of ideas—large general ideas, which overthrow small particular ideas about particular persons." [40] Perhaps he meant in part that the war was helping him to forget his troubles with Marguerite. Once he recovered from the initial shock caused by the outbreak of the war, a spirit of release, almost of relief, is present in his correspondence and in his journal for the early war period. That spirit is expressed in a letter to André Gide: "*Bref, je suis très occupé, et très interessé, et plein d'espoir.*"

Despite the excitement generated by events, Bennett continued to work on *These Twain*. He had been writing the novel since the end of May with very little interruption by other writing. By August he had some 25,000 words; and eight days after the declaration of war, he wrote in the journal that he was in "*full* work, and that only a defeat of the allies" would halt him. By the 17th of the month he had written another seven thousand words of the novel.

Why did he go on writing the novel when it appeared, at that particular moment, that there might be no market for it? Aside from contractual obligations with Methuen and others, he had several reasons for continuing. For one thing he had invested considerable time in the book and to complete it would be a more reasonable gamble than to abandon it. A more personal consideration that cannot be assessed with great precision is the probability that he was exploring his own marital relations

[40] *Letters*, II, 353. Elsie Herzog was the wife of Paul M. Herzog, George Doran's legal advisor at the time of Bennett's visit to the United States in 1911. Bennett was a guest of the Herzogs in New York and became a close friend of Mrs. Herzog, with whom he established a correspondence lasting from November 20, 1911, to her death in February, 1919.

through Edwin and Hilda's marriage. That the experience was painful can be guessed by his almost complete silence on the subject of the book, except for infrequent references to pages written or sections finished. At the end of October he said, "On Wednesday I finished the second part of *These Twain*. This afternoon I wrote my contribution to *King Albert's Book*—Hall Caine's scheme." [41] Nothing more. No comment on the novel; no hint of his feelings about the book. By the first week of December, he was "*in* the last part" of the novel. But the writing dragged. On the 19th he noted in his journal, "from Thursday in last week to last Thursday I did nothing on my novel. I was fairly free to go on with it on Wednesday, but I had neuralgia. I wrote 2500 words of it yesterday." It is difficult not to believe that the book was becoming a burden to him. In the greater excitement of the war, he had become bored with it. And, if he had originally hoped to find in the writing answers to his marital dilemma, that hope was now dead.

Whatever he thought about *These Twain* or whatever emotional pressures were generated by it, his writing was a release from the tensions of the war. On August 21 he noted the fall of Brussels: "Great spectacular depressing fact of the surrender of Brussels to the Germans this morning. But by the afternoon I had got quite used to it and was convinced that it was part of the Allies' preconceived plan and that all was well. But before getting this reassuring conviction I had gone upstairs and written 1200 words in two hours." [42] What was the relationship between the writing and the dawning conviction that "all was well"? Perhaps there was none. On the other hand, the writing probably shored up his confidence in himself, a confidence which he may have transferred to affairs in general.

He was unwilling, however, simply to bury himself in writing. The *Daily News* offered him one thousand pounds for the British serial rights to an eighty thousand word article on the intrigue and the negotiations leading up to the war. The paper was will-

---

[41] *King Albert's Book* was written to raise funds for the *Daily Telegraph's* Belgian Relief Fund. Bennett's contribution was "The Return," which contained an account of his first visit to Belgium and suggested how returning Belgians would feel when they went home after the war.

[42] *Journal*, 521.

ing to provide a great deal of the background information and raw material. The money must have been a temptation, but Bennett refused the offer. His excuse was that his American commitments were too heavy. He did have American contracts for two serials; and it is also possible that he was working on a very slight story called "The White Feather," which *Collier's Weekly* published in the fall. There were two stories due the *Metropolitan Magazine* which he may have had under construction. But it is more likely that Bennett did not want to engage in an evaluation of the government's diplomatic maneuverings. He had already characterized European diplomacy in *Liberty*. He had whitewashed Grey and the Foreign Office, and he would not have wished to reverse his position and admit that England had contributed, diplomatically, to the outbreak of war. Of course it is only conjectural to suggest he knew that a close study of the "intrigues and negotiations" would show that England's conduct had been, at times, less than exemplary.

Another fact that may have contributed to his refusal to write the study was Methuen's decision, conveyed to Bennett on the day before the *Daily News* offer, that *The Price of Love* would be published in book form on October 2. The publishers' panic was abating. The book trade was discovering that the war had created an increased demand for reading material, rather than curtailed it. Methuen reported to Pinker on October 11 that *The Price of Love* was selling extremely well and that it was "currently his best selling title."

It was much to Bennett's surprise that the novel was so well received by critics as well as the public. As early as July he told Pinker that while he was pleased that Methuen liked the story and that others found it good, "no one has yet been able to inspire me with enthusiasm." He did not say what he objected to in the book, but his doubts about it did not slacken. "The best judges I know," he wrote to Elsie Herzog, "are of the opinion that *The Price of Love* is A₁. This rather surprises me, but it relieves me." [43]

In the *Daily News* interview published on July 30, Bennett

[43] *Letters*, I, 207; II, 358.

said that his intent in *The Price of Love* was "to produce an interesting story—a story that would carry the reader on by its events whether he wanted to be carried on or not—in other words, a serial." He added that he also intended that it should be a book and that it should be a good book. He distinguished, however, without defining the difference, a book written for single volume publication from one written for serial publication. "In writing the serial," he insisted, "the author should conceive it primarily as a serial." He then emphasized that *The Price of Love* contained "the sincerest realism and the least crude psychology" that he was capable of producing. He expressed the conviction that a serial did not have to be "merely sensational" or without "psychological effects" to be a success. "*The Price of Love,*" he pointed out, "does not begin with a stab in the dark, or a sanguinary finger-print on the mudguard of a mysterious automobile."

He had not, at that point, had the advantage of Henry James's views on the novel. Pinker asked James what he thought of the story, and James replied,

> I read it with great interest, rather wondering all the time why I *was* so interested in it. [He had made somewhat the same observation about Bennett's work in general in "The New Novel, 1914."] It is an example of Bennett's amazing talent. I do not quite see why he should want to do it, but for what it sets out to be it is excellent. . . . It is wonderfully interesting to see how he can after apparently squeezing his own particular orange so dry, come back to his original inspiration, and find us something fresh.[44]

That something fresh may have been a result of the fact that by the time he came to write *The Price of Love* in 1913, Bennett's preoccupation with the provincial novel was nearly at an end. He probably feared that his audience was losing interest in the Potteries. Perhaps of greater importance, however, was his weariness with the moral and ethical values dominating the Five Towns. He was anxious to explore in the novel new ap-

---

[44] Butler Collection, December 2, 1914. James was later to describe *Hilda Lessways* to Max Beerbohm as "the slow squeezing out of a big, dirty sponge." [David Cecil, *Max* (Boston, 1964), 330.]

proaches to life, to bring his writing up-to-date with the shifting interests and patterns of behavior that were beginning to reshape English society even before the onset of war.

He was also taking his first steps in *The Price of Love* toward a serious examination of marriage and, more broadly, an exploration of relationships between men and women that were not based on a conventional marriage contract. This new concern was to be a major theme in Bennett's novels for the next twelve years. Appropriate as a beginning, *The Price of Love* concerns itself with the problems of two people who force themselves to maintain the conventional marriage contract in spite of severe strain. The careful reader is not convinced that Bennett's hero and heroine would live happily ever after. The novel closes with Rachel bent on martyrdom and Louis prevented by her sacrifice from ever growing up. Their problems are not so much resolved as postponed.

The novel is a very important effort in Bennett's attempt to reshape his fiction and is worth examining in some detail. His choosing to begin with familiar material was probably a mistake, since the finished book proved to be very much like the novels he had writing for the past thirteen years and was clearly not the breakthrough he was seeking. While the Five Towns shaped the personalities of the main characters, they did not give to the action that quality of inevitability which is present in *The Old Wives' Tale* or, to a lesser degree, in *Clayhanger*.

The plot is very simple, even thin. Too much depends on some irritating business about dropped bank notes. The simple story involves a maid and companion to Mrs. Maldon, an elderly widow. Following the old lady's death, Rachel Fleckring, the maid, marries Louis Fores, Mrs. Maldon's nephew. Louis is a polished and dishonest young man whose carelessness with other people's money has lost him two jobs. When the story opens, he is working for Horrocleave's pottery and stealing from the company's petty cash. He also contrives to rob his aunt, but by a misadventure the money is burned in the coal grate. After the marriage, Rachel learns that he is a thief. Instead of leaving him, however, she resigns herself to his weakness and by appearing unexpectedly at Horrocleave's at the moment when Horrocleave has made up his mind to have Louis arrested, averts that disaster. The story ends with Louis still a free man, but the problem of his dishonesty and its threat to the marriage remain unsettled.

Though the plot is thin, characterization in the novel is excellent. Mrs. Maldon; Rachel; Louis; his misogynist cousin Julian; and especially Mrs. Tams, the charwoman, are finely and vividly drawn. Councillor Batchgrew, Julian, and Mrs. Tams are worthy of Dickens. But Bennett holds his characters in check. They are never allowed to run away with the story. He trots them through the pages until they have made their contribution to the plot and then whisks them away. Although they are presented in less detail than are the characters in *The Old Wives' Tale* or Anna and her father in *Anna of the Five Towns*, they are astonishingly convincing. They have sufficient vitality to give the impression of living outside of their roles in the story. One can believe that they have lives of their own, that the novel does not contain them. If any of Bennett's characters refute Virginia Woolf's charge that he never really looked at his characters, never captured them—in fact, never looked at human nature at all—it is those in *The Price of Love*.

Bennett saw Mrs. Tams. Dickensian though she may be, she is not a caricature. He saw her life steadily enough without becoming either maudlin or bitter. His introductory description of her is masterly:

> Mrs. Tams was a woman nearly sixty, stout and—in appearance—untidy and dirty. . . . Human eye so seldom saw her without a coarse brown apron that, apronless, she would have almost seemed (like Eve) unattired. . . . She was thoroughly accustomed to the supreme spectacles of birth and death, and could assist thereat with dignity and skill. She could turn away the wrath of rent collectors, school inspectors, and magistrates. She was an adept in enticing an inebriated husband to leave a public-house. She could feed four people for a day on sevenpence, and rise calmly to her feet after having been knocked down by one stroke of a fist. . . . Her one social fault was a tendency to talk at great length about babies, corpses, and the qualities of rival soaps.[45]

45 Arnold Bennett, *The Price of Love* (London, [1914]), 82.

She never acts out of character. She is the embodiment of the serf mentality, but she is not without dignity. Her single act of independence—she leaves her job with Rachel because she has been forced to interfere between Rachel and Louis in a manner contrary to all her notions of a servant's proper behavior—is in keeping with her idea of her own dignity. But it is an action more quixotic than noble.

Rachel is another convincing character. Her decision to stand by her dishonest husband has the ring of truth to it. She is one of Bennett's "good" but complex characters. She is strong, high spirited, and possessed of common sense. And she is almost panting to resign herself to something unpleasant, something which Bennett called duty. Such a willingness to sacrifice one's self should be inspiriting. Rachel's is not. There is something unpleasant in Rachel's willingness to become a martyr. Perhaps it is the almost religious ecstasy with which she prepared herself for that "everlasting vigil" which she is going to have to maintain in order to protect Louis from himself. With Rachel, as with some in his other novels, it is almost as though Bennett were conducting an experiment to discover the lowest level of self-gratification at which his strongest characters can still endure life.

Several of Bennett's recurring motifs are present in the novel. The contrast between youth and old age is represented in the figures of Rachel and Mrs. Maldon. The harshness and the intransigence of the aged are embodied in Thomas Batchgrew, who broods over the novel like a bearded Mephistopheles reduced in rank and denied the power to be as mischievous as he would like to be. Mrs. Maldon dies of an embolism, providing Bennett with yet another opportunity to paint a death scene. Her dying is spread over some sixty pages, the high point of which is a description of her stertorous breathing, which fills the entire house with its awful noise. Measured against some of the other deaths in Bennett's novels, it is a sketchy treatment, but it is still chilling in its details.

Bennett's success with *The Price of Love* was followed by less fortunate attempts to satisfy Henry James Whigham, editor of the *Metropolitan Magazine*. In April, Whigham had contracted with Pinker for three of Bennett's short stories. By December he had received two of them, "The Muscovy Ducks" and "The Life of Nash Nicklin." "The Muscovy Ducks" had gone to Whigham the previous spring, and he had not been very enthusiastic about it. In December he got "The Life of Nash Nicklin" and liked that story even less than the first.

These two stories, which were to cause Bennett so much trouble in the ensuing months, were set in the Five Towns and were the last strictly Five Towns stories Bennett was to write. "The Muscovy Ducks," however, was more than just another Potteries tale. It contained a great deal of biographical material; and because its characters are such thinly veiled representations of Bennett, Marguerite, and others in the Comarques household, it justifies the search for biographical comment in earlier stories.

The story is set in Chamfreys Hall, a country house at the southern edge of the Five Towns. The house is owned by Stephen and Vera Cheswardine, who figure in several earlier stories. Stephen is now past fifty and Vera is almost forty. They had been young in 1907 when they appeared in *The Grim Smile of the Five Towns*. Now they are mature, prosperous, fixed in their ways. Their house is clearly Comarques. Vera is Marguerite; Stephen is Bennett; Ingestre is Lockyer, Bennett's head gardener; and the Muscovy ducks are a pair from Marguerite's flock of ducks which she kept on the ornamental pond at Comarques.

The story involves an episode in the continuing battle between Vera and Ingestre, who are described as enemies, a term that characterizes the relationship that existed between Marguerite and Lockyer. Marguerite, for example, on one occasion insisted that green beans intended for canning should be picked before they were ripe. It was Lockyer's view that such a practice was wasteful. Bennett came into the disagreement on Lockyer's side, and Marguerite retired to the house to nurse her wrath and her injured pride. In "The Muscovy Ducks" Vera and Ingestre quarrel over precisely the same thing, but Vera wins, a victory that must have galled Marguerite if she ever read the story.

The central episode in the story is the disagreement which

arises between Vera and Ingestre over a pair of Muscovy ducks which Vera intended to present, alive, to a neighbor. Her maid, who carried the message to an undergardener, misunderstood her mistress's instructions and ordered them killed. Vera accused Ingestre of having deliberately killed the birds against her wishes in order to mortify her. Stephen manages to vindicate Ingestre by adroit handling of the maid and at the same time preserve his wife's dignity.

Of particular interest in the story is Bennett's description of Vera. While it cannot be stated flatly that he is describing Marguerite, there is no doubt that he had his wife in mind when he took up his pen. We are introduced to Vera as she stands in front of a cheval glass admiring herself:

> She was an attractive creature, without an idea in her head save for her own advancement. Some serious persons said that she was not attractive; that, indeed, she was insufferable. But other persons still more serious found pleasure in her company. She had no culture, no spirituality, no artistic taste . . . and assuredly her facts were nearly always wrong. She was not charitable. Her sparkling eyes did not sparkle with angelic benevolence. . . . She was a snob. . . . Many said that she was an empty-headed little fool and would be so until her dying day.[46]

Bennett was fully aware of the extent of Marguerite's pride in her culture, spirituality, and artistic nature. She once told Frank Swinnerton, "I am the real artist in the family." She seems to have believed it, and it is difficult not to conclude that Bennett was getting his own back by way of Vera. Marguerite's egotism, folly, and perversity are all in the story. There is even a grim chuckle at Marguerite's expense in the fact that Vera has a "lifelong adorer" in the character of Charlie Woodruff, who stands for Rickards. Stephen Cheswardine, grown middle-aged and fat, is almost certainly a half-humorous self-portrait of Bennett. Stephen's quiet defense of Ingestre and his underplayed victory over his wife allow Bennett to win vicariously a skirmish in his long matrimonial war. The story is, of course,

[46] Arnold Bennett, "The Muscovy Ducks," *Metropolitan Magazine* (July, 1915), 24.

amusing in its own right and does not depend on the reader's being aware of the biographical content for interest. But the biographical content of the story provides a valuable clue to the method Bennett employed in converting personal experience into fiction.

"The Life of Nash Nicklin" is also a Five Towns story. It is a character study of a man who is crossed in love and who in the depth of his bitterness lashes out at a sick man and hastens the man's death. Denry Machin figures in the story, first as a young boy living with his mother in a house next to Nicklin's and later as a young man; but he has no great importance to the story beyond helping to settle Nicklin into the Five Towns context and to fill in a chapter in his own life not given in *The Card*. The story, in certain ways, looks back to an earlier period in Bennett's short story writing and would not be out of place in either *The Grim Smile of the Five Towns* or *Tales of the Five Towns*.

In any case, Whigham refused to be pacified. He demanded to be released from his contract for the third story, making what Bennett called a "veiled threat" to do his best to spoil Bennett's American market if he were not released. In the same letter Whigham said that his "whole experience" of Bennett's work had "been unfortunate."

He referred particularly to two sets of essays, "The Case of the Plain Man" (*The Plain Man and His Wife*) and "The Story Teller's Craft" (*The Author's Craft*), published by the *Metropolitan* in 1912 and 1913 respectively. He originally praised Bennett for the first series, but was less enthusiastic about the second. In his letter to Pinker, however, Whigham forgot his initial enthusiasm for "The Case of the Plain Man" and condemned all the Bennett material which he had published. As a matter of fact, the *Metropolitan* had even issued one section of "Plain Man" as a pamphlet at the end of 1913. But Whigham had frightened himself with the belief that Bennett's popularity was waning and that he could not appeal to the heterogeneous tastes of the audience buying a wide circulation magazine. He had forgotten that in 1913 he wrote to Bennett praising him for his success in having learned to appeal to just such an audience.[47]

Pinker sent Whigham's letter to Bennett, and Bennett responded at once with a long letter to his agent. He was angry, and he took the occasion to unburden himself about Whigham and about editors and publishers in general. "It is of course quite impossible for an author to argue with an editor about the quality of his stuff. If the editor does not like his stuff, there is no more to be said. All that I have to remark is that I think 'The Life of Nash Nicklin' one of my best short stories. . . . I should certainly not dream of holding Mr. Whigham to his contract as regards the third story."

He went on to review the problems he had faced in trying to get some of his best short stories, such as "The Death of Simon Fuge" and "The Matador of the Five Towns," accepted by editors. He had experienced the same trouble, he said, in finding publishers for *Buried Alive* and *The Old Wives' Tale*. If I have made myself a commercially successful writer, he added, "I have done so . . . in the teeth of practically all the editors and publishers in America and in England." [48]

However ready Bennett was to release Whigham from his contract for a third story, he was not going to release him from his agreement to buy a serial. The *Metropolitan* had paid $15,000 for it, and Whigham was now complaining that he had been cheated. The price, he said, was exhorbitant. Bennett disagreed. Pinker had already sold two serials to Munsey for $17,500 each, and Bennett said that he could immediately sell the *Metropolitan* serial for $16,600.[49] The serial in question was unwritten, and at the time of the exchange of letters between Bennett and Pinker a synopsis had not been composed, nor was Bennett yet working on one.

In November, Bennett's mother died. He first referred to her illness on the 20th: "On Wednesday afternoon I went to Burslem to see Mater, reported to be past hope." She had, apparently,

[47] *Letters*, I, 219–22.
[48] *Ibid.*, 219–20.
[49] *Ibid.*, 223*n*.

been ill for some time. She died on November 25 of arteriosclerosis and congestion of the lungs. Bennett said that she "suffered such constant and acute physical pain that her death was a deliverance. . . ."[50] He told Naomi Alcock (she and her husband were old friends) that his mother's suffering was so great that in her letters to him she frequently "expressed a wish" to be freed from it by death.

She did not have an easy death. "Her condition," Bennett said, "was very distressing." He was moved to ask if life "couldn't always end more easily." He had helped to nurse his father through a long, degenerative, and ultimately fatal illness. As bad as his mother's death was, though, it was far less protracted than his father's had been. It would be easy to suggest that his preoccupation with deathbed scenes is traceable to his experience with his father's death and later reinforced by his mother's were it not for the fact that in his first novel *A Man from the North* (1898) there is such a scene; in it Richard Larch, sitting at the bedside of the dying Aked, reflects that "Life was sublimer, more terrible, than he had thought. . . . Art was a very little thing."[51] Perhaps the challenge of death was the supreme test of Bennett's art. Perhaps he tried to capture it wholly and, by so doing, render it comprehensible. Perhaps he also hoped to find some meaning in death and thereby discover meaning in life.

Bennett recorded in his journal a remarkably detailed description of his mother's sickroom: "Amid tossed bedclothes you could see numbers on the corners of blankets. On medicine table siphon, saucer, spoon, large soap-dish, brass flower bowl (empty). The gas (very bad burner) screened by a contraption of Family Bible, some wooden thing, and a newspaper. . . . Gas stove burning. Temperature barely 60 degrees. Damp chill penetrating my legs. . . ."

He made notes on the behavior of those who had gathered around the dying woman. The nurse, dressed in black, was "decent, but not over sympathetic." There were "little frictions and

---

[50] *Ibid.,* II, 361.
[51] Arnold Bennett, *A Man From the North* (New York, 1898), 145.

jealousies" among his sisters and sister-in-law. The servants "were obviously having a fine time." His sister Florence remarked with some acerbity that "they ate what they liked." Florence also told Lizzie, one of the servants, that she would give her a sixpence if Mrs. Bennett were dead in the morning, doubting that the patient was as weak as was being assumed. It makes odd reading to find in the same entry a sudden shift to Frank Maddox, someone quite outside the family, who, Bennett said was "in grip" of a correspondence swindle to teach drawing through the mail. He also recorded having gone into Burslem, where he met another acquaintance who told him that the life of a horse at the front was five days.[52]

Bennett and Marguerite went "down" to Burslem for his mother's funeral, which he reported in some detail in the journal. "Funeral. Too soon. . . . Coffin in center on two chairs. Covered with flowers. Bad reading and stumbling of parson. Clichés and halting prayers. . . . Sham brass handles on coffin. Horrible lettering." At the cemetery he took note of "John Ford's vault next to Longson, with records of his young wives ("The flower fadeth," etc.)." He thought a fine story could be made out of John Ford's vault.

Bennett's treatment of his mother's death and of her burial is so cool that it borders on indifference. Was he untouched by the events? It does not seem likely. That he was relieved that she was at an end of her suffering is understandable. That he wrote not a single word of affectionate regard for her—beyond wishing she could have had an easier death—is less easy to understand. Reginald Pound, one of Bennett's biographers, called his extensive note taking "a formula for checking imaginative indulgence," which might be interpreted to mean either a way of holding the emotions in check or a device for purging sentimental claptrap.

It must also be remembered that Bennett intended his journal to be published, and in *Mental Efficiency* (1911) he defined the role of a journal as giving "the large spectacle of life." In a letter to Pinker in January of 1914 he wrote, "My Journal is now in its 18th volume, and almost the whole of it is yet in

[52] Unpublished Journal, November 20, 1914.

manuscript. Whenever I look at it, it seems to be rather interesting. . . . Some day sooner or later it ought to be a valuable source of profit." [53] He had originally modelled his own journal on those of the Goncourt brothers. He may have felt that his account of his mother's death should include his objective impressions, not his personal feelings. In any case, most of the funeral turns up in *These Twain*, even to the detail of the joke, "The flower fadeth." Bennett was always reluctant to bare his heart to public view. But in the exercise of such total restraint there is the disturbing suggestion of powerful feelings repressed so totally as to be unacknowledged.

A few weeks after the funeral, Bennett and Marguerite entertained at Comarques two officers of the North Devon Hussars. The men told Bennett that a young subaltern of engineers named Grant Michaelis was living in town alone and feeling extremely lonely. Bennett said that he set out at once with the two officers to find the lieutenant. Michaelis was found and invited to dinner on Sunday. The following Tuesday he moved to Comarques on a permanent basis. Bennett seemed to like Michaelis, finding him "very intelligent and with a sense of humor." [54]

Marguerite gave quite a different account of how the young man came to stay with them. According to Marguerite, it was General Fitzgerald, Head of Staff at Frinton-on-Sea, and his aide-de-camp Lieutenant Trotter, who came to tea that Saturday and introduced the subject of the lonely lieutenant. Marguerite said that it was she who suggested that Michaelis come to Comarques, having first gotten a silent nod of consent from her husband.

When the visitors were gone, she said to Bennett, "I am so happy, Arnold; you do not mind that officer coming?" He said that he did not and that "it will give you something to do!" They both agreed that he was a pleasant companion. He stayed eight months at Comarques, was sent to France, and was killed shortly thereafter. He was eighteen years old. [55]

Bennett's strong affection for Michaelis is apparent in "Confi-

---

[53] *Letters*, I, 204.
[54] *Journal*, 538.
[55] M. Bennett, *My Arnold Bennett*, 122.

dence," a *Daily News* article published on December 31, 1941. "I reckon that I came close to a realization of war when I made the acquaintance of a certain youth from Australia," he wrote. "He was a subaltern of engineers in a Territorial Field Company. . . ." Bennett praised the young officer's sense of responsibility, his energy, and his courage. "His dream was to be pontooning at the front in the middle of winter," Bennett recalled. "And when he got the chance of pontooning on an English river, his face showed that the gates of heaven were opening." The note of personal wistfulness in the description shows that Bennett was aware of his own physical liabilities. In spite of Michaelis's worrying existence, Bennett said, "nothing whatever prevented him from sleeping soundly all night and every night." Bennett would have, indeed, seen the gates of heaven opening had he been able to sleep half as well.

Michaelis's arrival was an indication of the degree to which Bennett's private life was being invaded. He was already devoting at least a day and a half a week to war work and was contributing to the Belgian Relief Fund at the rate of fifty pounds a week. Other officers came to stay at Comarques, and their presence was distracting. Marguerite was delighted to have them and devoted a considerable amount of time to their entertainment. She undoubtedly found their attentions flattering and a welcome relief from being ignored or treated with cool civility, which had become Bennett's manner.

The military intruded on his life in other ways. In September he complained of a "constant flow of one or two military officers in and through this house. . . ." They were coming to see two young women, a Miss Hatchett and Mimi Godebski, wife of the artist Cepa Godebski, who were guests of the Bennetts. In the same entry he complained that the women's "latest move" was "a night excursion in car to see searchlights playing on the sea off Frinton." He was also meeting socially a succession of officers and their wives, with whom, a few months earlier, he would have had nothing in common and who could have been of little interest to him. Miss Nerney became so occupied with hospital work that her work for Bennett came "to a standstill." "I gave notice," he said, "that it [her hospital schedule] would have to be altered."

In mid-November, Major General H. N. C. Heath, Commander of the South Midland Division, asked Bennett to be "military representative" on the Thorpe Division Emergency Committee. Bennett said that he would take the post but that he was "regularly criticizing the War Office in the press, and might continue to do so." He was writing against conscription. Heath invited him to a meeting at the nearby Crown Hotel. At the meeting he told Bennett that his journalism need not affect his appointment. He then asked if Bennett were in favor of civilians sniping at enemy soldiers. Bennett said emphatically that he was not, a view which coincided with the General's. H. G. Wells had written a letter to the *Times* advocating civilian attacks on soldiers. Heath had read it and been upset with Wells as a consequence, but he was pleased with Bennett's attitude, and Bennett's appointment was confirmed.

The purpose of the Emergency Committee was to act as an organizational center for evacuating civilians in the event of a German invasion. There was widespread fear along the Essex coast that the Germans were planning an invasion. Bennett claimed not to believe that it was a genuine danger, and he was both amused and irritated by the invasion rumors which ran up and down the country. Connected with the scare were repeated rumors of spy activity. Marguerite became very spy conscious.[56] Bennett recorded several instances of individuals being suspected of spying, but all were found to be quite innocent. On one occasion a police inspector arrived at Comarques to make inquiries about Read, the chauffeur, whom someone had turned in as a spy. On December 1, he complained to Pinker that "special local work in connection with preparations for the raid is now occupying so much of my time that my own work is being seriously interfered with. The notion of a raid is to me entirely absurd. Nevertheless, one cannot help feeling that the preparations ought to be done." [57]

56 *Ibid.*
57 Pound, *Arnold Bennett*, 253.

It was not always easy, however, for Bennett to keep his balance. Officers whom he knew and trusted continued, even through December, to bring him fresh reports of invasion threats. There were constant false reports of troop movements. One such report had it that 160,000 Russian troops were to be landed in Britain and then shipped on to France, where, some feared, they would immediately join the Germans and sack Paris. "This rumor I think took the cake," Bennett wrote. He had, apparently, not heard the ultimate refinement on that story which was that the troops had disembarked at a Scottish port, and that they had come ashore with snow still on their boots.

He seems to have been less suspicious of a story printed on December 15 in the *Daily Telegraph* describing German "trains of the dead." These trains, according to the article, carried the German dead back from the front "tied together like bunches of asparagus, and stacked upright on their feet." These trains had, supposedly, been seen passing through Brussels, apparently carrying their grisly cargos back to Germany to be burned in blast furnaces. Bennett copied out the report in the journal but made no comment on it.

On December 30 he wrote that he had spent the previous day trying to write his *Daily News* article and managed to finish it after being interrupted twice by visitors. On Sunday and on Tuesday of the same week he managed to write two thousand words of his novel; and on Christmas Day he interrupted the holiday festivities by driving through the surrounding parishes delivering the code word that, if issued, would mean that the Germans had invaded. There was no particular reason Bennett had to deliver the message rather than someone else, but he probably got considerable pleasure being driven from village to village, carrying the code word to his committee captains. "Official" action had a great appeal for him. As an added benefit of being away from Comarques on that particular afternoon, he did not have to sit through one of Marguerite's boring recitals.

Since the outbreak of the war, despite the output of articles and his increased vigor, he had begun to turn inward on Comarques, Thorpe-le-Soken, and local issues in a dangerous way. Cut off from the stimulation that association with writers and artists gave him, he was running the risk of losing himself in a round of petty, semi-official activities. And although his journal entries and his correspondence between August and January give the impression of a man busy and content, a closer look reveals worn places in that garment of contentment. He did not always find his life as interesting as he had told Mrs. Herzog and Gide that he did. For example, he was forcing himself to attend dozens of charity concerts in the Frinton area, put on for one sort of war relief or another. Following one of the concerts, which had been slightly more dreadful than the others, he burst out in desperation, "The ordeal is too much." One can believe that he meant it.

Except for *These Twain* he was writing no fiction, and *These Twain* was dragging painfully. After August his journal became increasingly concerned with issues and events unlikely to provide him with story material. He was spending considerable time with men like General Heath, who had developed a fixation about civilians shooting soldiers and even managed to infect Bennett with his mania. In its opening months the war had stimulated Bennett's journalism, but there was, as yet, no corresponding flourishing of his fiction.

The year ended with financial problems pressing in on him. Pinker was sending monthly statements to Bennett, but these statements often arrived as late as the second week of the month. By the first of each month, Bennett was in need of cash, and delays in receiving it made him impatient. On December 15 he acknowledged receiving the November statement—he was scrupulous in making such acknowledgments—and wrote, "I shall probably require all this money early in the New Year for purposes of income tax." Two days later he wrote again: "I have now learned the worst as to my income tax and super-tax due on 1st January. The total is just one thousand pounds. Next year it will be more than two thousand pounds." Then, two days later: "Can you send me the latest sales of *The Price of Love?*

. . . I should like a December statement of accounts on the 1st of January if it is not inconvenient." [58]

Bennett closed his journal for 1914 without any reference to his year's work. He had not done so in 1911 either, but that year he was just returned from his American visit and made no entry at all after December 8. It is unusual for him not to make a summary of the work done in any year, sometimes even to the number of words written and the money earned down to the exact penny. But in looking back over 1914, he could have seen little to cheer him, especially if he compared the year with the two preceding it. One novel, *The Price of Love*, published; fewer than half a dozen short stories sold; one book on writing, *The Author's Craft*, published; no plays produced and only one new one written. It was his journalism that was keeping the pot boiling, but it was not enhancing his reputation as a novelist. As a curiously appropriate close to the journal, he chose to describe a local maltster's plan for closing the highway and the railway to Harwick in the event of an invasion. It was the brewer's intention to set fire to his brewery (having first assured himself that the government would reimburse him for his loss) and by that action put both the road and the railway out of commission. Bennett thought it would work. The account is dull in the extreme, and as a concluding comment on his year, it is, to borrow one of Bennett's favorite words, "wistful."

[58] Ogden Collection, December 1, 15, 17, 19, 1914.

# III

# EACH FOR HIMSELF

Pauline Smith, who came to Comarques in the spring of 1915, remembered Bennett, in the midst of alarms and confusions, remaining "his ordinary, everyday, well-balanced self." She said that he was supported by his "blunt Five Towns grit and sincerity" and that he "doggedly" pursued his own course through the tremendous pressure of events swirling around him—the war, trouble with Marguerite, disruption of the orderly managing of his house, financial pressures, mounting demands of committee work, and the increasingly heavy burden of journalism. She found him interested in life, although somewhat detached from the people and the events he so carefully observed. And it was her conviction that he was, as he had always been, deeply sympathetic to the problems of others.[1] His niece Mary Kennerley and his friend Olive Glendinning remember him as being cheerful and accepting events with philosophic calm.

Frank Swinnerton, who came to Comarques at about the same time as Pauline Smith, saw Bennett in quite another way. Swinnerton came to Essex to continue a friendship which had begun in the previous summer. He was recovering from a long and severe illness, during which the H. G. Wellses, and then the Bennetts, were keeping a careful watch over him. Within a short time Bennett was saying of Swinnerton, "He and I are awfully intimate."[2] Swinnerton and Bennett understood each other and were in many ways temperamentally alike. "We laughed at the same jokes, some of which we made ourselves; and at the same people; and we took a very professional view of the art of letters, which we nevertheless practiced in all innocence." From the outset the relationship was a warm and sympathetic one and must have been a source of satisfaction to Bennett, whose personal

---

[1] Pauline Smith, *A.B.* (London, 1933), 42–43.
[2] Frank Swinnerton, *Swinnerton: An Autobiography* (New York, 1936), 146.

relationships were, at this time, growing more and more formal and superficial. There was little opportunity for him to select his company, thrown as he was among the host of people brought his way by the war.

The picture which Swinnerton gives of Bennett differs sharply from Pauline Smith's and that of Mary Kennerley and Olive Glendinning. Instead of a man in command of himself and his affairs, a man confident in his powers and happily engaged in the work he loved, Swinnerton has portrayed a lonely, melancholy Bennett:

> He was at that time a discontented man. He had enjoyed and was enjoying great success; but he was living sixty-five miles from London (it seemed as if it must be two hundred), which did not suit him; and he was bored. To see him trudging along a country lane, alone, in order, he said, to "get some ideas for his work . . . was to receive a shock; and to hear him say, at meeting: "We-ell, Mr. Swin' . . . I am delighted to see you. I have been . . . extremely *gloomy*," was to feel that something was seriously wrong.[3]

What was wrong, in Swinnerton's view, were Bennett's recurrent attacks of neuralgia, his insomnia, the weight of assumed responsibilities, much overwork, and "a profound disillusion with what he might have called the power of decency in human affairs." All of these stresses were concealed, at least from the casual observer, by a carefully maintained facade of imperturbability—even Pauline Smith missed or else chose not to record their presence. Marguerite said nothing of them. Attempting to explain why Bennett was so dangerously close to collapse, Swinnerton said that Bennett's strength was gradually being destroyed, that his constitution was unequal to the task of supporting such massive labors as were being demanded of it.

What was more burdensome, however, was the strain of supporting a marriage that was gradually becoming intolerable. And it was Bennett's relationship with his wife more than the strain created by the war that was wracking him. One of the symptoms of their incompatibility was the incessant quarreling over do-

---

[3] *Ibid.*, 147.

mestic arrangements. It was much fought-over ground. As early
as 1907, only two years after the marriage, Bennett wrote to his
sister Tertia from Les Sablons, where Bennett and Marguerite
were staying: "The only worm gnawing at the root of my mind
is that this business of being married cannot possibly last as it is.
It can last perfectly well on my footing; but it can't last on *her*
footing. However, it is no use trying to explain facts about
human nature which that body is not rife for receiving." [4]

Seven years later Bennett and Marguerite were still not "rife"
to receive "facts" about one another—or, perhaps more accurately stated, neither was prepared to compromise regardless of
"facts" concerning the other. Marguerite had ideas about how
the house should be run, but Bennett invariably overruled her.
They could not even agree upon the time to have a child, although they may have been incapable of having one in any case.
Such seems to have been Marguerite's view of their childless
state. When a daughter was born to Bennett and Dorothy
Cheston Bennett years later, Marguerite burst out, "In his heart
Arnold knows it is not his child." Virginia was, in fact, very
obviously his child.

The sketch which Swinnerton gives of Bennett's daily routine
is a frightening one. Up early every day, he spent the mornings
writing. Then in the afternoons he worked for an hour before
tea and after that pause returned to his desk until eight or nine
o'clock in the evening. In the intervals between journalism, novel
writing, and correspondence, he read almost without pause.
Much of this reading was done late at night when he could not
sleep. Swinnerton said that one gained the impression of "incessant" activity, "appalling" activity. At the same time Bennett
remained methodical. He ordered his life ruthlessly perhaps, yet
in such a way as to get the maximum returns for the energy
expended. Swinnerton denied that Bennett insisted on method
because he cared "grossly and desirously for money," but because order, routine, and punctuality were essential to him.[5]

[4] From a letter in the possession of Bennett's niece, Mary Kennerly.
[5] One way of determining which of Bennett's characters are, from the
author's point of view, sympathetic is to ask whether or not they are punctual.
Bennett nearly always tells, and in telling he judges with a Jehovah-like finality.

Undoubtedly Swinnerton is right as far as he goes, but he has not wholly accounted for the origins of Bennett's depression. At this time Bennett had two principal sources of anxiety. One was his wife and the other his lack of money. It is impossible to say to what degree, if at all, Marguerite was responsible for the money problem, but she was clearly a major cause of his dissatisfaction with his life. Both Pauline Smith and Frank Swinnerton noted the strain between husband and wife. Pauline Smith, however, minimized its significance and Swinnerton passed rapidly over it. He noted in a rather puzzled way that Bennett and Marguerite "had many matters to debate" and that they "were engaged in an endless argument by correspondence." [6]

The very fact that they found it necessary to discuss their differences by letter is in itself a measure of their troubles. According to Swinnerton, they wrote to one another because Bennett was incapable of arguing with Marguerite without having his stammer render him helpless. Faced with a quarrel, Bennett would tell Marguerite to write down her grievances. He would then write his reply. On one occasion Marguerite forced a drawer in her husband's desk and discovered a number of her letters unopened. She was, of course, furious to learn that Bennett had been simply ignoring her side of the arguments. Her original purpose in forcing the drawer was to find love letters which she suspected him of receiving. There were none.

The strain between Bennett and Marguerite was not new. Marguerite's feeling of neglect and lack of sympathetic understanding were described by Pauline Smith as early as 1909 when she visited the Bennetts at Fontainebleau and later when she travelled with them to Florence.[7] The war, however, increased the tension. Marguerite threw herself into the task of arranging entertainment for the officers in the surrounding camps, filling Comarques with guests for parties of various kinds. In addition to the added strain of entertaining on such a large scale, she was also struggling to master her own nerves. Pauline Smith hinted

---

[6] Swinnerton, *An Autobiography*, 148.
[7] Smith, *A. B.*, 28–29.

that Marguerite was, at this period, having trouble maintaining her sense of proportion.

Always of an explosive and impetuous disposition, she caught hold of every war rumor, especially those concerning spies, and allowed her imagination to run away with her. She peopled Thorpe-le-Soken with German agents and felt herself in danger. Her nervous excitement welled over in the entertainment which she arranged at Comarques for the local officers. The programs were, at times, extremely painful for the audience to endure, especially when Marguerite rose to recite from the works of Baudelaire or Verlaine. She began these performances by repeating three times, with a dramatic pause between the utterances, the word *silence*, accompanied by a slow lifting of her extended right arm. The effect was dreadful in the extreme; and although Bennett encouraged her in her recitations, on one occasion when she had gone on an unusually long time, he leaned over to Frank Swinnerton, who was seated beside him, and whispered, "If that damned woman doesn't stop soon, we shall be late for dinner." Such outbursts were rare. He almost never made a spoken criticism of Marguerite.

A full understanding of their quarrels will not be possible until certain letters and papers, which are not now available for study, are made public. But Dudley Barker has made reference to the content of one such letter written by Bennett to his wife, in which he criticized her at length for moving the piano a few inches without asking his approval.[8] And Miss Mary Kennerley, who has read the letters, described them as dealing principally with disagreements over domestic arrangements and other trivial matters. In all likelihood their quarrels were safe ground for differences more profound than either was prepared to face. One is reminded of Edwin Clayhanger's quarrel with Hilda over the arrangement of furniture for their "musical evening" and the anger with which Edwin returned the room to its original arrangement after finding that Hilda had altered it against his wishes.

[8] Barker, *Arnold Bennett*, 188.

It is generally held that *These Twain* is the principal document in Bennett's fiction dealing with his marriage. But there are other pieces of his writing which are, to a degree, at least, autobiographical. In *The Glimpse* (1909) the marital difficulties which Loring and Inez experience are the same as those that Bennett felt in his own marriage. As Barker has pointed out, it is significant that Bennett frequently employed a persona named Loring in place of the first person (there are several short stories, particularly "The Matador of the Five Towns" and "The Death of Simon Fuge," in which Loring appears as narrator) and that Inez is obviously drawn as a portrait of Marguerite.[9] Bennett himself acknowledged a degree of autobiography in *The Glimpse*, and there is an element of autobiography in "The Death of Simon Fuge."

In *The Lion's Share* marriage and domesticity, English style, are sharply satirized. The detective has a Burslem kind of marriage, and Bennett's judgment of it is given to the detective to pronounce: "When a wife is strongly convinced that her sphere is the home . . . you're tempted at times to let her have the sphere all to herself. That's the universal experience of married men. . . ." The absurd marriage of Lady and Lord Southminster is also exposed to ridicule. "So that's love!" Audrey says at one point of the couple's behavior. "No," Miss Ingate replies, "That's marriage. And don't you forget it."[10] *The Price of Love* also makes a comment on marriage, although less explicitly than do *These Twain* and *The Lion's Share*, both of which reveal the nature of Bennett's marital dilemma.

Although Bennett was living extremely well and spending a great deal of money without apparent regard for economy, he was existing at the extreme outer edge of his income. Despite Marguerite's assertion that money was not a problem—and she may have believed that such was the case, since Bennett was not likely to have taken her into his confidence—he must have been keenly aware of his position. He had been unable to pay back a penny of the almost £1,000 borrowed from Pinker in the pre-

[9] *Ibid.,* 154.
[10] Arnold Bennett, *The Lion's Share* (London, 1916), 209, 361.

ceding September. In addition to his regular expenses, he learned in early May from his income tax advisor that he owed the government nearly £2,500 in back taxes.[11] The blow was softened, however, by the fact that in the same week his earnings for a seven-day period came to just the amount of his debt.

He was no longer maintaining the *Velsa*, but his other costs had risen. Expenses for entertaining were up as were those for travel to and from London and the everyday maintainance of Comarques. The war had pushed up the price of most things, but it had depressed real estate values along the east coast. The selling price of Comarques had declined sharply, making the house a financial liability in addition to the emotional liability it had long been. Whatever he earned in addition to the £5,000 accounted for in the records covering the period January 1 to June 30, 1915, it was certainly less than the £4,000 necessary to bring his income for the period up to the £9,000 which he had earned in the first six months of 1913.

In this atmosphere of tension and worry, intensified by the war and its uncertainties, Bennett completed *These Twain*. On Saturday, the 6th of March, he wrote in his journal, "I finished *These Twain* yesterday. Doran came for the weekend." It would be difficult to say which event gave him the greater satisfaction. One thing is certain. He never had any difficulty controlling his enthusiasm for "Clayhanger III." In fact the entire history of the novel from its inception to its publication is puzzling. "Clayhanger III" was the name which Bennett first attached to the story, visualizing it as the third volume of the Clayhanger trilogy.[12] By August, 1913, however, Bennett decided that he wanted to "change to another sort of novel" and to write something more autobiographical than he had as yet done.

The following May he began actual composition and by June 7 had written the first chapter, which he thought to be "fairly good." At the end of June he recorded that he had completed 20,000 words of the novel and that it seemed "all right." He

[11] Unpublished Journal, May 15, 1915.
[12] *Journal*, 476.

added that it had been written with ease. By the time of publication in November of 1915, Bennett had gone so far beyond his original idea of completing the trilogy that he refused to put any front matter into the book saying that the volume completed the Clayhanger series. The reason that he gave Pinker for declining to do so was that readers might imagine the novel was not "complete in itself." He did later write a preface to the serialization done by Munsey.

Between June, 1914, and March of the following year, when he completed the novel, Bennett made only four written references to the book. On October 30 he noted that he had finished the second part of *These Twain*. In November he wrote to Elsie Herzog, "I can't spoil the simplicity of my novel by letting Edwin and Hilda procreate. They have young George and he's quite enough for my purposes." [13] On Sunday, December 6, he recorded in his journal that he was "now fairly *in* the last part of the third *Clayhanger*." And in one of his last entries for the month, Bennett said that in two days he had written four thousand words of the novel. But during the last six months of the novel's composition, Bennett said nothing of how he thought it was progressing or of his satisfaction with it.

Dudley Barker has said that with *These Twain* Bennett "turned abruptly aside from his childhood, his native towns, his marriage and any further autobiography. . . ." [14] Available evidence supports the view that Bennett did, indeed, turn away from the Five Towns. But the turning away was not particularly abrupt. He had been in need of a new source of inspiration for some time, at least since the end of 1913. That Five Towns orange, to which Henry James was so fond of referring, was very nearly squeezed dry; and *The Price of Love* contained the last of the juice. *These Twain* is, of course, set in the Five Towns; but it is set there because that is where Edwin and Hilda must live if they are to be the kind of people who will have the kind of marriage Bennett is interested in describing. In addition, the Five Towns had long provided Bennett with the basic meta-

[13] *Letters*, II, 358.
[14] Barker, *Arnold Bennett*, 191.

phor for exploring the mystery of life. In *These Twain* he turned once more to that familiar material.

By 1915 Bennett was probably bored with the Towns. He was also bored with the people in them and with their way of looking at life. And he had, with the passage of years, grown away from them. The death of Auntie Hamps in *These Twain* is, probably, fully as significant in marking the end of an era as the death of Mr. Baines in *The Old Wives' Tale*. Her death closes a period in Bennett's life. Its ending corresponds in a rather dramatic way with the closing of a period in the national life brought about by the outbreak of war. The fact that Bennett described her funeral in terms very close to those with which he recorded his mother's burial suggests that he may have wished to impart to her death a significance greater than that which the fictional circumstances of her death warranted.

There is in the entire novel something of that overburdening which Eliot found in *Hamlet*. Bennett gave to events and to the emotional states of his characters, particularly Edwin and Hilda, an intensity of implied meaning which was in excess of the intensity suggested by the fictional circumstances. He seems to have wished desperately to say something about his personal experience with marriage that he could not express, either because of reticence or because Hilda and Edwin were an inadequate metaphor.

To a greater degree than in his earlier writing, Bennett allowed himself in *These Twain* the freedom of being critical of his relatives. It has been suggested that his mother's death gave him that freedom. It is also possible that his mother's death cut him free from the last vestiges of sentimental attachment to the Towns. And with the severing of that emotional tie came the release necessary for him to be able to express directly his hostility toward the people of the Five Towns. The hostility had been there in a latent form from at least as early as the writing of "The Death of Simon Fuge" in 1907; but it was masked by a narrator who was at least partially sympathetic toward the Potteries, as Loring is in "Simon Fuge" and "The Matador of the Five Towns."

The war, his mother's death, and his inability to make his marriage function smoothly are linked to his rejection of the Towns, although his drift away from them certainly began before 1914. In a *Daily News* interview for July 30, 1914, Bennett announced that *These Twain* would be the last novel he would ever write about the Five Towns.[15] "I am going to write about London," he said, with a touch of combativeness. "London is a far better subject than the Five Towns. And I'm also going to write about the Continent—or rather about the English on the Continent. There's a rich subject for irony." He was tired of the Potteries, and he was tired of their values. How intense this reaction was will become clear a little later.

His attempt in *These Twain* to picture his marriage, and perhaps solve its riddle in the process of writing about it, is the most severe test to which he ever submitted the Five Towns material. Of course, it failed. He did not succeed in writing a successful novel about marriage, and he did not find in the material a solution to his own problems. He had exhausted the material both artistically and emotionally. It is possible to conclude that he no longer found a vital relationship between life as he now saw it and the fictional life of the Five Towns as he had been depicting that.

Connected with Bennett's loss of interest in the Five Towns is the change in the type of woman he wrote into his novels after *These Twain*. Rachel Fleckring in *The Price of Love* is the last strictly Five Towns woman to be a heroine in his novels. Hilda Clayhanger stands outside that group. Hilda is the mother of an illegitimate child; she has lived away from the Towns; and she is not willing to submit to the clannish ways of the Clayhanger tribe. Rachel, however, is directly in the tradition of Constance Baines. But both Hilda and Rachel share the view that marriage is a struggle in which the stronger wins, and both have a middle-class respectability which determines their social behavior. Hilda's child, it must be remembered, was the product of a biga-

[15] In the same issue the *Daily News* offered a prize of £25 "together with other valuable prizes" for the best postcard criticism of *The Price of Love*, which the paper began serializing the following Tuesday.

mous marriage, not of a liaison. Hilda had supposed her marriage to be a legal one.

With *The Lion's Share*, which Bennett started writing in the spring of 1915, he began to deal with women who were entirely different in character from Rachel Fleckring. He also shifted the setting out of the provinces to London and Paris. For the first time in his fiction he dealt with modern Paris. He also determined that the book would deal with more "sentiment, love, and advanced civilization" than he had put into *The Card* and *The Regent*.[16] But despite his insistence that the book was to be light and humorous in character, Bennett allowed a substantial amount of personal comment to find its way into the writing. In his descriptions of Frinton and of Mr. and Mrs. Spatt, he is savagely satirical. He became a member of the Frinton Tennis Club in May of 1915, but that did not prevent his making fun of the Club in the chapter on Frinton. His ridicule of Mr. and Mrs. Spatt is directed against their provincialism and their stuffiness and their ignorance, characteristics which he had, in the past, excused in his Five Towns people. But in *The Lion's Share* he was clearly done with finding excuses for provincialism.

The novel is set in the period immediately before the war, but a reference to the approaching catastrophe occurs at the end of Chapter XLIV. Mr. Ziegler, a German with a singularly repulsive character, informs Audrey that within a year the German army will be in Paris and the work of imposing German culture on Europe will have begun. Only Miss Ingate is sufficiently interested in the remark to ask Mr. Ziegler what he means by it, and he repeats that everyone in Germany knows that war is coming and that Germany will win. The rest of the group simply ignores Mr. Ziegler's remark. Bennett was giving fictional life to what had been not only his but a general unwillingness to see that war was on its way. Of course he allows Mr. Ziegler to represent the nastiness of Germans; but considering that the book was written in war time, Mr. Ziegler might well have been drawn with more malice than Bennett usually employed.

The two leading women in the novel, Audrey Moze and

[16] *Letters*, I, 223.

Madame Piriac, are drawn in strong contrast to Bennett's earlier fictional heroines. Both of these women are unconventional. Audrey poses as a widow in order to gain the freedom necessary to see life and indulges her fancy for excitement by toying with the suffragist movement. Madame Piriac, who is the older and more sophisticated of the two, is married and happy in her marriage; but her marriage does not confine her. She and her husband have a very great deal of individual freedom. Neither attempts to circumscribe the other's actions or invade the other's privacy. And although Audrey eventually marries Musa, she does not sink into domesticity as do Rachel Fleckring and Constance Baines. She retains her individuality.

Madame Piriac and Audrey are drawn with a vivid, lively interest. Bennett enters the story himself disguised as Mr. Gilman, the millionaire yacht owner troubled by seasickness and a recalcitrant liver. Mr. Gilman is on the verge of proposing to Audrey when she runs off in search of Musa. But he finds solace in Miss Thompson and is not at all a ridiculous figure. He is attracted to the young suffragists by their youth, their beauty, their dash, and their unconventionality. They in turn find him attractive, and he goes out of the story bearing away one of the young ladies and complaining about his liver. It is all done in the greatest spirit of good fun, but there is a certain residual seriousness. Audrey and her friends have a genuine appeal for Bennett.

Whatever attraction the strong and domestic women of the Five Towns once had for him, by 1915 it had been dissipated. "Advanced civilization" and its principal creation, the emancipated woman, were his new interests. There is no doubt that he was responding to commercial opportunities in writing the novel. The book is, in one sense, escape reading, despite Bennett's insistence that it concerned itself with a serious social problem. The reading public wished to be diverted from the pressures of the war, and *The Lion's Share* provided that kind of distraction and may be one of the first novels to treat the Edwardian period with nostalgia. Bennett was also escaping himself. He was escaping from the stresses of his own marriage by projecting himself into an entirely different kind of marriage and was having fun with yachts, foreign ports, beautiful women, and unlimited wealth.

Another important shift in Bennett's writing which occurs after his completion of *These Twain* is the sympathetic treatment he gives to those of his characters, particularly the young men, who are sensualists and who act outside of the code of morality operating in Burslem. In *The Old Wives' Tale*, by way of contrast, Gerald Scales persuades Sophia Baines to run away with him first to London and then to Paris. He is forced to marry Sophia in order to possess her, but the marriage proves to be a disaster for both of them. Scales is a cad and becomes a wastrel. And in keeping with the Five Towns ideal of justice, he comes to a bad end; that is, he dies penniless. In his degradation he is punished for his treatment of Sophia and for mishandling his inheritance—the sins in Burslem being about equal, one would judge.

In *The Price of Love*, however, Louis Fores, who is a thief as well as a sensualist, is allowed to escape the consequences of his acts. He goes out of the novel on his wife's arm, and the reader has the feeling that he may go jauntily through the rest of his life coolly avoiding punishment. Ironically, it is his cousin Julian, the man of conscience and of "common sense," who suffers. Frank Swinnerton has written that the war disillusioned Bennett, and Bennett's treatment of Louis Fores bears out the conviction. Louis Fores's escape from justice amounts to a moral revolution in Bennett's serious writing. The revolution begins with *The Price of Love* and is completed in *The Lion's Share*. *These Twain*, which comes between the two novels, tests the doctrine of respectability and finds it wanting. Under its aegis, for example, George Cannon is denied the knowledge that he has a son. Edwin and Hilda live together under such a condition of strain that their continued relationship is, perhaps, more unnatural than Hilda's bigamous marriage to George.

Bennett struggled to find a solution to Edwin's problems within the limits of respectable behavior, as Edwin understands that term and as the Five Towns understood it. But there is no solution; there can be none. Edwin can compromise, resign himself to the fact of injustice, or with unconvincing bravado insist that he will not be beaten by his marriage. But he is beaten. He is beaten because marriage between Hilda and himself is unceasing war. As long as they see their marriage as a contest, they must go on living in armed camps with scouts and skirmishers maintaining an everlasting vigil. Their respectability, their renunciations, their good intentions are nothing in the face of their marriage, a marriage, one cannot help feeling, that has been dictated by their social rank and is only preserved by dread of a scandal.

It has been suggested that *These Twain* ends with Bennett determined to resolve the problems of his marriage. What is more likely is that in *These Twain* he admits its failure. "I am a happy woman," Hilda says. "But still—*each is for himself in this world*, and that's the bedrock of marriage as of all other institutions." Women, Edwin observes, "are a foreign race encamped among us men." In another place Edwin "dwelt sardonically upon the terrible results of family life on the individual, and dreamed of splendid freedoms." The examples could be multiplied with ease. But they all say essentially the same thing: Life between Hilda and Edwin—like that between Bennett and Marguerite—is an unending contest of wills in which every kiss is qualified by the search for an advantage; and the kiss itself, which is offered, withheld, or exploited for sexual gratification, is a deadly weapon.[17]

What kind of marriage produces such a living hell? Bennett described it in *These Twain*. Can there be any other kind? He answered that in *The Lion's Share*. Madame Piriac and her husband have a marriage in which neither attempts to devour the other. Madame Piriac would never be so barbaric as to say in respect to her marriage "each is for himself in this world." In fact, the reason to do so would not arise. In the "advanced civilization" in which the Piriacs live, there is too much urbanity, too

---

[17] Arnold Bennett, *These Twain*, in *The Clayhanger Family* (London, 1925), 986, 1003, 1057. Mary Kennerley has said that Edwin speaks for her uncle and that to hear Edwin's speeches read aloud is to hear Bennett speaking. Frank Swinnerton believes that many of the quarrels between Hilda and Edwin were taken almost verbatim from quarrels between Bennett and Marguerite.

much humanity, too much respect between husband and wife for them ever to think of their relationship in such violent and ultimately destructive terms. Audrey and Musa's marriage has the same free structure and is, if anything, less individually limiting than the Piriacs' marital ties. Bennett seems to have said in the course of the two novels that a particular kind of people will make a particular kind of marriage. Provincial people will have marriages like Edwin's. Emancipated people will have marriages like Madame Piriac's. He adds a further comment: Emancipated people do not live in the provinces, neither in Burslem nor in Frinton.

The movement in Bennett's writing away from a preoccupation with Five Towns respectability toward a more liberal view of human behavior is sufficiently in evidence in *The Price of Love* and *The Lion's Share*—and by default in *These Twain*—to suggest that Bennett was either undergoing a personal reevaluation of his life style or had sensed in his reading public a desire and a readiness for more experimental subject matter than he had been writing. Probably both explanations have a share in the truth. But a change certainly occurs. Looking forward to *Lilian* (1922), one discovers that the transition has been made. Respectability, in the form of Miss Grig, goes to the wall; and Lilian, the typist-mistress who runs away with her boss, triumphs, against all the rules of Burslem and Militant-Methodism.

Georges Lafourcade found a "gentle, insidious cynicism" in *Lilian* and "a quiet voluptuousness" which imparted a unique warmth to the style.[18] Hints of that cynicism are to be found in *The Lion's Share*, but they are more in the form of a preparation or a prophecy than a genuine part of the tone of the work. The closing lines of the book are given to Miss Ingate and to Madame Piriac. Speaking of Audrey's behavior, Madame Piriac, who observed that Audrey wants the lion's share of life, said, "I was never young like that." "Neither was I! Neither was I!" Miss Ingate responds. "But something very, very strange has come over the world, if you ask me." In Bennett's view women like Audrey were one of the strangest and most exciting symp-

[18] Georges Lafourcade, *Arnold Bennett: A Study* (London, 1939), 165.

toms of that change. In order to accept them and in order to enjoy what they offered, it was necessary to stop measuring morality with a Burslem yardstick.[19]

Without suggesting that Bennett decided on New Year's day, 1915, to reshape his life, it must be pointed out that in early January he began travelling to London with greater frequency and occasionally extended his London visits to as much as ten days, and the inconsequential and occasionally silly conversations with local people about spies and schemes to hamper the Germans fade out of the journal in early 1915. In their place are references to writers, editors, and men connected with the government. E. V. Lucas, Edward Knoblock, Frank Swinnerton, Pauline Smith, Hugh Walpole, and H. G. Wells, among others, began visiting Bennett at Comarques or became his guests at lunches and dinners in London. He met Pinker regularly and lunched with editors at the Reform Club, his favorite London haunt. He went to the theatre, to concerts, and to the galleries; and he learned to dance—but not with Marguerite.[20]

At the same time, an enormous amount of his time was being given to committee work. In part his increased responsibilities to the various war-related committees on which he was serving accounts for the additional time he spent in London. There were regular meetings in Colchester of the Thorpe Division Emergency Committee and weekly meetings in London of the Wounded Allies Relief Committee (WARC), of which he became permanent chairman in May. He managed to get Pinker to serve on the WARC, much against Pinker's wishes. Pinker's letters to Bennett, in which he tried to explain how busy he was

[19] At about this time he confided to Frank Swinnerton that he had recently met at a social occasion in H. G. Wells's flat several of the "new" women. "They are all impure," he said, summarizing his impressions of them. "They have all been seduced." Frank Swinnerton felt that Bennett had been deeply shocked by their amorality. On the basis of his treatment of sexual freedom, however, in The Lion's Share, Lilian, The Pretty Lady, and Lord Raingo, it is possible to conclude that he was less shocked than he pretended to be.

[20] Olive Glendinning taught both Bennett and Marguerite to dance. It was a difficult task. Bennett had grown very stout, and he stood stiffly erect with his stomach thrown out and moved with a kind of flat-footed ponderousness. Oddly enough, he became quite a good dancer. Marguerite was an even more difficult student. She could not be taught to follow. She insisted on leading.

and how unprepared to devote his time to the work as he would wish to do, are a portrait of a man being outgeneralled.

As a consequence of the committee work, he occasionally found himself in the most bizarre circumstances. In early January, for example, he wrote to Hugh Walpole asking him to buy a ticket to a boxing match to be held at the National Sporting Club. The event was called the Wounded Allies Relief Committee Ladies' Night, proceeds to go to the WARC fund. Bennett also asked Walpole if he would like to take Marguerite to the affair. Bennett said that he would be late himself, because he had to attend a dinner, connected with the Ladies' Night activities, which he was giving to a group of ex-pugilists.[21]

In May he told Elsie Herzog that he was devoting three days a week to "war work." This was primarily with committees—he had, for example, begun to plan a London concert for the WARC—but he was also still concerning himself with issues connected with the government's conduct of the war. It is probable however that he did include in his estimate of three days the time spent writing his *Daily News* articles. Days and weeks drained away. By a conservative estimate, based on journal entries, between January 16 and June 20 he spent eight full weeks in London, not counting the two-and three-day visits. Meanwhile, at Comarques there was a steady flow of guests. Among his visitors were Edwin Rickards, the Sharps, George Doran and his wife, Edward Knoblock, and Betty Lilley, who, according to Bennett, sang one Sunday evening in February "jolly well."

In the midst of such distractions, Bennett contrived between January and June to complete *These Twain* and to write the first half of *The Lion's Share*. By the end of February he had begun the job of cutting *These Twain* from 128,000 to 100,000 words, a task which he completed on March 6. The Munsey Syndicate had bought the American serial rights to *These Twain;* and Doran, the book rights. It was probably in connection with the serial publication that Bennett did the cutting, although it was to Doran that he sent the shortened version first.

[21] *Letters,* II, 363.

As a professional writer Bennett had come a long way from the days when he had been appalled to learn that Eden Phillpotts cut his novels at the request of editors. It seemed to Bennett in those early days that a carefully planned book could not be cut without destroying it.

He had told Pinker on January 5 that he was unable to provide the *Metropolitan Magazine* with a synopsis of the novel he was to do for them but that it would be definite by the end of February. "All that I can say now," he continued, "is that the action will be in modern Paris . . . and that the tale will be light and humorous in character.[22] He was as good as his word. On the second of April he wrote in his journal, "I decided yesterday to get ideas into order and begin my new novel, *The Lion's Share*, today." Eight days later he had written 12,500 words, enough for a first instalment. He thought that what he had written was not deeply imagined but that it was fairly good and interesting.[23] He wrote swiftly and by April 28 had completed the third instalment.

The quantity of his writing in his short period seems to contradict the assertion that he was busy with war work, but the number of committee meetings did not lessen. He continued to go to London. The only explanation that can be offered is that the first half of *The Lion's Share* poured out of him, almost as though a dam had been broken. The speed with which he wrote is an indication of the sense of release that the novel appears to have given him. It is almost as though he were purging himself mentally and emotionally of the preoccupations of *These Twain*. In May, however, the writing slowed; and Bennett recorded that on the 14th he spent most of the day alone at the Royal Thames Yacht Club (RTYC), "all afternoon in bed" trying to get ideas for the novel.[24]

He had arranged to deliver the story in two parts to the *Strand Magazine* for English serialization and to the *Metropolitan Magazine* for American serialization. The first half was to be

22 *Ibid.*, I, 223.
23 *Journal*, 552.
24 Unpublished Journal, May 14, 1915.

delivered in June and the second in December. *The Metropolitan* was to pay £1,500 for each of the two instalments at the time of delivery. Pinker had also sold the novel to Munsey and to Cassell, but Cassell asked Pinker to resell their rights in the novel, and Pinker agreed to the proposal, selling the novel to the *Strand Magazine*.

H. J. Whigham of the *Metropolitan* was delighted with the novel, despite the rather harsh exchanges he had had with Bennett and Pinker over the three short stories. But the *Strand* editors were not at all happy. In June, Greenhough Smith reported to Pinker that the Board of Directors had decided that it was very dangerous for the *Strand* to publish a women's suffrage novel. They had no wish to offend either the suffragists or the antisuffragists.[25]

The war had by no means killed the women's suffrage movement in England. Its militancy was put somewhat in abeyance out of consideration for the state of national emergency, but what it lost in visibility from its abandonment of mass rallies, marches, and attacks on government leaders it more than made up for in the good will and respect generated by women's readiness to step into the jobs left vacant by the mobilization of men. But that good will had little immediate political effect.

One of the difficulties facing the suffragists was that their cause was not a party cause. No party could endorse it without losing the support of half its members. In Asquith's Cabinet in the spring of 1913, for example, Lloyd George and Sir Edward Grey were resolute supporters of the suffragists while Harcourt, the Secretary of the Colonies, and the Prime Minister himself were vehement opponents. In the confusion and uproar created by the women's suffrage bill introduced early in 1913 by the Government but never brought to a vote, the Liberal government was at least temporarily discredited by having gone back on its word to support such a bill; and the English people were brought to a realization that women's suffrage was a genuinely serious issue.

Feelings on the question of women's suffrage tended to be

[25] Butler Collection, June 9, 1915.

antipodal and violent. Emotional rather than rational responses characterized argument on the subject; and, for that reason if for no other, any newspaper or magazine which printed an article or a story either defending women's suffrage or attacking it could absolutely rely on offending half of its readers. Bennett heard from Pinker about the *Strand*'s doubts and concluded that he would be able to reassure the editors. But his first reaction was one of surprise and irritation.

"It was yesterday morning after a bad night," he wrote on June 12, "that I had news the *Strand* would not use my *Lion's Share* because it had to do with suffragettes! Incurable people. Still I think I can beat them." [26] On the same day he wrote to Pinker protesting the *Strand*'s action and attempting to demonstrate that the novel was not a women's suffrage novel. Having pointed out that Madame Piriac is definitely antisuffragist and that Audrey marries Musa and settles down, he went on to condemn any editorial policy that prevented a writer from treating "the most generally interesting scenes of modern public life." He closed the letter by saying that since there was always "something real, some vital question," behind his stories, the *Strand* had set him an impossible task if they expected him to write a novel without even touching on a vital question.[27]

He was not able to calm the fears of the *Strand*'s Board of Directors which finally turned down the novel entirely, and Pinker disposed of the English serial rights to the *Grand Magazine*. Dudley Barker has suggested that the *Strand*'s real reason for turning down the story was the novel's poor quality. Barker called it magazine fiction of the dreariest kind; [28] and Reginald Pound listed it among what he called the rent-paying novels, "which increased his fame and diminished his reputation." Pound placed it in the same class as *The Pretty Lady*, *The Roll Call*, *Lilian*, and *Mr. Prohack*.[29] But its value as a document recording Bennett's changing attitudes would be difficult to over-

[26] Unpublished Journal, June 12, 1915.
[27] *Letters*, I, 229.
[28] Barker, *Arnold Bennett*, 191.
[29] Pound, *Arnold Bennett*, 279.

estimate. In any case, *The Lion's Share* is a lively story, well told, and—at least in the first half—brimming with life. It makes a pleasant and healthy change from *These Twain*.

In early January the ghost of *Don Juan* rose briefly, only to sink swiftly again into obscurity. Frank Vernon, writing to Pinker from New York, asked if Bennett would like to have *Don Juan* produced in New York "this season." Bennett declined on the ground that before there could be much hope for an American success for the play, it would have to succeed in England. Pinker agreed, adding that there was "no chance" of its succeeding in England until the war was over.[30] Perhaps Bennett was reluctant partly because Vernon was suggesting production. Vernon's handling of the play in the spring and summer of 1914 had not satisfied Bennett. And the aborted production undoubtedly left Bennett somewhat distrustful of Vernon's methods, despite the fact that it had been, presumably, the war which prevented the play from being performed.[31]

Despite a reawakening of the theater, which was matched by a corresponding boom in music hall entertainment, none of Bennett's plays were in production in London. The Esmé Percy and Kirsten Graham's Company arranged to do three performances of *The Honeymoon* and of *Cupid and Commonsense* in Birmingham. Pinker sold the American vaudeville rights in *A Question of Sex;* and Alice Kauser, Knoblock's film agent in the United States, wrote to Pinker, saying that *Milestones* ought to be put into a stock company because the chances of touring were very poor.[32] In March, Methuen and Company sent Bennett his share in the year's royalties on the published version of *Milestones.* The sum was one pound, sixteen shillings, and four-

[30] Ogden Collection, January 11, 1915.
[31] A letter from Bennett to Pinker (Butler Collection, January 11, 1915) reads in part: "Many thanks for your wire. I answered it in the negative. I don't think Vernon could possibly produce it right without me. And I certainly don't want to go over. We have not discussed the production at all in detail. . . . Further, I think the play has little chance of success in New York unless it begins with a success in London. It certainly is not everyone's play. . . . My notion . . . is a postponement till after the war. I quite expect to write another play in the autumn."
[32] Butler Collection, April 26, 1915.

pence, a sad decline from 1913 when the total income from his plays had amounted to something close to £8,000.

Because *Milestones* did not retain its audience appeal into the war and failed in its winter, 1914, revival, it is not surprising that Bennett did not at this time have much incentive to write a play. Pinker, however, thought that he should be working on one. In late May he wrote, "My dear Arnold, I wish you would take the war play idea seriously. You ought to do one, for I'm sure you could do one and I don't know anyone else who could." [33] But Bennett was not tempted. Throughout the spring he maintained a careful silence on the subject of plays.

More disturbing, perhaps, since there was a market for them, was his failure to produce any short stories during this period or to make any firm contracts to write any in the future, although he had assured Pinker early in the year that he "had several ideas for short stories, and intended to write one immediately after completing *These Twain*." [34] In January and February he and Pinker continued to wage a kind of guerrilla warfare with H. J. Whigham over "The Life of Nash Nicklin," which had been sent as the second of three stories contracted by the *Metropolitan Magazine*. Whigham did not like the story and did not wish to publish it. Bennett had agreed to let the *Metropolitan* out of its contract for the third story, but Whigham couldn't make up his mind what he wished to do.

With what appears to have been a genuine talent for raising the hair on Bennett's neck, Whigham paused in one of his letters to compare English short story writers unfavorably with American short story writers. Bennett replied ironically in a letter dated January 26 that Whigham's remarks were interesting "as a disclosure of critical standards." It is worth quoting Bennett at some length on the subject of Whigham's contention; and even allowing for the exaggeration which anger may have produced, his comments probably reflect with some accuracy his attitude toward both American and English short story writers:

[33] *Ibid.* (This letter from Pinker is undated but was probably written in late May.)
[34] Ogden Collection, January 4, 1915.

I have read a great deal of American literature, and I have also heard a great deal about the American short story. But I have never read any American short story, except one or two by O. Henry and Ambrose Bierce, which in my opinion would rank with even the secondary short stories of Kipling, Wells, Hardy, Galsworthy, Conan Doyle, Phillpotts, George Moore, Frank Harris, Gilbert Chesterton, or Percival Gibbon, not to name sundry others. Nor do I know any American short story writer (with the few exceptions aforesaid) who has made the slightest impression as a short story writer outside his own country. Certainly I know of none who has aroused any interest whatever on the continent, where the works of the above-named English writers are much read both in the original and in translations. I wish you would send me a specimen of what you consider to be a first-class American short story. That I should try to imitate it is improbable, but I like to understand.[35]

On February 19 Whigham seemed to have made up his mind to drop the third story, but on the 24th he wrote what Bennett called a "letter of the boot-licking variety." When Bennett left for the front, the issue was still not settled. The only further mention of it that Bennett made in the spring of 1915 was done in connection with a request from *Century Magazine* for an eight-thousand-word story. Bennett said that he would do the story with pleasure and that "it would be a good one." [36] Nothing more was said, however, and the arrangements for the story appear to have fallen through. Bennett had not, of course, written the "third" story for Whigham, a fact which accounts for his readiness to allow Whigham to cancel the contract for it.

Edward Knoblock came to visit Bennett in March. He had not been at Comarques since November of 1913, when he and Bennett had made a fruitless attempt to find a subject for a new collaboration. While riding down from London on the train, Knoblock had gotten the idea for the play which became *My Lady's Dress*, but he made up his mind to write the play himself and said nothing to Bennett of the idea. He had sketched a scenario of the play on the cuffs of his shirt and was in a state of

[35] *Letters*, I, 225–26.
[36] *Ibid.*, 224.

terror after arriving at Comarques until he could change his shirt
for fear that Bennett would see the writing and ask about it.[37]

It was not really hope for a new collaboration that brought
Knoblock to Essex on this occasion but rather a plan for turning
some of Bennett's sensational novels into films. He had managed
to interest Alice Kauser in one or two of Bennett's stories, and
Bennett was sufficiently encouraged by what Knoblock said to
write to Pinker asking him to talk with Alice Kauser about agent
relations before negotiations went any further.[38] Unfortunately,
the project died. After recording that he and Knoblock had met
once more in London for lunch, Bennett dropped the subject.

The war had stimulated the book trade to the point that publishers were finding it profitable to issue cheap editions of books
which had either been out of print for some time or were selling
slowly in expensive editions. In February, Methuen asked to do
a shilling edition of *Buried Alive*, having sold out a two-shilling
edition issued shortly before. At the same time Hodder and
Stoughton were preparing a sixpence edition of the same book.
Pinker agreed to all of the new editions, including a further
proposal by Methuen that his company do a two-shilling edition
of *The Regent* in July. Doran found it worthwhile to do a fifty-
cent edition of *The Gates of Wrath*, one of Bennett's early
dreadfuls and a novel he had been trying, unsuccessfully, to forget since its original appearance in 1903.

But Bennett's chief concern in this period was with his
journalism. Committed to writing at least one article a week and
frequently called upon to do more, he was under constant pressure to find subjects about which he could write and which
would interest a national audience. The *Daily News* and the
*Sunday Pictorial* were the chief publishers of his articles and
both were "popular" publications in the sense that they addressed themselves to a very large and very mixed group of
readers.

Bennett was obliged to collect his information and his impressions from a variety of sources. An omnivorous newspaper

---

[37] Edward Knoblock, *Round the Room* (London, 1939), 187.
[38] *Letters*, I, 227.

reader himself, he used the newspaper to keep up with the general news. But since the government was imposing a fairly strict censorship on war releases of any kind, he had to supplement his newspaper reading with information from other sources. The officers billetted at Comarques and those who visited the house brought Bennett masses of semi-official information. His task was to sort out the facts from what was simply rumor or distortion. Major F. G. Danilsen, an intelligence officer stationed in the neighborhood, frequently confided in Bennett, giving him current estimates about the chances of invasion and related military matters.

Of greater use were men connected with government who were willing to talk freely with him. His friend C. F. G. Masterman, who in the spring of 1915 lost his post at Wellington House in the course of a Cabinet shake-up, had intimate knowledge of the processes of government. So did G. H. Mair of the Ministry of Information, who, Bennett said, was always "full of authentic information on things." Both of these men saw Bennett regularly and gave him information which he could have acquired in no other way.

Bennett was also on familiar terms with Charles Philips Trevelyan, a sharp critic of the government, who had resigned his government position in protest against the policies which had led to bringing England into the war. Ernest McKenna, brother of Reginald McKenna, the Liberal politician, was another who knew a good deal about what the government was doing and was glad to share his knowledge with Bennett. Oddly enough, Pinker frequently gave Bennett material which he could turn into copy. Pinker got his information chiefly from Henry James, who was on close terms with Walter H. Page, the American Ambassador.

Not everything that Bennett wrote for the *Daily News* and the *Sunday Pictorial* had to do with the war itself or with the activities of the government. His article for the March 14th issue of the *Sunday Pictorial* was "War and the Future of Women," an interesting topic considering the subject matter of *The Lion's Share*, which he was soon to begin writing. He had a great deal

of freedom as to what he would write. The degree of his freedom is indicated by a letter from Pinker in late March. "If there
is anything particular that you would like to write about this
week," Pinker said, "I think I could arrange it with the *Sunday
Pictorial* for another article." [39] The titles of articles written by
Bennett for the *Daily News* between January and June show the
variety of his offerings: "Foreign Policy," "Pensions Officers,"
"Prejudices," "Punishing Germany," and "Being Ourselves."
His articles for the *Sunday Pictorial* were of the same sort:
"Eyewitnessing," "The Hard Case of the Poor," "Men and
Their Leaders."

Nowhere else in his writing does Bennett show himself so
wholly committed to defending the rights of the worker as he
does in these articles, and the three subjects which most occupied his attention between January and July of 1915 were the
hardships suffered by the poor because of rising prices and the
inadequate compensations paid to the dependents of servicemen
and the threats to justice and social democracy which he saw
gathering force in the nation. In "An Act of Patriotism" he
pointed out that the country was telling its poor "when we want
you to work, you must work. When we don't, you and your
families can starve." [40]

Pointing out the injustice and the danger of a situation in
which large numbers of the population are allowed to remain in
misery, he wrote, "Our rulers are so ignorant, the employing
class is so stupid, the whole nation is so apathetic, that this condition of affairs is allowed to persist. . . ." [41] From that condemnation he moved to a second. There had been a howl of
protest in the press against the munitions workers in the North
when they went out on strike.[42] Bennett defended their action,

---

[39] Butler Collection, March 30, 1915.
[40] Arnold Bennett, "An Act of Patriotism," *The Daily News and Leader,*
April 8, 1915, p. 4.
[41] *Ibid.,* 4.
[42] Bennett's brother Septimus worked in a northern munitions factory during
the war and provided Bennett with much of his background material for these
articles.

hammering home the incontrovertible truth that profits had increased for everyone in industry except the laborer, who was asked to go on working for his prewar wage and to pay for goods and services at inflated war-time prices. As for the demand that unions should give up their privileges for the duration, he asked rather sardonically what the result would be of asking the members of the Church of England to give up their "hieratic privileges" in order to gain some national end. "They would," he thought, "want a deal of persuading." [43]

He also reminded his readers that there had been a sixty percent rise in coal prices over an eight month period but no rise in miners' wages. In April, Charles Hobhouse, Postmaster General, refused to give the postal employees a wage increase, defending his refusal by saying that all classes must bear the war burden equally. Bennett was outraged. "If Hobhouse does not know," he wrote with withering scorn, "that the burden of high prices always falls more heavily on the poor than on the rest of the country, he ought to retire and consent to be exhibited in the British Museum as a truly remarkable specimen." [44]

Having made a visit to a National Relief Fund house near Park Lane in which unemployed girls were being trained for future employment, he made the observation that "one's first impression is that there must be something wrong with a civilization in which girls so young have to earn their living." [45] Of other workers he said, "I have never believed that Waterloo was won on the playing fields of Eton. But I am quite ready to believe that the present war will be won in the workshops of Great Britain." [46]

Nothing angered him more than the pervading apathy of the government toward the poverty in which so many soldiers' de-

[43] Arnold Bennett, "The War Within the War," *The Daily News and Leader*, February 11, 1915, p. 4.
[44] Shortly after Bennett's article appeared in print, Hobhouse relented and granted the pay raise. What effect, if any, Bennett's article had on his decision is not known.
[45] Arnold Bennett, "Eye Witnessing," *The Daily News and Leader*, January 7, 1915, p. 4.
[46] Bennett, "The War Within the War," 4.

pendents were obliged to live because of the niggardly compensation granted to them. "Nothing is more certain," he warned in January, "than that after the war whole regiments of men, women, and children will be made desolate by the ingratitude of a saved nation." [47] It was a theme to which he returned over and over again. And his concern with it was of a dual nature. Not only did he insist that common justice and humanity demanded a fair treatment of the poor in general and of soldiers' dependents in particular but he also attempted to waken the public to the danger of allowing a large segment of the country to feel cheated and disenfranchised. There would be a reckoning he warned, and if those who practiced suppression suffered in it, they would have no one to blame but themselves.

His articles dealing with the laboring classes usually dealt with the influences under which they lived, but on occasion he turned on the wealthy and attacked them for their antidemocratic practices. "Foreign Policy," published on January 14, was such an attack. In it Bennett directed his criticism against the "privilege" of the  Foreign Office to choose its men outside the bounds of the Civil Service. The article was occasioned by the publication of the Royal Commission on the Civil Service report, which, Bennett lectured his readers, was not receiving the wide attention it deserved: "To make an outcry is so natural; to educate oneself on the subject of the outcry is so unnatural."

Although he had defended Sir Edward Grey early in the war, Bennett was not at all sympathetic toward the Foreign Office itself. It was to him, like the War Office, a place where special influence was most deeply entrenched. Underlining the exclusiveness of the corps, he noted that sixty-seven percent of all candidates had been to Eton and that almost without exception their recruits were graduates of either Oxford or Cambridge. He dismissed the argument that the qualities most needed for the service were most likely to be found among the wealthy and the educated classes. The real reason that recruiting practices went unchanged, he insisted, was that the wealthy and aristo-

[47] Arnold Bennett, "To Jog the Memory," *The Daily News and Leader,* January 7, 1915, p. 4.

cratic classes wished to keep the diplomatic service as a preserve of their own.[48]

Not satisfied with challenging their motives, he called their capabilities into question. Arthur Boutwood, a member of the Royal Commission, put himself on record as having said that men of the other classes lacked the skill to deal on terms of equality "with considerable persons." Bennett dismissed the assertion with derision. Has Boutwood ever run up against a post office girl or a policeman or anybody with the moral support of the state behind him? he demanded.

"The very last quality possessed by our ruling classes," he continued, "is the capacity to mix freely with foreigners of all classes. Such a capacity demands imagination, and there is no class in Britain with less imagination than the ruling classes." By way of illustration he referred to Lord Curzon and Lord Milner and asked his readers to "reflect on the amount of blundering and suffering which the world might have been spared if either of these men had possessed a spark of imagination, or the least capacity to understand a point of view other than their own." [49]

His hostility toward the aristocracy never led him to the point of actually blaming the war on their folly, but he did express with considerable disgust his belief that the theory of balance of power was chiefly responsible for most of "the existing mess," and that as a working theory it would have to be abandoned. Balance of power, in his view, meant simply "the balance of dynastic, aristocratic, and military forces, none of which has any real vital relation to the progress of a European country in these days." His alternative was a foreign policy based on the will of an educated citizenry. In order to make his scheme workable, he knew that there would have to be a revolution in public education which would provide effective courses in modern history in secondary schools and in evening schools. Until people were willing to make an effort to educate themselves in the subject of international relations they would get the treatment they

[48] Arnold Bennett, "Foreign Policy," *The Daily News and Leader,* January 14, 1915, p. 4.
[49] Bennett, "Foreign Policy," 4.

deserved—"that is to say, the treatment accorded to children."

In March with "Men and Their Leaders" Bennett returned again to the subject of the Foreign Office. He defended the Foreign Office against the "inaccurate and prejudiced" attack made on it by a left-wing pamphlet, *How the War Came*, and said it should be ranked with "the miserable effusions of Frank Harris in *The New York Sun*," [50] but he insisted again that the public should familiarize themselves with the workings of the department. It seems certain that it was his determination to assist in the education of his readers that led him to visit the Foreign Office in April with a view to collecting data on its operation. As is pointed out elsewhere, however, whatever plans he had for writing about the Foreign Office were shunted aside by the invitation extended to him to visit the fronts.

Bennett found it necessary to write his articles when and where he could. Frequently he was overtaken by an article deadline while he was in London. When that happened, he usually wrote at the Reform Club, finding the surroundings congenial. He also did some of his writing at the RTYC, which he had begun to frequent. But writing these articles late at night or when he felt ill or overtired, as was frequently the case, was a strain. And he appears not to have had any reserve energy for extra writing. No plays or short stories were in progress; he did not even take up Pinker's offer to place an extra article with the *Sunday Pictorial*. He appears to have had only sufficient strength to meet the demands of his journalism and fulfill his commitments to his book publishers.

His virtual retreat in the spring of 1915 to the Reform Club and the RTYC during his London trips became a regular feature of those trips. He and Marguerite generally had rooms at the Berkeley or another hotel, but Bennett seems to have left them to

[50] Frank Harris wrote a series of articles for *The New York Sun* which were collected in *England or Germany?* (New York, 1915). The essays were anti-English in sentiment and a strange mixture of personal spleen and remarkable insight. In June, Bennett reviewed Harris's essays, concluding that Harris had never forgiven the English people for not having liked his short stories (Bennett had praised them). Bennett made no effort to deal with the issues raised by Harris.

Marquerite for her use. At least until the middle of June, when Read drove the car to London for the last time to have it laid up for the duration of the war, Bennett frequently went to London by automobile while Marguerite went on the same or the following day by train. They occasionally met in the city for lunch or dinner or a theater engagement, and on one occasion he spent the afternoon with her shopping for clothes. She bought two dresses at Selfridge's. Bennett remarked that the women along Oxford Street were very *chic*.[51]

Judging by Bennett's journal for the period, it was more common for him to dine with his friends while Marguerite dined with hers than it was for them to eat together. Bennett frequently noted that he had eaten alone or gone to the theater or a concert alone or not in Marguerite's company. Even at Comarques the two were not always at the same table. On the night of his arrival at Comarques in April, Frank Swinnerton and Bennett dined together alone while Marguerite and two other guests went out for dinner to the Grand Hotel in nearby Clacton.[52]

Although Pauline Smith gives what is, on the whole, a sympathetic picture of Marguerite during this period, she does reveal aspects of the Frenchwoman's personality which must have grated constantly on her husband, given his temperament, and made it essential for Bennett to have periods of rest from her. Pauline described Marguerite as vehement and enthusiastic in her approach to her own affairs. She flung herself wholeheartedly into whatever she did, expending the same energy, apparently, in her pursuit of spies as in singing songs of her own composition for the local officers.

Pauline Smith also wrote that Marguerite's ardor "was at times delightful in its simplicity, and at others embarrassing in its French vehemence." Frank Swinnerton, her friend Olive Glendinning, and her niece Mary Kennerley all attest to the explosive character of her temperament and to her consuming need for flattery and affection. When she did not get the atten-

51 *Journal*, 554.
52 *Ibid.*, 552.

tion which she felt was her due, she would burst into an angry attack on Bennett in loud and abusive tones. Seen through unfriendly eyes, Marguerite's manner could be brutally satirized. Lytton Strachey, at a somewhat later date, attending what he called "an incredibly fearful function in Arnold Bennett's establishment [in London]," described Marguerite reading poetry "with waving arms and chanting voice . . . till everyone was ready to vomit." [53] Bennett was not present at the "fearful function," and one scarcely need ask why. For Bennett, who disliked every sort of emotional excess, his wife's behavior must have been almost intolerable.

On the other hand, Marguerite felt herself mistreated by her husband. At any moment in company he was likely to interrupt her with, "Marguerite, that is not *true!*" The contradiction, always provoked by Marguerite's violent attacks on him, was spoken so frequently that Frank Swinnerton recalls it as one of the things Bennett said most frequently in his wife's company in those days. (Another favorite remark was "We-ell, I've written one . . . thousand and sixteen words this morning—all . . . of the best." [54]) Marguerite responded to the contradiction by crying out, "My de' Arnole! That is so rude of you." But she did not easily throw off his harshness. She complained repeatedly to Pauline Smith of Bennett's lack of tact and understanding, but she was still able to end her complaints with "*mais il-y-a des moments,*" indicating that she had not, at this time, utterly despaired of their relationship. [55]

Bennett practiced petty deceptions against Marguerite, and both the deceptions and their failure, for they rarely succeeded, must have irritated her. They probably helped to plant the suspicion in Marguerite's mind that her husband was being unfaithful to her, a suspicion that grew as the war advanced. But Bennett's deceptions were, in fact, almost silly and appear not to have increased with time. For example, he enjoyed buying paintings, and Marguerite objected to the expense. As a ruse

[53] Michael Holroyd, *Lytton Strachey: A Critical Biography* (New York, 1968), II, 440.
[54] Swinnerton, *An Autobiography*, 148.
[55] Smith, *A.B.*, 48.

he bought pictures and hid them under his bed for six months, then hung them on the walls. When Marguerite remarked on the new purchases, he would say that they were not new, that he had had them for a long time. Marguerite carefully explained to Swinnerton that she was aware of what Bennett was doing. Bennett had as carefully explained to his friend how he managed to go on buying new pictures without appearing to be doing so.

At the end of March, G. H. Mair asked Bennett if he would like to visit the French and the English fronts. The offer was a unique honor. Made at a time when censorship was exacting and becoming sterner almost by the week, the Foreign Office invitation gave Bennett an opportunity to have what amounted to a Cook's tour of the Western Front. Bennett was sent out only two months after the first newspaper correspondents were allowed to follow the army to France. The correspondents who were permitted to take up a conditional position at army headquarters were carefully limited in their reporting, although their exclusive right to the news releases gave them an enormous advantage over those who were forced to remain in England. The opportunity was so flattering, on the one hand, and so challenging that Bennett accepted at once, subject to the condition that he be provided with a guide.

It may never be possible to say precisely why the Foreign Office decided at that particular time to launch an official tour of the fronts. It is equally difficult to say why Bennett was chosen from among all of the journalists available. There are, however, two reasonable explanations.

In January, Pinker wrote to Bennett, saying that he was glad Bennett had "taken up the question of the Diplomatic Service." [56] He said also that if the public ever developed an interest in foreign affairs, they would be shocked. What Bennett had in mind is not definitely known, but on March 31 he went to see Mair at the Foreign Office. An official showed Bennett around the offices and explained how the ministry worked. That same day, after lunch, Mair went to the Reform Club and extended to Bennett the Ministry's invitation to go to the Front.

[56] *Letters*, January 13, 1915.

It is tempting to conclude that the Foreign Office made the invitation in the hopes that Bennett's attention would be diverted away from itself. It would be flattering to Bennett to think so, because such a decision implies that he had managed through his journalism to become a potential threat to the government. And it cannot be doubted that he had acquired a vast reading public. He had become something of a public figure. He reported in his journal that when he entered the theater for the March 22 premiere of James Barrie's *Rosy Rapture*, he was greeted with cries of his name from the pit, something that had never before happened to him.[57] It was the journalist and not the novelist or the playwright who was being cheered.

On March 7 he became a member of the Board of Directors of the *New Statesman*, a position which gave him the power to influence the editorial policy of one of the country's liveliest Socialist journals.[58] Bennett had never belonged to the Fabian Society or been one of the intimates of the Webbs, but the radical character of some of his *Daily News* articles, matched with his reputation for conservatism and "commonsense," must have made him palatable to the *New Statesman* group.

Mair and others in the government may well have decided that Bennett might become a formidable adversary if he ever chose to make an all-out attack on the Foreign Office. On the other hand, Bennett had, in general terms, been a supporter of Asquith and the Liberal government. He was not a pacifist; he accepted the seriousness of the military situation, but he was still capable of solid optimism. He was a man of "common sense" and

---

[57] *Journal*, 550.

[58] Bennett went onto the board of the *New Statesman* and put an unknown amount of money into the paper at a time when the journal was in something of a financial crisis. It also appeared that G. B. Shaw was about to withdraw from his position on the board. Shaw and Cedric Sharp, the editor of the *New Statesman*, were in violent disagreement about the attitude the paper should be taking toward the Asquith Government. Shaw, of course, wished to denounce the war and the policies of the Liberals. Sharp was determined to follow a supporting line as long as the war lasted. Bennett's arrival not only shored up the paper's shaky financial structure but also provided Sharp with an ally. Bennett became a regular contributor, writing a column headed "Observations" and signing himself Sardonyx.

had proved it by defending the government against Shaw's virulent attack of the previous year. In many ways he was the perfect choice for the job of reporting, in a semiofficial capacity, on
the state of affairs at the front. Taken that way, there was
nothing sinister in Mair's offer. Mair was simply exploiting an
opportunity to give the government and public morale a boost.
If in the process Mair kept Bennett from annoying the Foreign
Office, so much the better.

Whatever else the assignment meant to Bennett, it was an opportunity to do some valid reporting and to make some much
needed money. Throughout April he and Pinker discussed the
business of the trip, opening negotiations for articles with *The
New York Times*, the *Saturday Evening Post*, and later the
*Daily News* and the *Illustrated London News*. By May 18 he
had settled with the *Saturday Evening Post* for a series of "war
sketches." The *Post* agreed to pay £300 each for six or fewer
articles and £200 each for seven or more articles up to a maximum of twelve. He eventually settled with the *Illustrated London News* for six articles at £250 each. Pinker was disappointed
with the price but thought it better "from every point of view"
that the pieces should appear there rather than in a daily paper
or a penny weekly.[59] He skirmished with Gardiner of the *Daily
News*, who wanted him to represent that paper at the Front.
Bennett's refusal was based on the fact that he was already committed to the *Post* and could not be expected to do two different
sets of impressions.

Mair had begun by insisting that Bennett should not let it get
around among the newspaper offices that a trip to the front was
being planned. There was vague talk on Mair's part about departmental jealousy, but Mair may have been laying on a little
secrecy simply to impress Bennett. A real problem, however,
was that of censorship. As late as May 13, Bennett cautioned
Pinker not to contract for any articles on the English Front for
the present as there might be trouble getting the English authorities to permit publication. The French were less exacting,

[59] Butler, May 18, 1915; June 25, 1915.

and Pinker was able to go ahead with contracts for articles on the French Front.[60]

Bennett wrote little about his preparations for going to the Front and very little about his emotional reactions to the approaching journey. He confided to Elsie Herzog in late May, "I think that I shall shortly be going to the Front, at least as near the Front as a civilian who respects his vitality may go." [61] He eventually became reconciled to making the trip with Mair, who had determined to go with Bennett; but in April he noted that he was "rather disturbed by the prospect" of having Mair for a companion. He may have felt that the presence of a Ministry of Information official would hamper his freedom of observation.

In the midst of preparations to leave for France, Bennett continued to be positive in his comments on the progress of the war. Talking with Norman Angell, an author and lecturer who had become very upset over the gravity of the national situation, he said that there was no point in worrying about the war as worrying did no good. In any case, he thought that things were going well for the Allies; and to give point to his optimism, he laid bets amounting to £125 that the war would be over by the end of July.[62]

As mentioned earlier, in Bennett's fiction there is a tendency on his part to deprive his characters of some freedom or happiness and to associate that deprivation with the performance of a duty. On the first of April, Bennett wrote to Hugh Walpole, who was on the Russian Front, and said, among other things, "the drink question is now agitating us, I have suggested that total prohibition should begin first in the Cabinet, the Reform Club, and the National Liberation Club!! I met three Cabinet Ministers at dinner on Tuesday, and this scheme seemed to please them. I doubt if they will adopt it. Personally, I should be in favor of prohibition as a national act of self-discipline." [63]

[60] *Letters*, I, 227.
[61] *Ibid.*, II, 365.
[62] *Ibid.*, 363.
[63] *Ibid.*, 362.

His preoccupation with the need to abolish drinking appears in several articles written in the spring of 1915. "Sobriety," published in the *Daily News* on March 10, is an example of his public stance on the subject. After summarizing the difficulties facing the nation, he said that the two virtues most wanted in the crisis were conscientiousness and sobriety. Of the two he felt that sobriety was the more important. He said that beer and whiskey "ought to be ostracized" and urged the government to do what it could, short of abolition, to control their sale and consumption. He then went on to talk about the need for sobriety in word, deed, and judgment.

Bennett may have thrown off the outer forms of the evangelical Protestantism from which he had sprung, but many of his gut-level reactions were still Methodist in character. In at least one part of his nature, self-denial and duty were still marching shoulder to shoulder. His preoccupation with drinking was probably a manifestation produced by other tensions and anxieties deriving from unacknowledged causes. The same may be said about his preoccupations with time, but it is only fair to point out that the "drink" question had become one of national concern and was the subject of many "Letters-to-the-Editor" and of periodical articles.

His preoccupation with time continued to show up in the journal, although the total number of complaints concerning other people's lack of promptness or disregard for schedules was smaller than for the final six months of 1914. Nevertheless, he nearly always entered in his journal the times at which his trains arrived and departed. He was particularly disgusted with the 10:07 train to London, which, he lamented, he had never known to be on schedule. At a meeting of the Queen's Fund, he met a Mrs. MacArthur who impressed him very favorably because she had drawn up a "timed programme . . . with times in it for leaving, like 2:48." On the same day that Mair asked him to go to the front, Bennett attended a Bach recital at St. Paul's. He had yet another appointment following the recital, and he recorded with stern disapproval that the man who was to meet him was thirty seconds late.

On the whole, however, despite Swinnerton's testimony to Bennett's unhappiness in the spring of 1915 and to the stresses and pressures to which he was constantly exposed, during this period his emotions appear to have been reasonably stable. His journal reflects a widening interest in the world. His health, though occasionally bad, did not altogether break down. In the spring of 1915 he seemed to be less concerned with the petty distractions of the Comarques neighborhood than he had been earlier. His circle of acquaintances was growing, and he was meeting men capable of stimulating his imagination rather than subverting it. Undoubtedly, he was neglecting Marguerite. He had found staying at the Reform and at the RTYC pleasant; and as *The Lion's Share* makes obvious, he was struggling to adjust his attitudes to fit the new world which was emerging with such speed under the whip of war.

# IV

# VERY DECIDEDLY UNDER FIRE

On Friday, June 18, Bennett collected his passport and his police clearance from the Foreign Office. The police pass, however, had been made out to Havre instead of Boulogne, and Bennett had to return to Mair's office three times before that as well as other difficulties with his travel documents were resolved. "Godfrey's calm under these provocations," Bennett recorded somewhat sardonically of Mair's secretary, "was remarkable." Considering Bennett's own compulsion to be accurate, his restraint in recording these delays is also remarkable.

At 7:45 on the following Monday morning, he was at Victoria Station waiting for his train. Having checked his luggage, he walked around the station, studying the people. They were mostly soldiers, officers, and "shabby, respectable girls."[1] His own forthcoming adventure was made more real and, perhaps, more romantic by a chance comment which he overheard. A general and another officer passed close to Bennett. The general said, "What I should really like to know is how they relieve those trenches at night." For Bennett the remark was charged with drama, but he seems not to have been struck by the oddity of an army general's not knowing how trenches were relieved. The war had, after all, been in progress for nearly seven months. He might well have been both amused and horrified by such ignorance, but he gave no indication of such feelings.

His initial observations, however, once he was actually on his way, were prosaic enough. Folkstone impressed him chiefly by the quantity of shipping in the harbor, and he was pleasantly surprised to find the Channel crowded with ships of every kind. Admiral Jellicoe and the Grand Fleet were keeping the Channel relatively safe for ships, and Bennett recorded no anxiety about the crossing. The weather was pleasant, and a few miles off the

[1] *Journal*, 559.

French coast Bennett entered in his Notes, "Melancholy of voyage gradually wearing off. Wind on port bow." [2] The entry is at once unusual and yet entirely in character. Although his laconic reference to his emotional state is a rare disclosure, his snapping off of the subjective line with "Wind on port bow" is wholly in keeping with the brusque objectivity that is a hallmark of the journals.

At Boulogne he found, to his relief, that the police pass allowed him to move swiftly through the various security checks and on into the city. Once in the streets he immediately noticed many men of military age who were not in uniform. On his way to the Paris train he saw a "bevy" of nurses in "white starched muslin, blue and red-edged." He also recorded with a straight face that an Army Postal Van arrived at the station with "legends about YMCA and Kaiser written with a finger in white dust on the sides."

Although Bennett did not mention it, Boulogne was one of the three ports, along with Rouen and Havre, to receive the first 80,000 men of the British Expeditionary Force sent out from Portsmouth and Southampton on August 9, 1914. An irony apparently overlooked by Bennett was the fact that these same troops, disembarking at Boulogne, first stepped onto French soil at the foot of a column erected to the memory of Napoleon— just at the place from which he had hoped to launch his invasion of England. [3]

What, in fact, Bennett knew of the military situation as it existed at the time he landed in France is not certain. Judging from what he wrote, however, it can be assumed that despite his long talks with Mair and others he knew relatively little. Oddly enough, he was to display a remarkable lack of curiosity about it. With his passion for organization one might have expected him to have kept battle maps, charts, and so on in the greatest detail. Such was not the case. Occasionally remarking on the fall of a

[2] Arnold Bennett, "Notes Made at the Front 21st June–13th July, 1915. France, Belgium," entry for June 21, 1915. These bound notes are in the Berg Collection, New York Public Library. Hereafter they will be cited Notes and date of entry. (Pagination in the Notes is confused.)

[3] Barbara Tuchman, *The Guns of August* (New York, 1965), 229.

city or the outcome of an engagement, he displayed in his journal and letters little interest in campaigns.

Although Bennett was not particularly concerned about the situation, Britain's military position in June of 1915 was not a cause for celebration among either her military or her civilian leaders. Thanks to the government's strict application of the Defense of the Realm Act, passed in August, 1914, the English public had only the haziest ideas about what was actually happening to their armies and no idea at all of the character of the policies being pursued by the government. Bennett had protested repeatedly in his articles against the censorship of news, insisting that it was too often being used as a means of keeping Englishmen in ignorance of what their government was doing and of preventing criticism of individuals and of policy. But the censorship actually was being applied with increasing vigor despite all protests.

The truth was that Britain's military effort was floundering. The tragically abortive Dardanelles expedition had been launched in January; but after weeks of delay and more weeks of bickering among Cabinet members, admirals, and generals, the forcing of the straits had not been accomplished. Instead, thousands of lives had been lost pointlessly, and British prestige in the East had received a damaging blow.

Affairs were not much better in France. Joffre, the French Commander, was at odds with Sir John French,[4] the Commander-in-Chief of the British forces in France; and French was at odds with Kitchener, his nominal superior in England. Following the battle of Mons on August 23, 1914, French had withdrawn his army in a remarkable thirteen day, two hundred mile retreat. Halted by Kitchener, French reluctantly threw his army into the French counteroffensive on the Marne in September.

[4] Sir John Denton Pinkstone French was replaced by Sir Douglas Haig in the fall of 1915, who remained in command for the duration of the war. Generalship did not rest easily on French's shoulders. On one occasion he said to Lord Esher, "It is a solemn thought that at my signal all these fine young fellows go to their death." French was shockingly incompetent, but no hint of that incompetence entered Bennett's articles or found its way into his letters or journal.

Again his army was spared, this time by a German tactical error which had divided their First and their Second Armies. French found himself in the gap between them, with his cavalry reconnoitering, at times, forty miles behind the German lines. No advantage was taken of the situation, however; and the Germans, discovering what had happened, withdrew to the Aisne and dug in, too tired to retreat further, and by their defensive actions establishing the pattern for the trench warfare that was to characterize the fighting from that time forward.

Within a few weeks the B.E.F. was withdrawn to Flanders. It reached its new positions just as a more powerful German force, freed after the fall of Antwerp, was advancing to outflank the Allies. The resulting collision was the first battle of Ypres, which lasted from October 12 to November 11. The B.E.F., outnumbered and outgunned, held the Germans until October 31, when they succeeded in piercing the British line. But the Germans were so exhausted that they were unable to follow up their advantage quickly enough to prevent French troops from sealing the breach. The first battle of Ypres stopped the German advance, but it also marked the end of the B.E.F. and the end of the old British Army. More than half of the men who had crossed to France in August were casualties; one in ten was dead. Kitchener's New Army became, aside from the Territorials, England's only significant land force.

By November the English government acknowledged that it had been mistaken. The war would not be short. Kitchener was talking of a three-year war with armies numbering in the millions. And those who had counted on a swift British victory at sea were disappointed. The German Fleet remained in port and Admiral Jellicoe sat at Scapa Flow and waited for his enemy to come out and fight, knowing that a single mistake by him involving the loss of his armada would mean England's defeat.

With the turn of the year the English government found itself almost helpless to deal with the military situation. Lord Esher described the wretched state of affairs existing in the War Council: "It is like a game of nine-pins," he wrote on January 13, 1915, following a lunch at the Admiralty with Admiral John Fisher and Arthur Balfour; "one plan is knocked over, and, in falling, knocks over the next one, and so on until the board is clear; the result is a total want of initiative of any kind." [5]

On the Western Front, General French was preparing an independent action against the Germans which was to be remembered as the battle of Neuve Chapelle. In it the situation of the first battle of Ypres was reversed. French pierced the German line but could not bring reserves up in time to consolidate his advantage. Had Joffre been taken into General French's confidence, and had French troops been ready to act as reserves, something might have been gained. A month later the Germans attacked again at Ypres, this time with gas, but were beaten back after very heavy British losses. Then in May the French and British struck the German lines together at the battle of Festubert or Aubers Ridge, as it is sometimes called. The outcome was indecisive, but losses on both sides were again heavy.

French blamed his failures on the shortage of ammunition. There is no doubt that such a shortage existed. In a letter to Lord Kitchener, dated March 21, 1915, Lord Esher wrote, "If we are beaten in this war, it will be on account of a shortage of ammunition." He went on to say that French offers to show how ammunition could be produced rapidly were ignored.[6] But Kitchener remained unmoved in his insistence that all was being done that could be done. French grew increasingly irritated.

Then Lord Northcliffe, who had a correspondent in French's headquarters, in defiance of the War Office ban on correspondents, managed to bring the whole ammunition scandal into the daylight of print. Charles à Court Repington, the "Playboy of the Western Front," a retired Lieutenant-Colonel turned journalist, who was also at French's headquarters, released to Lord Northcliffe the text of a communication by French protesting against the shortage of shells. The story broke in The Times on the morning of May 14.

Coupled with the Gallipoli debacle, the exposure undermined the Asquith government to the extent that Asquith was forced to shuffle the Cabinet in favor of the Tories and accept a coali-

[5] Reginald, Viscount Esher, *Journals and Letters of Reginald, Viscount Esher,* ed. Oliver, Viscount Esher (London, 1938), III, 203.
[6] Esher, *Journals and Letters,* III, 223.

tion government as the price for avoiding a Parliamentary debate on the shell issue. Northcliffe, who had intended to bring down the government and Kitchener with it, published an attack on the old soldier in the *Daily Mail* on May 21; but so popular was Kitchener that the circulation of the *Daily Mail* immediately fell from a daily circulation of 1,400,000 to fewer than 25,000 copies.[7]

The new government was even less decisive than the old one had been. It had nothing that could be called a coherent policy for conducting the war and was reduced to suppressing debate on any issues in Parliament and exercising as strenuous public censorship as possible. Kitchener, uncertain and indecisive, continued to find himself at odds with French. Strategy, such as it was, seemed to be dictated more by German actions than by an Allied scheme for achieving victory. English Generals in France organized fox hunts and occasional raids against "local objectives." The fox hunts outraged the French, who said that the British were not taking the war seriously; and the raids succeeded in killing large numbers of English soldiers without accomplishing anything useful.

It was in the midst of this depressing muddle that Bennett was to make his inspection of the Fronts. It is difficult to believe that he did not know what a mess things were in; but all the evidence of his Notes, journals, and correspondence indicates that he had no clear idea of how the war was being conducted. It is certain, however, that he was familiar with Belloc's articles in *Land and Water* and with what was being written in the *Times* and other newspapers. His refusal—and it is difficult to characterize his response any other way—to admit that the government was managing things badly and that the war was being prosecuted chiefly by stop-gap measures can be explained only by assuming either that he had chosen to ignore the facts or

_____

[7] On August 14 Bennett recorded in his journal that he had lunched with Clifford Sharp and had learned from Sharp that Northcliffe himself had dictated the article and that it had originally been even more savage than the printed version. Northcliffe's personal animus toward Kitchener, according to Bennett, stemmed from Northcliffe's loss of several nephews in the war. When remonstrated with about his attitude toward Kitchener, he was reported to have said, "But he's murdered my nephews!"

concluding that nothing was to be gained by dwelling pessimistically on them.

Bennett reached Paris by train from Boulogne, travelling by way of Étaples, where he saw an army camp and hospitals. From his compartment the scene struck him as being "as English as England." Further on at Abbéville he reported that "the whole line, station and scene makes an impression like perpetual Sunday, except for soldiers and camps." The entry is his first reference to the peacefulness of the countryside, which was to become such a consolation to him as he moved through successive war zones across France and into Belgium. His ties with France were strong. He knew her to be threatened, and it is as though he were saying in relief as the train bore him toward Paris, "Well, there are soldiers here and camps and hospitals; but France, after all, is still France."

From the taxi which he took to the Hotel Meurice at 228 Rue de Rivoli, he looked out on the streets of Paris and was disturbed to see so many of the shops closed. Then he remembered that it was after closing time and immediately felt better. Later that evening he and Mair, who may have crossed to France ahead of him, went to visit Cepa Godebski, an artist and a very old friend. Bennett also called on Émile Martin, another old friend whom he first met in 1904 and who had helped him to settle in Paris years before. Martin's mother, Bennett observed wryly, was "still firing cooks." She said to him, "If you are coming to lunch, Bennett, come before Monday, because on Monday my cook takes herself away, and as for the new one I should dare to say nothing." [8]

His first recorded impression of Paris was that there were a surprising number of young men not in uniform.[9] He also found the city darker than London and pervaded by a "peculiar feeling." When he had time to digest these and other impressions,

[8] Notes, June 22, 1915.

[9] Bennett was preoccupied with the conscription issue. He opposed conscription on the grounds that it was pro-German (meaning that it was a Prussian device for raising and maintaining an army) and that it was part of a larger plan on the part of the radical Tories to undermine the democratic processes in England. He knew that the presence of large numbers of men of military age out of uniform greatly strengthened the conscriptionists' cause.

he recorded them at length in his first article for the *Saturday Evening Post* and the *Illustrated London News*. There is a remarkable degree of emotion in his description of the city as he viewed it from the hotel balcony: "Nobody who knows Paris, and understands what Paris has meant and still means to humanity, can regard the scene without the most exquisite sentiments of humility, affection, and gratitude." His gratitude sprang from the fact that the city had been spared.[10]

The absence of autobusses and trams and the poor showing of taxis [11] along the streets gave the city, he thought, the "perpetual aspect of Sunday morning" with only the sound of church bells lacking. He was also struck by the fact that many of the most expensive shops were shut. "But the provision shops and all the sturdy cheap shops of the poor go on naturally, without any self-consciousness, just as usual." With a sense of pride and something of a sense of triumph, he wrote, "Never was Paris so disconcertingly odd. And yet never was it more profoundly itself. . . . Paris is revealed under an enchantment. On the surface of the enchantment the pettiness of daily existence exists queerly." [12]

In general Bennett's tone in "The Zone of Paris" is sincere. He described experiences which he felt deeply. Only occasionally in the opening paragraphs of the article does the propagandist and special pleader make himself felt. When he does appear, he speaks in an unmistakably official voice of the sort heard in the following account of Parisian widows: "The number of young girls and women in mourning, in the heavy mourning affected by the Latin race, is enormous. This crape is the sole casualty list permitted by the French War Office. It suffices. Supreme grief is omnipresent; but it is calm, cheerful, smiling. Widows glance at each other with understanding, like initiates of a secret and powerful society. . . ." [13]

---

[10] Arnold Bennett, *Over There: War Scenes on the Western Front* (New York, 1915), 4.

[11] The French had used the Paris taxis to move their Sixth Army out to meet the advancing Germans in a maneuver which was instrumental in turning the German attack.

[12] Bennett, *Over There*, 7.

[13] *Ibid.*, 7.

On the 22nd he gave André Gide, Godebski, and Mair lunch at the Meurice. "Gide," he remarked with quiet humor, was "intellectually more than ever like an orchid." That evening he dined at Nisia Edward's flat—Nisia was another friend from his early days in Paris—with Philippe Berthelot, a French diplomat; Gide; Mair; the Godebskis; and Legrix, a young French novelist. Berthelot had been invited for the purpose of helping Bennett to secure permission from the French government to go to the front. The permission had been mysteriously delayed and both Mair and Bennett were becoming restless. Berthelot was not a stranger. Bennett had known him years earlier and had not liked him very much. He found that he still didn't care for him, although he had considerable respect for Berthelot, who was soon to become Clemenceau's trusted advisor.[14] Bennett was particularly disturbed by the way Berthelot dressed. Several days after the party he inserted in his Notes (which he kept during his stay in France and Belgium and later had bound) the confession that he had been thinking rather "often of the badly-fitting grey alpaca suit and worse-fitting boots" which Berthelot had worn.[15]

The after-dinner talk had swung away from the war to literature; and Legrix asked Bennett what he thought of *The Way of All Flesh*, which Legrix had just been reading. Bennett did not record his answer, but he did observe that it was "singular how that ruthless book makes its way across all frontiers." Legrix was also interested in Gissing; but before Bennett could respond to the young novelist's questions, the conversation was turned back to the war and specifically to England's attitude toward the Germans. Bennett's French friends were convinced that the English simply did not hate the Germans sufficiently to be really passionate about the war. It was a characteristically Gallic objection and Bennett responded to it with what he described as a rather awkward laugh, "as any Englishman would."

There was one unnamed friend whom Bennett had hoped to meet at the party, but he did not show up. "He was engaged with a Countess," Bennett wrote, adding cryptically, "Naturally."

[14] *Journal*, 197.
[15] Notes, June 25, 1915.

But even in the warm glow of after-dinner conversation Bennett was unable to maintain his lightness of mood. Looking around at the guests, he was again astonished by the number of men who "had escaped active service." With rather heavy-handed irony he noted that "one or two who might have come failed to do so because they had perished." [16] He leaves it to the reader to decide whether or not they died in the war and also whether or not he was making a comment on those out of uniform.

Despite Berthelot's intervention, the government continued to delay in giving Bennett permission to go to the front. Tired of the inactivity and troubled by morning headaches, he arranged to go on his own to Meaux, Barcy, and Chambry, towns outside Paris which marked the closest approaches of the German army to the capital. In his description of Meaux, Bennett established the pattern he was to follow in the articles when dealing with towns that had been overrun by Germans and retaken or else subjected to heavy shelling by the German guns. He gave a brief history of Meaux, concentrating on the successive battles and massacres which had occurred there from the time of the Normans to the present crisis and then filled in details of the town's present circumstances.

His purpose in giving the history was at least twofold. In the first place he wished to fix the place in his readers' minds and to place it in a context. Secondly, he wished to contrast the intermittent periods of violence and bloodshed which the town had undergone with the more enduring peacefulness of the place. In a lesser way, he may have wished to make the point that the present trouble was temporary as all those of the past had been. It was a neat journalistic device, but its effectiveness in the articles was reduced by repetition.

On the outskirts of Meaux, Bennett saw his first soldier's grave. Located on a hillside close to the road, it was marked by a white cross of painted wood and was surrounded by a low barbed wire fence. The dead man had belonged to the 66th Territorials, a British battalion, and Bennett thought he must be the soldier who had fallen closest to Paris. His description of the grave is very

[16] Bennett, *Over There,* 19.

effective, but in an effort to give additional dramatic force and significance to the grave he fell back into the near-bathetic: "It [the grave] marked the last homicidal effort of the Germans. . . . This tomb was a very impressive thing." [17]

The simple fact of the grave with its inscription was enough, but he could not leave it to speak for itself. He felt compelled to "milk" the situation—and to make it "count." Such inflated writing, rather than any misrepresentation of fact, makes the articles propaganda. Marguerite stated, and others have taken her at her word, that Bennett was psychologically shattered by his experiences at the Front. Since nothing shattering is to be found in the articles he wrote about the Front, it has been assumed that he had not told the truth in them, that he engaged in deliberate distortion of fact, and worse.

But his distortions are of the kind described above and almost always intrude when Bennett feels the need to write more emotionally than his own feelings justify. The Notes are not substantially different in content or in tone from the articles which grew from them. The Notes, however, never descend to a straining for effect. There is not the slightest evidence to suggest that he falsified his reports to cover up horrors which he could not or would not describe. Neither are the Notes themselves edited to exclude anything unpleasant. Written for the most part in pencil and while he was riding in an army car or walking along trenches, they are a series of jottings of what he saw, heard, and smelled.

Although John D. Gordan called the Notes "the most poignant of all the Journals," there is nothing in them to suggest that Bennett was exposed to scenes which sickened or horrified him and which he later determined to suppress.[18] That is not to say that he was never shocked by what he saw. He was and, as will be shown later, he wrote about those things which did upset him. But it is the wildest speculation to say that Bennett was psychologically damaged by his experiences at the front. In fact, con-

[17] *Ibid.,* 22.
[18] John D. Gordan, *Arnold Bennett: The Centenary of His Birth, An Exhibition in the Berg Collection* (New York, 1968), 45.

sidering his age, the state of his health, and the great physical strain to which he was subjected by the hard walking and rough riding, he appears to have remained surprisingly cheerful throughout his stay. There is no evidence of a declining spirit in the Notes. They remain uniformly calm and objective to the end.[19]

The articles are not, of course, simply reproductions of the Notes. But there is a remarkable similarity between them and very few instances of unpleasant facts being suppressed. A comparison of the Notes made on the battlefield between Chambry and Barcy with the later description given in "The Zone of Paris" demonstrates the relationship between Notes and articles. The Notes on his observations read as follows:

> Many tombs in wheat, and hidden in wheat. Barbed wire and four stark posts (bird on post). . . . On every side in these open fields, the gleam of cross or flag, as far as you can see. Scores and scores. General impression: How little is left [of signs of war]. How cultivation and civilization have covered the disaster over! Wheat growing out of a German.[20]

In "The Zone of Paris" this was expanded into four overly literary paragraphs:

> We made towards Chambry. Chambry is a village, which, like Meaux, lies below the plain. Chambry escaped glory; but between it and Barcy, on the intervening slope through which a good road runs, a battle was fought. You know what kind of battle it was by the tombs. These tombs were very like the others—an oblong of barbed wire, a white flag, a white cross, sometimes a name, more often only a number, rarely a wreath. You see first one, then another, then two, then a sprinkling; and gradually you perceive that the whole plain is dotted with gleams of white flags and white crosses, so that the graves seem to extend right away to the horizon marked by a line

---

[19] Bennett was severely limited in what he could publish. Both the English and the French censorships were very strict. No war correspondents had accompanied the English Army to France, and it was not until May of 1915 that six English correspondents were allowed to go to the General Headquarters for "a limited period," as the official permission stated. In fact, the correspondents remained there throughout the war under the strictest supervision by Army censors. The Press Bureau released news bulletins, and the War Office censored all cables and foreign correspondence.

[20] Notes, June 24, 1915.

of trees. Then you see a huge general grave. . . . Much glory about that spot!

And then a tomb with a black cross. Very disconcerting that black cross! It is different not only in color, but in shape, from the other crosses. Sinister! You need not be told that the body of a German lies beneath it. The whole devilishness of the Prussian ideal is expressed in that black cross. Then, as the road curves, you see more black crosses, very many. No flags, no names, no wreaths on these tombs. Just a white stencilled number in the center of each cross. Women in Germany are still lying awake at nights [sic] and wondering what those tombs look like.

Watching over all the tombs, white and black without distinction, are notices: "Respect the Tombs." But the wheat and the oats are not respecting the tombs. Everywhere the crops have encroached on them, half-hiding them, smothering them, climbing right over them. In one place the wheat is ripening out of the very body of a German soldier.

Such is the nearest battlefield to Paris. Corporate excursions to it are forbidden, and wisely. For the attraction of the place, were it given play, would completely demoralize Meaux and the entire district.[21]

The day after his visit to Meaux, he wrote in his Notes that the trip was successful and was "a proper introduction to a seeing of the war." The same day he began writing "The Zone of Paris" and finished it the following morning. The French Foreign Office broke its long silence and sent word that he and Mair could go to Rheims. That evening he and Mair dined at Meaux; and when, while they were eating, Lord Esher came into the dining room, Bennett's reaction was unusual.[22] Having described Lord Esher as wearing a "fancy military costume" with a star "depending from his neck," he added that Esher looked like "a very debased and bad man, and his voice told the same tale." [23]

[21] Bennett, *Over There*, 28–29.
[22] Viscount Esher (Reginald Baliol Brett) was a somewhat shadowy semi-political figure whose position in society and whose intelligent interest in the Empire made him a man of considerable influence in Edwardian England and during the war years. He was a close friend of the King and the advisor and confidante of nearly all the major political personalities in England. Since he was also on intimate terms with French diplomats and generals, he was very valuable as a liaison between the French and the English governments. In the summer of 1915 he was in Paris as the informal "eyes" of Lord Kitchener.
[23] Notes, June 25, 1915.

The attack was not only out of character, it was, apparently, unwarranted. Bennett did not know Esher, probably had never met him. What moved him to condemn the man is not known, but at rare intervals his journals record similar unprovoked attacks, usually based on the individual's looks. Occasionally Bennett admits that a man is not responsible for his physical characteristics, but the condemnation is likely to stand unqualified. There is no doubt that Bennett harbored a deep dislike for privilege. He was, however, much too honest and magnanimous a man to judge those people he met on the basis of class, but occasionally his resentment appears to have flashed out at titled people whom he did not know for no better reason than that they were titled.[24]

On June 26th Bennett and Mair reported to the Foreign Office to work out the final details of the Rheims trip. There they met Walter Hale, the English illustrator who was eventually to do the drawings for *Over There,* and Owen Johnson, An American novelist.[25] Since Bennett knew Hale, it was settled that the four men should make the journey together under the supervision of a French Army Officer, Captain D'Arenberg, who was to act as chief guide as well as official censor of any written reporting done by the group. Bennett was favorably impressed by D'Arenberg, finding him "charming and witty."

He was equally pleased by the elaborateness of the preparations which the French had made for them. Equipped with three motor cars to accommodate the passengers and a fourth for luggage, the four civilians started on their way, carefully shepherded by four Staff officers and six chauffeurs. "Every facility was given," Bennett wrote to Pinker. "Every available general explained things to us himself, and we were treated like princes."[26] What Bennett seems not to have noticed was that

---

[24] In a journal entry for April 11, 1912, Bennett wrote, "By the way, at the Princess's Restaurant, I saw Lord X. He looked a vulgar and damned scoundrel. Not his fault, of course."

[25] In referring to Johnson in a letter to Pinker, Bennett put "bestseller" in parentheses after his name. Bennett was probably referring to Johnson's *Stover at Yale,* published in 1912.

[26] Ogden Collection, June 28, 1915.

while he and his companions were being protected, they were also being kept from almost any unplanned contact with conditions at the Front. They were being given an official tour, and they were allowed to see only what the French Army Staff wanted them to see.

"Never once," Bennett was to write later, "at any moment of the day, whether driving furiously along somewhat deteriorated roads in the car, or walking about the land, did I lack a Staff Officer who produced in me the illusion that he was living solely in order to be of use to me." [27] He was more pleased than he should have been by the attention, and more flattered. But it was precisely this sort of official recognition that most tickled his vanity. At times his self-satisfaction prevented his seeing clearly what was actually happening to him. It was not so much that he distorted in his front articles what he had seen as that he tended to accept without question that he had, in fact, seen the reality of war.

A revealing example of how he was led astray is found in his account of the relationship existing between the officers and the men in the French army. Among the noncommissioned officers in Bennett's party were a corporal and a sergeant, who dined with the officers. Bennett was greatly excited by such a show of equality: "Talk about an ideal democracy," he wrote happily. "It is here realized." He seems not to have made any connection between the way they were treated and the facts that the corporal was a playwright and an interpreter and the sergeant, the son of a French general. It was enough for him that a corporal and a sergeant ate with commissioned officers. "We are all equal," he explained in "On the French Front." "The French Army is by far the most democratic institution I have ever seen." Such uncritical acceptance of surface appearances on Bennett's part amounts almost to a deliberate act of self-deception. Given his experience as a novelist and as an observer of life, it is difficult to accept his blindness as being wholly ingenuous.

There were those, however, who considered the kind of thing Bennett and other "official" observers were writing a deliberate

[27] Bennett, *Over There*, 34–35.

traducing of the public. Siegfried Sassoon, for example, was an uncompromising critic of the propagandists. "What was this camouflage war which was manufactured by the press to aid the imaginations of people who had never seen the real thing?" he asked in *Memoirs of an Infantry Officer*.[28] In the same book he recorded an interview with Markington—who was really Henry W. Massingham, editor of *The Nation*—in which Markington said,

> Quite a number of middle-aged members of this club [the Reform] have been to the front. . . . After a dinner at General Headquarters and a motor drive in the direction of the trenches, they can talk and write in support of the war with complete confidence in themselves. Five years ago they were probably saying that modern civilization had made a European war unthinkable.[29] But their principles are purchasable. Once they've been invited to visit General Headquarters they never look back. Their own self-importance is all that matters to them. And any lie is a good lie as long as it stimulates unreasoning hatred of the enemy.[30]

Douglas Goldring, writing in 1920, said, "To many men of the younger generation who fought in the war, it now seems incredible that during their absence the inciters to hatred and slaughter could ever have contrived to get such a stranglehold on public opinion.[31]

Does *Over There* put Bennett among the "inciters to hatred and slaughter"? Was any lie a good lie as far as Bennett was concerned? Had his principles been purchased by the English government? Had his own self-importance become his greatest preoccupation? It cannot be denied that Bennett supported a policy of rigorously prosecuting the war. He was also a supporter of Asquith and the Liberal government. But as will be seen later, he never at any time defended a policy of suppressing the truth in order that the government might escape embarrassment. As for his having abandoned his principles or become the victim of his

[28] Siegfried Sassoon, *Memoirs of an Infantry Officer* (London, 1969), 186.
[29] Bennett had, of course, said the same thing as late as July, 1914.
[30] Sassoon, *Memoirs*, 194.
[31] Douglas Goldring, "Mr. Wells and the War," *Reputations* (London, 1920), 83.

self-importance, there is no evidence in the records of his trip to France and to Belgium that anything of the sort took place. His judgment may sometimes be questioned but never his basic honesty. He was guilty of inflation in his articles, and he strove to present both officers and men in a near heroic light. But he was not guilty of a dangerous duplicity.

From the Chateau Pommary, situated on a hill near Rheims, Bennett had his first glimpse of the German lines, which he mistook at first for a level road. It was a moment of great excitement for him, but the excitement was accompanied by the painful realization that all of France beyond those lines lay under the "insulting tyranny of the invader." Below the Chateau and between him and the German lines there were eighty thousand French troops, hidden from sight. There was little to see, but he could hear the sound of guns firing in the distance. At his feet, however, the land fell away along the slopes in vineyards of such luxuriant growth that he was moved to record that "the whole of the earth seemed to be cultivated and to be yielding bounteously." His overriding impression was one of "peace, majesty, grandeur; and of the mild, splendid richness of the soil of France." [32]

Once again Bennett was deeply moved by the tenacity with which the French peasants clung to their land. "The earth was yielding fabulously," he wrote in a lyric fervor. "It was yielding up to within a mile and a half of the German wire entanglements." [33] Despite the danger of being killed, the women, clad in blue, moved through the fields, bending patiently to their tasks. The French officers had warned them repeatedly of the risks they were running, but they went on quietly with their work. When the Germans began raking the countryside with their artillery, which they did at intervals, the women simply lay down and waited for the firing to stop. Then they would get up and go on with their work.

While he was lunching at the Chateau, Bennett insisted on drinking water, much to the horror of the "champagne propri-

[32] Bennett, *Over There*, 34.
[33] *Ibid.*, 37.

etor," whom Bennett suspected of wanting to sell his wines. It seems probable that Bennett's illness following his return to England should be traced to this and similar indiscretions with doubtful water. Bad water had nearly killed him in 1912, when in the southern part of France he was stricken with an undiagnosed attack of typhoid fever, which left him a semi-invalid for months afterward.[34] It is even possible that it was a mild form of typhoid that he struggled with on his return home, although it is more likely that he had contracted dysentery. There was the same intestinal flare-up as had occurred in 1912 and the same slow recovery, marked with relapses. He never learned to distrust water on the Continent, and it was a typhoid infection that killed him in 1931.

Coming down from Chateau Pommary, Bennett was driven to an "engineers' park" where he inspected stacks of barbed wire and other materials of trench warfare in "unimaginable quantities." He then went on to the town of Merval, where he had his first look at German prisoners. A small group of them under a guard were collecting muck in a courtyard. His description of them in the Notes is brief, but in "On the French Front" he expanded the event, using it as an excuse to attack German militarism. "They were men in God's image," he wrote of the prisoners, "and they went about on the assumption that all the rest of the war lay before them and that there was a lot of it. To me they had a brutalized air, no doubt one minor consequence of military ambition in high places."

He had other encounters with prisoners. On one occasion he saw a young German being brought back from the lines. He was, Bennett recorded, "a miserable tuberculous youth with a nervous trick of the face, thin, very dirty, enfeebled, worn out." In an attempt to be hard hearted or, perhaps, sardonic, Bennett wrote that the wretched, half-starved youth had "had just about enough of world dominion. . . ." Continuing in the same vein and with less success at keeping up the jocular tone, he concluded his account of the prisoner by saying, "No doubt, some woman was his mother! It appeared to me he could not live long, and that the

34 Pound, *Arnold Bennett*, 366.

woman in question might never see him again." Bennett's attitude is assumed for the occasion and is worn rather poorly. He came closer to revealing his true feelings about prisoners of war when he wrote, "Some people can go and stare at prisoners, and wreck an idle curiosity upon them. I cannot. A glance, rather surreptitious, and I must walk away. Their humiliation humiliates me, even if they be Prussians of the most offensive variety." [35]

Although the facts presented in Bennett's "Front" articles are essentially the same facts recorded in his Notes, an exception must be made in his description of the French field hospital at Merval. Interestingly enough, he did not put a description of the hospital into his Notes until he had returned to Paris. The haste with which they moved through their itinerary may have prevented his doing it sooner; but he may, on the other hand, have preferred to write up his impressions of the place at a time when there was no possibility of the description's falling into the hands of men who were responsible for the hospital.

The hospital was called an *ambulance de premiere ligne*. Wounded were brought to it directly from the front line dressing stations to undergo surgery. In "On the French Front" Bennett confined himself to giving an account of how the hospital functioned, the principle on which it and others like it were set up, and so on. As to the character of the hospital, he said only that "the worn face of the doctor in charge showed that vast labors must have been accomplished in those somber chambers." [36]

Bennett's description in the Notes is quite different. Under the heading "Back from Chateau-Thierry," he wrote, "The only bad thing we saw during the trip was *ambulance*. Badly and inefficiently arranged. Dirty. Many flies. Dirty attendants. Dirty linen. Patients seemed chiefly depressed. Commanding officer and other officers seemed very second rate." [37] Of course, it is a certainty that the French censor would never have passed such a description for publication. And Bennett might well have suppressed

[35] Bennett, *Over There*, 111.
[36] *Ibid.*, 42.
[37] Notes, June 28, 1915.

such a piece of information, in any case, feeling that to submit such material for approval would only offend the authorities and perhaps curtail his future movements.

Bennett was back in Paris by the 28th, and in a long letter to Pinker he said that three days at a time [at the front] was all that he could stand. The program was full, and the strain of being driven at high speeds along bad roads exhausted him, often before he had begun the hard work of looking at trenches, ammunition dumps, supply depots, and so on. He was not, however, too tired for business. In the same letter he gave Pinker permission to make the final arrangements for selling the "front" articles to the *Illustrated London News* at forty-five pounds per article. "I would rather have the articles in the *I.L.N.* at forty-five pounds," he wrote "than with the *Sunday Chronicle* at seventy-five pounds." [38]

He also set the number of articles at six, adding that there might be fewer. Although he denied that he was limiting the number to six because there was a lack of material, he may have felt that the pressure of the French censorship coupled with the limited experiences he was having made it impossible for him to write more than six effective articles. He finally wrote seven pieces, but left the seventh out of *Over There*, publishing it finally in the *Daily News* on September 30, 1915. In view of the fact that *The Saturday Evening Post* was prepared to accept twelve articles, Bennett must have felt his reasons for limiting the number to six to be unassailable. He certainly could have used the money that the extra pieces would have brought him.

It pleased Bennett to be able to tell Pinker that he had been under fire, "very decidedly under fire." The circumstances of the incident are given with considerable verve in "On the French Front." Having approached the French lines at Merval, he was greeted by a general and his staff in a demolished village and treated to a *vin d'honneur*. The Germans saw the unusual activity in the village and laid down an artillery barrage on it. The party and their guides retreated along a communication trench, which also came under fire, and then fled in their automobiles.

Before the *vin d'honneur* Bennett examined some of the

[38] Ogden Collection, June 28, 1915.

French trenches, which he found "very remarkably swept and dusted and spotless. . . ." Since he was not given the opportunity to talk to any of the soldiers whom he passed, he was obliged to rely on what he saw and what the officers told him about the spirit of the men. Even granting the distance he was forced to maintain between himself and the soldiers, it is still difficult to fully understand just what he intended in his description of one French soldier, whom he seems to have chosen to stand for all French enlisted men.

The soldier was in one of the firing line trenches. At the appearance of the Commandant the man sprang to attention. "He threw his head back," Bennett wrote, "and slightly to one side, and his brown beard stuck out. His eyes sparkled. Every muscle was taut. He seemed to be saying, 'My Commandant, I know my worth; I am utterly yours—you won't get anything better.' " The description is forced and unconvincing to the point of being irritating; but whatever else may be said of the portrait, it is in keeping with the closing lines of his description of the trenches: "We had been to the very front of the front, and it was the most cheerful, confident, high-spirited place I had seen in France, or in England either." [39]

The French authorities kept Bennett in Paris until August 8 before making a decision about where to send him next. His Notes for the ten days he spent waiting show that he was often bored, but he did manage to write two and a half articles of the series. They were sent to D'Arenberg to be censored and were promptly passed, a development which proved that Bennett had judged accurately the temper of the French military censorship. He lunched with Mair, Godebski, and the composer Maurice Ravel, who was in the army and disappointed at not being in the air corps; but he had been unable to secure an appointment to the air corps because his friends refused to help him get a commission, insisting that flying was too dangerous. On one occasion Gide said that Bennett's presence made him want to work. Bennett replied complacently that he often had that effect on people.

The weariness of waiting for something to happen, made more burdensome by what Bennett called the "Russian disaster . . .

[39] Bennett, *Over There*, 52, 60.

and the prospect of a fierce and perhaps successful attempt to break through the French line and reach Paris," was lifted by the news that they were to go to Amiens and from there to Arras. Bennett later added his experiences in Amiens and Arras to those at Rheims and from them wrote his third article "Three Ruins," which he had half written before leaving Paris. The ruins he described were Rheims and its cathedral, Arras and its cathedral and its town hall. Bennett was able to write with genuine sincerity about Rheims and Arras, dropping the brittle liveliness he had assumed in his descriptions of the French trenches and the democracy of the French Army. What he saw in Rheims and Arras shocked him deeply. In their shattered streets he came face to face with the violence of war and the callous indifference with which it is waged.

Driving through the shelled quarters of Rheims, Bennett was impressed by the reminders of domestic life that were exposed by the shattered buildings. In the Notes he wrote that the wind blew through the ruins continually, so that there was an almost constant sound of things falling—pictures, objects left standing on shelves and tables, mirrors, and bits of rubble. Some quarters of the city were nearly deserted, their inhabitants having saved what they could from the wreckage of their homes and gone away. "Each knows his lot in the immense tragedy," he wrote, striving to make what had happened to Rheims comprehensible and then abandoning the attempt as hopeless. "Nobody can realize the whole of the tragedy," he continued. "It defies the mind; and, moreover, the horror of it is allayed somewhat by the beautiful forms which ruin—even the ruin of modern ugly architecture— occasionally takes." But he could find no consolation here in the ripening wheat or the tenacity of purpose of the French peasants. He was outraged by what had happened to Rheims and by the senselessness of the destruction. "It is desperately cruel," he wrote in anger. "But it is far worse than cruel—it is idiotic in its immense futility. The perfect idiocy of the thing overwhelms you." [40]

He was obviously touched, as he had not been by the trenches and even by the sea of crosses, with an awareness of the immense

[40] *Ibid.*, 65, 66.

folly of the war, of any war: "And to your reason it is monstrous
that one population should overrun another with murder and
destruction from political covetousness as that two populations
should go to war concerning a religious creed. Indeed, it is more
monstrous. It is an obscene survival, a phenomenon that has
strayed, through some negligence of fate, into the wrong century." [41] How extraordinary it is that the destruction of buildings
should have aroused in him a passionate revolt against war when
the graves of the dead soldiers served only to provoke in him
hackneyed expressions of honor, glory, and patriotism.

A partial explanation of what appears to be an insensitivity in
his responses to the war is that he actually saw almost nothing in
the trenches to excite his imagination with horror. Guns fired,
shells exploded; but no one seemed the worse for that. It cannot
be denied, however, that he never allowed himself to speculate
on the possibilities for individual suffering which trench warfare
held for those caught up in it. He was shaken by the sight of
shelled towns, but he remained strangely unmoved by the sight
of men shooting at one another. He may have suppressed his feelings because he found them intolerable; or, what is more likely,
he may have refused to allow his imagination to work in a way
that would have diminished his powers of observation. He dis-
trusted the fanciful and in reference to it had written to Mrs.
Herzog in September of 1914 that "as no good purpose can be
served by letting the imagination loose, it is best to keep it in control." On that occasion he was referring to fears about the war.
It is possible that he continued to be guided by that principle.

He described the destruction of Rheims Cathedral with more
restraint than he had employed in writing about the city itself,
but the trembling sense of injustice was still present. He turned
his anger directly against the Germans and what appeared to him
to be their total lack of justification for shelling the Cathedral
and in his condemnation made the structure a symbol of French
resistance. "The Cathedral stands," he wrote, "high above the
level of disaster, a unique target, and a target successfully defiant."

Arras was, if possible, even more staggering to him in its deso-

[41] *Ibid.*, 66.

lation than Rheims: "Every house in it [Arras] presents the same blighted aspect. There is no urban stir. . . . Not even a cat walks. We are alone. . . . We feel like thieves, like desecrators, impiously prying." He found streets paved with powdered glass and tangled in twisted coils of wire. Houses with their roofs blown off but with the furniture in place and potted plants blooming on tables and window ledges stood like museum exhibits. Over the city was the continual sound of the firing of the French and the German guns.

As for Arras Cathedral, it had been riddled by shells and was in flames when he saw it. The Town Hall, which had been built in the sixteenth century and had once boasted the tallest bell tower in France, lay with scarcely one stone on another. Faced with this destruction, Bennett lost that objectivity which was so distinctly his and became, for the moment, one with those who were demanding in the English press that Germany be made to suffer for her acts: "I am against a policy of reprisals, and yet—such is human nature—having seen Arras, I would honestly give a year's income to see Cologne in the same condition. And to the end of my life I shall feel cheated if Cologne or some similar German town is not in fact ultimately reduced to the same condition. This state of mind comes with seeing things with your own eyes." [42]

He continued, however, to exercise a selective sensibility in expressing outrage. Certain things, horrible in their own ways, did not move him either to anger or dismay. On one occasion, when he was inspecting some trenches under the guidance of a general, German guns began pounding the road along which he had ridden shortly before. They completed their inspection and were ready to move on, but the bombardment was still in progress with 77mm shells falling on the road at two minute intervals. "We naturally decided not to go up that road in the car," he wrote. However, the general, "a very seasoned officer," turned to the driver and said, " 'You may as well go at once. . . . We will assist at your agony.' " He then "laughingly" asked one of his junior officers what he thought. The man was noncommittal.

[42] Ibid., 89.

Fortunately for the driver the general finally postponed the departure. There was not a breath of criticism of the general in Bennett's account. That a man's life was on the point of being sacrificed foolishly did not appal him. His only comment was that the general "regarded all military duties as absolute duties. The car must go along that road. Therefore, let it go."

On another occasion he was inspecting French artillery and antiaircraft guns when it was suggested by one of the group that it "would be proper to try to kill a few Germans for our amusement" with one of the seventy-fives.[43] The request was granted and two rounds were fired to gratify the warrior blood in the visitors. "The shell was put into its place," Bennett wrote. "A soldier pulled a string. Bang! A neat, clean, not too loud bang! The messenger had gone invisibly forth." It was all very tidy, and the consequences, if there were any, did not have to be viewed at close range. Bennett found the incident amusing. Compton MacKenzie, on the other hand, has recalled in *Gallipoli Memories* an occasion when he was on the receiving end of an artillery bombardment and a soldier near him was killed by a bursting shell. The soldier's companion, whose nerves were nearly gone, turned to the shocked and frightened MacKenzie and said, " 'Beg pardon, Sir, you think it's funny at first, but it's serious, really.' " [44] MacKenzie did not find it at all funny, not even "at first."

By July 9 Bennett reached St. Omer and settled in at the Hotel du Commerce, which he found to be excellent. The principal reason for his rise in spirits was that he was now in the English lines and feeling more and more at home. One of his first social engagements was with Brigadier General Macdonough, Director of Military Intelligence GHQ, whom Bennett found *"tres sympathetique."* There was, he recorded with satisfaction, "no military talk at dinner. No gestures. Terrific contrast with the French meals." In the Notes he stated flatly that in the British lines he found "everything very superior to [the] French." In "The British Lines," the fifth of the articles, he employed a circumlo-

[43] *Ibid.*, 45.
[44] Compton MacKenzie, *Gallipoli Memories* (New York, 1930), 121.

cution to express his feelings: "The British occupation—which is marked, of course, by high and impressive cordiality—is at once superficially striking and subtly profound." [45] It is doubtful that his readers caught his meaning.

Once he was established at St. Omer, he made a list of items which he intended to check—"discipline, flying, communication, food, billetting, shelter, ammunition, horses, relations with the populace." What he learned in nearly every instance, since his exposure to conditions at the front was, if anything, more limited and more "official" than it had been at the French front, was that conditions under which the men fought were nearly ideal. Equipment, food, transportation, and ammunition were of the best and existed in staggering quantities. After a brief tour of the trenches, he was forced to conclude that one could "find everything in the British lines except the British Army." The comment and what follows it is the only hint in the Notes or the articles that he was not being allowed to see what he had come to the fronts to see. The French had been more subtle in keeping things out of his sight. "I went for a very long walk, up such hills and down such dales as the country can show," he wrote, "tramping with a General through exhausting communication-trenches, in order to discover two soldiers, an officer and his man; and even they were not actual fighters." [46]

The journalistic high point of his tour at St. Omer was an interview with General French. Bennett made every effort to exalt the General in his description of the meeting, but the drama of the event was exaggerated, forced, and unconvincing. " 'The Commander-in-Chief will see you,' " Bennett wrote, describing his entrance into the General's Offices. "You go forward, and I defy you not to be daunted." Bennett gave a short description of French's room and then turned to the man himself: "There he is, the legendary figure, a thick-set man, not tall, with small hands and feet, and fingernails full of character. . . . When he talks of the Germans he has a way of settling his head and neck with a slight defiant shake well between his shoulders. . . . From the

---

[45] Bennett, *Over There*, 124.
[46] *Ibid.*, p. 139–40.

personality of the man there emanates all the time a pugnacious and fierce doggedness." Bennett was given a formal welcome, treated to a few "general observations," and dismissed. "As you pass out of the building," Bennett wrote, "the thought in your mind is: 'I have seen him!' " One almost expects to find the *h* in *him* capitalized. The intention to flatter shows through the passage so clearly and the writing is so trite and artificial that it must be almost the worst piece of Bennett's prose in print.[47]

Bennett was certainly aware of the problems that French was having with Kitchener and the government as well as French's failure to communicate successfully with the French leaders. He was obviously writing as "official observer" and feeling very strongly his commitment to uphold civilian morale. The role did not suit him. He did not have the gift for simulating sincerity; and, perhaps, that is to his credit. Whenever he attempted to generate a false enthusiasm in his readers, an enthusiasm which he did not genuinely feel, the results were embarrassingly bad.

In response to questions about discipline, Bennett was told that there had been "some executions" of British soldiers for infractions of military laws. He recorded in the Notes that about half of the offenses were committed while the men involved were drunk. There had also been a number of desertions. "In retreat," he wrote solemnly, "men got lost and went to live with French grass widows. Some not yet caught." Presumably it was the men and not elusive "grass widows" who remained uncaptured. He made no mention of the executions in his articles—undoubtedly the censor would have suppressed the material—and made no comment on them in the Notes, where the suppression, if it was suppression, was his own. He remained silent about the rigorous application of discipline in the ranks.

The last city he visited before returning to Paris was Ypres. It was, of course, in ruins and totally deserted. He described the

---

47 The intention to mislead was not exclusively Bennett's on that occasion. Bennett reported in the article in which the description of French appears that he complimented the General on his fine garden. French replied that he had never been in it. However, French told Lord Esher that he enjoyed his headquarters because there was a small garden where he could walk unmolested.

experience in his sixth article, "The Unique City," and seemed unaware that he and his group had been set the harmless task of seeing one of the "sights." The city had been systematically defeated by German artillery and for some unknown reason, was being totally destroyed. Even while Bennett walked through its battered streets, the city was still under fire.

Having reached the Grand Place, which was the city's central square and which had been under intense bombardment because of the Cloth Hall and the Cathedral fronting it, he sat down and began to sketch. No sooner was the rest of his party out of sight, however, than he discovered that he was afraid. Sitting alone in the ruined Place he was struck with the thought that "a shell might quite well fall here at any moment." But that fear, he found, was not his strongest feeling. What most disturbed him was the loneliness: "Every street was a desert; every room in every house was empty. Not a dog roamed in search of food. The weight upon my heart was sickening." [48]

Although his fear subsided with the return of his companions, the resulting depression lingered for hours afterward. Here, as at Rheims, he was deeply disturbed by what he saw; and he denounced the German policy of destruction as "mean, miserable, silly, childish, and grotesque." But he found consolation in his belief that Germany already regretted having begun the war and "that she would be crushed." He left Ypres on the 12th of July, closed his Notes, and two days later was back in London. His tour of the fronts was over.

It is, perhaps, understandable that Marguerite should have come to the conclusion that the trip upset him, since he made almost no further references to his experiences in France and in Belgium in his writing—and, apparently, in his conversation— once the last of the articles were written. But she was, in all probability, mistaken. He was not deeply wounded. Except for the single outburst in "Three Ruins," he never demanded that Germany be subjected to reprisals. It is true that he continued to demand the smashing of her military machine and the deposing of her Junker ruling class, but no more than that. He did not lose

[48] Bennett, *Over There*, 165.

his balance or that prized quality of common sense, which he considered to be the surest means by which a policy or an action could be judged. It is probably fair to say that he was not, on the whole, deeply affected by what he saw at the front, if one makes an exception of the ruined cities. He returned from France essentially the same man who had crossed the Channel three weeks earlier.

What remains difficult to understand is the fact that Bennett made so little use of his experience at the fronts in his subsequent fiction. He was a writer who generally used all of the material at his disposal in the most thorough way, wasting almost nothing. He drew heavily on personal experience for his characters and settings, but no novel or short story of his written after his trip to the fronts was placed in a distinctly war setting. No significant character was drawn from the officer with whom he came in contact in France and in Belgium. None of the incidents recorded in his Notes ever found their way into his fiction.

# V

## ALL THE D-DAMNED GAMES

"I returned home from the Front yesterday, after two nights in London at the Savoy," Bennett wrote in his journal on July 16, adding with a flourish of self-congratulation, "By the evening I had dealt with all arrears." But there was no following sigh of pleasure at being once more at Comarques or home again with Marguerite. He made no mention of Marguerite or of what she had been doing in his absence. With the observation that the *Strand Magazine* remained obstinate in its objections to *The Lion's Share* and that there was a considerable movement of troops in the Frinton area in response to a new invasion scare, he quietly picked up his affairs where he had left them three weeks before.[1]

Almost immediately after reaching Essex, however, he succumbed to an illness which put him to bed for nine days and left him convalescent for another two weeks. The illness was diagnosed, according to Bennett, as inflamation of the colon, brought on by fatigue and nervous excitement at the Front.[2] The diagnosis was almost certainly incomplete. On July 22nd, in the first entry in his journal for six days, Bennett said he had been "mysteriously and intestinally ill for a week." Later he called the malady colitis and added a liver complication to account for symptoms not attributable to colitis. A reasonable guess is that he came down with either dysentery or a mild form of typhoid. For the rest of the year he suffered relapses and frequently felt sick. When he was in London, where the relapses sometimes occurred, his favorite medication to counter the general malaise brought on by the slump was a "tonic" at Hepples', which, he felt, "did him good."

The most serious effect of the illness on his writing was a delay

[1] Bennett, *Journal*, 563.
[2] Bennett, *Letters*, I, 229.

in completing the Front articles. On July 25 he warned Pinker that Lorimer at *The Saturday Evening Post* should be told not to expect delivery of the articles on schedule and that if the magazine planned to run the articles in immediate sequence, it would have to alter its plans. Fortunately, his arrangements with the *Illustrated London News* were more flexible and did not produce the same complications.

He was, of course, still facing deadlines with the *Metropolitan* for *The Lion's Share*. The first half of the book had been submitted to Whigham in June. The second half was not due until December, but he had already lost three weeks of working time at the Front. Now he was losing another three weeks. He expressed his concern in a letter to John Squire, who was standing in for Sharp at the *NS*, in which he said, "although I am now getting up for a few hours each day, I am absolutely off work."

Besides the perennial worry about money added to the irritation of being "off work," the civil courts decided against the *Daily News* in a case stemming from one of Bennett's articles in the newspaper in which he deplored the stoning of a German chemist's shop. In the article Bennett gave the name of the firm and its London address. He made a mistake in either the name of the street or in the name of the firm; and the English chemist located at the address given sued and received a settlement of one hundred twenty-five pounds, ten shillings, and tenpence plus costs. "Such," Bennett ruefully observed in the journal entry of July 22, "is the law of libel." [3]

By the 6th of August he was sufficiently recovered to begin once again making trips to London, and he resumed them with obvious pleasure. His first piece of business in London was a conference with Masterman and J. Alfred Spender, editor of the *Westminster Gazette*, with whom he had a long and jolly talk about the corruption of the Russian administration. The real subject of the interview, however, was the distribution of his Front articles on the continent. On the 18th he was able to inform

[3] The article in question was "The Pogrom" (*The Daily News*, Tuesday, May 18, 1915). In it Bennett made a blunt attack on people who assaulted German shop owners and on the yellow press for fomenting such trouble.

Pinker, "in confidence," that the articles were to be published in France, Russia, and Sweden "under the auspices of the Foreign Office, who are [sic] arranging the thing themselves, unofficially." [4]

He appeared to be moving toward a full recovery, but the outburst of anger with which he rejected Methuen's proposed dust jacket for *These Twain* was an indication that his health was still undermined. The book, which had been a burden to him throughout its composition, continued to be a trouble even after its completion; and his irritation can be partially explained by the problems he had had in getting the book properly set up in type, with one version going to Munsey and another to Doran and to Methuen. These difficulties, however, do not adequately account for the vehemence of his objection to the wrapper.

In the first week of August, Bennett received the dust jacket in colors from Methuen, and on the 5th he wrote to Pinker refusing to accept it, calling it "hideous." Pinker apparently carried Bennett's objections to Methuen but failed to persuade Methuen to order a new design. Pinker told Bennett what had taken place, and Bennett reacted to the news with almost hysterical fury. He began his response in a reasonably calm tone, but the letter soon turned into a bitter tirade against publishers in general and perhaps Methuen, who is not named, in particular:

> Many thanks. I return the design. What I object to in it is the horrible ugliness of the whole thing—coloring and drawing. I will not agree to it in anything like its present form. Also it is utterly misleading. I draw in the book a man refined and artistic, especially with refined features, and the artist gives a man like a bookmaker or a moneylender. Edwin has plenty of hair and beard. The artist makes him half bald and beardless. He is always very quietly dressed in blue with a black *bow* necktie and a stand-up collar. The artist gives him a grotesque waistcoat, a green suit, a low collar and a sailor's knot-necktie. This man would have made Edwin sick. As regards the woman, the blouse is incredible. Also I particularly say that Hilda has *straight* and thick eyebrows, whereas the artist gives her eyebrows like a chinese. I am not going to give way to

[4] Ogden Collection, August 18, 1915.

commercial travellers. What do they know about it? If one had asked their opinion of *Clayhanger* at the start, they would have said that God himself couldn't have forced it on the British public. They are nearly always wrong. I don't mind the *idea* of the present design; in fact I think it rather good. But it will have to be completely altered in detail before I approve of it.[5]

While there was nothing unusual in Bennett's willingness to fight for his convictions, there is a petulance and a lack of moderation in the letter which suggests that he was not wholly in command of himself. He had fought against the "commercial" judgment of publishers before and would do so again, but seldom did he so wholly lose his sense of humor or power of ironic comment as he did in this case.

The exaggerated refusal to accept the wrapper also suggests the depth of his personal involvement in the novel and the closeness with which he identified himself with Edwin. That explains why the representation of Edwin as a man possessing the character of a "bookmaker or a moneylender" would have been deeply offensive to him—something of a personal insult. But whatever explanation is advanced for his reaction to the book jacket, it is plain enough that he was more disturbed than the circumstances warranted. He carried the day with Methuen, however. The design was changed.

He was well enough to complete his Front articles by August 26 and to send them off to the censor. On September 1st he had the first of them back again, and he remarked that "with the exception of about three words the whole of the censoring struck me as entirely futile." [6] He added that he was keeping the censored copy "as a curiosity." But he was still not free to turn to other writing. He had in mind a supplementary article on a hospital at the Front, which may have been "officially" inspired, although he had notes for it already in hand when he returned from France. The article was designed to reassure English readers that proper care was being given the wounded at a time when

5 *Letters*, I, 230–31.
6 *Journal*, 567.

the effectiveness of the Army Medical Corps was beginning to be questioned. Bennett knew very well that medical attention for the troops was often inadequate. He had deplored it in at least one of his *Daily News* articles that fall.

"A Hospital" appeared in the *Daily News* on September 30 and was a description of a hospital in a converted French chateau. Bennett stressed the efficiency and the effectiveness of the care given to the patients. In a sentence reminiscent of his description of the front-line trenches, he wrote, "what so deeply impressed me about this hospital was, first, its human, jolly spirit." The censor passed the article without deletions.

He completed the piece on September 8 and wrote with relief that he was "now quit of all this [the Front articles], except that I may write a preface for the book form." He was anxious to take up *The Lion's Share* again and to continue planning his "London" novel, which was eventually to take shape as *The Roll Call* and to have a very stormy passage before reaching the reading public. In addition to the novels, he had in mind a "war play." The idea for the play had been given to him in late August by Lee Mathews, with whom he was lunching at the Reform Club. The idea, which Bennett called "A₁," was for him to write a "prophetic play" about the condition in which the country would find itself two years after the war. He was confident that the play would "advance" every time he thought about it for an hour,[7] but the problem was that spare hours were becoming increasingly rare.

In addition to his weekly WARC meetings, which he attended as soon as his health permitted, he became involved again with the organization of defense plans for the east coast, which was, according to semi-official report, in imminent danger of a German raid. What was real was the Zeppelin threat. Zeppelin flights were passing nightly over the East coast on their way to London, and sporadic bombing of the East coast was causing concern in

[7] Despite Bennett's early enthusiasm for the play, it was never written. Continued ill health, the pressure of work in hand, and his own uncertainty about writing such a play combined to kill the idea. Bennett was no H. G. Wells; he knew that prophecy was not really in his line.

the area surrounding Comarques. Bennett recorded in the journal that he didn't believe a German raid was going to occur, but he threw himself into the work of organizing plans for civilian evacuation in the event of an attack. The work was tiring and largely futile.

Nothing is more indicative of the absurdity of the work Bennett was doing than the fact that a year after a code word had been chosen to signal an invasion and trigger evacuation procedures, the army officer in charge of emergency arrangements for the Frinton area had never even heard of the word. Bennett was shocked. "If I had not brought the matter up," he recorded in his journal, "the whole emergency scheme might have been vitiated if an invasion had suddenly taken place."

It does not seem to have occurred to him that the army was not taking the civilian preparations seriously, even though army officers were in charge of the civilian committee. Bennett showed a painful lack of humor regarding his involvement with the defense committee and with the military establishment in general. A few days after the code word episode, which he referred to as a case of "official negligence," he visited the army base at Harwich and ran into more trouble.

Harwich is located about fifteen miles north of Thorpe-le-Soken. When he stopped at the entrance to the base in order to present his credentials, he asked the sentry to search his car to be sure that nothing was being carried into the area contrary to the rules. The sentry refused and sent Bennett on. But later, when he was leaving, the sentry on duty decided to make a search and turned up a map. Bennett was sent back to headquarters with a soldier. "The attitude of the A. P. M. and another official, who both interviewed me," he wrote angrily, "was grotesque, and I have written formally to wake them up." [8]

It is sometimes difficult to tell from what he wrote whether Bennett was indulging in black humor or simply being solemn. He recounted a story in the journal about a soldier who, having lost all of his limbs as well as his eyesight, asked to be allowed to

[8] *Journal*, 567.

die. Bennett closed the account with the comment that "there is some exaggeration somewhere in this story." Having dined with a man and his wife who were what Bennett referred to scathingly as "colonials from Shanghai," he wrote without comment that after dinner the man "danced an imitation of Maud Allan's Salomé and ended by falling flat on the floor." [9]

But he was, on the other hand, unmistakably amused by the behavior of his friend Mrs. MacGregor, a young widow who lived in Frinton and who frequently entertained the Bennetts at her home. According to Bennett, Mrs. MacGregor, because she was a "young and attractive widow," was afraid of scandal. But her fears, he wrote, did not prevent her serving cocktails "to her assembled friends every Sunday morning in a place like Frinton!" He also recorded that "she was great on what women could expect from men. Doubtless owing to her widowhood." [10]

In his fiction Bennett was capable of making fun of organized religion; and, as *The Price of Love* was to demonstrate, his doing it sometimes got him into trouble. But he seldom wrote at the expense of churches and clergymen in his journal. In late August, however, he made a long entry in the journal which described with delicate irony an event involving an adulterous composer, a brigade concert, and an army chaplain, who told Bennett the story. The chaplain had been making the arrangements with the composer for the concert when it came out that the composer was living with a mistress. The chaplain felt compelled to give up his position as agent out of consideration for his calling.

But he was not unduly upset by what he had learned, and he asked the composer to explain things to the committee in charge of the concert as a means of avoiding any misunderstanding. The composer did, telling them that he could not write while living with his wife and that he needed the financial support which his mistress could give him. One man on the committee immediately offered the composer an income if he would leave his mistress. The offer was declined. Bennett asked the chaplain if the man were a communicant. "No," the clergyman replied, "He doesn't

---

[9] Unpublished Journal, September 22, 1915; November 20, 1915.
[10] *Journal*, 574.

quite know where he is. He's trying to find himself. I tell him to take his time." [11]

On October 4 Bennett accepted an invitation from the Wellses to visit them at Easton Glebe the following weekend. Marguerite, who had made plans to go to London that weekend, refused the invitation; and Bennett went alone. He left Comarques at ten o'clock Saturday morning and drove "over slippery roads in a Scotch mist" to Little Easton, where he met Wells for an evening walk in the park. It was stag rutting season; and the two men, walking through the park in the gathering dusk, were somewhat intimidated by the bellowing of the excited animals. But they were not prevented by the uproar from examining the park with critical eyes. The park, which belonged to Lady Warwick, was, Bennett wrote, "immense." He added that there must be "hundreds such" in the country, and Wells responded by saying that "it ought to be taxed out." [12] However, they seemed to have enjoyed their stroll despite the objections to private ownership of such large chunks of land.

There were eighteen guests at the Wells's house, and they were kept busy playing strenuous games in the best Wells tradition. Bennett remarked on Wells's "tremendous energy," and said that it was that quality in his host that made the place so entertaining. Among the guests were Newman Flower of Cassell's publishing house, with whom Wells was placing *Mr. Britling Sees it Through*.

Flower's account of the weekend, given in *Just As It Happened*, contains some amusing details of Bennett's experience with the Wellses' brand of entertainment. Everyone, Flower wrote, was compelled to play hockey, and eventually Bennett took a bad fall. He had to be carried into the house, but that evening he "came down to dinner . . . cursing all Sunday games and dressed in a wonderful evening suit." When Bennett left on Monday morning in his "ancient 'Tin-Lizzie,'" he shouted to Wells as he moved away, " 'I hate all your d-damned games.' " It was to Flower that Bennett sent the manuscript of *The Lion's*

[11] *Journal*, 566.
[12] *Ibid.*, 571.

*Share*, and Flower attributed that to the weekend they had spent together. "It was," Flower recalled, "the beginning of a literary partnership that went on smoothly through the years." [13]

Bennett's visit was, however, important to himself in other ways as well. For one thing, it was the first holiday he had had since August of 1914. Writing to Elsie Herzog after the visit, he insisted that the change had done him much good. He was probably right. Despite the shaking up he had suffered while playing back in the hockey game, he had been taken out of himself; and the pleasure he derived from the visit shines through everything he wrote about it.

He was glad also of the opportunity to reaffirm his friendship with Wells, who had been gradually growing away from Bennett over the years. Such a separating was probably inevitable, given their basic differences in temperament and outlook. Bennett's "common sense" response to life was not Wells's answer to the increasing complexities of existence with which the world was surrounding him. Wells's dissatisfaction had been expressed very early in their relationship when he criticized Bennett for being content with surface values and for failing to feel deeply the human predicament. In his response Bennett took refuge in the excuse that he viewed the world from above and that such a position was the proper one for an artist to assume.

The war had driven them even farther apart, although Bennett never publicly acknowledged the fact. There is even an indication in the letter which Bennett wrote in October accepting Wells's invitation to Easton Glebe that Wells had been inventing excuses for not having seen more of Bennett. "I like your remark about the Reform Club," Bennett observed wryly. "The R. C. has been closed for a month and only reopened last Friday, so that your attempt to persuade me that you have been practically living there during September fails. Up to September I regularly attended the said Club on Fridays." [14]

They had also fallen out with one another in print, although there was certainly no personal animosity on Bennett's part in

[13] Flower, *Just As It Happened*, 157–59.
[14] Bennett and Wells, *Arnold Bennett and H. G. Wells*, 189.

the exchange. In July, Wells wrote an article for *The Nation* attacking the wrangling of party politicians and suggesting that their behavior was threatening the democratic process of government. He also maintained that the democratic nations were less efficient than the Central Powers and that they had been less ready for war, weaknesses which he attributed to their form of government. Bennett wrote a piece for the *Daily News* contradicting Wells; and in a letter to Squire, written in early August, he remarked that he had "noticed the Wells phenomenon" [in *The Nation*] and that he had "got across him" in the *Daily News*.[15] But he hastened to add that he and Wells were "still intimate friends, and whenever I see him his talk is absolutely $A_1$, and seems to improve each time." [16]

That intimacy appears to have existed chiefly in Bennett's imagination. They were not meeting frequently, and a glance at the Wells-Bennett correspondence for the period in question shows that Bennett's correspondence was chiefly with Mrs. Wells and that Wells's responses to questions put to him by way of his wife took the form of brief notes written on the letters and given back to Mrs. Wells.

Wells's attitude toward Bennett found at least a partial expression in *Boon*, that strange work which Wells published in 1915. In the one place in the book where he is named, Bennett is described as "an aborted Great Man. [He] would have made a Great Victorian and had a crowd of satellite helpers. Now no one will ever treasure his old hats and pipes." [17] In Lovat Dick-

15 Bennett actually wrote two articles attacking Wells. The first, "Under Which Government," The *Daily News* (August 4, 1915), countered Wells's argument that democracy, in order to be saved, must be delivered from the hands of party politicians. He also denied Wells's assertion that the Central Powers had been better prepared to meet the exigencies of war than had the Allies. As for Wells's objection to political wrangling, Bennett said that the presence of it always encouraged him and that it was a good sign of healthiness in the democratic state. The second article, "Democracy *vs.* Oligarchy," The *Daily News* (August 11, 1915), refuted Wells's contention that the press ought not to be controlled by private ownership. Bennett argued that private ownership was not nearly so dangerous as state ownership, which he felt Wells was suggesting.

16 *Letters*, II, 369.

17 H. G. Wells, *Boon, The Mind of the Race, The Wild Asses of the Devil, and The Last Trump* (New York, 1915), 160. Wells published the book under

son's opinion Bennett also figures in the character of Reginald Bliss, who Dickson describes as "someone not unlike Wells's friend Arnold Bennett." [18] There is a certain prissiness in Bliss which may suggest Bennett, but in no other respect is there a resemblance. Bliss totally lacks that brusqueness and forthright, independent manner so characteristic of Bennett. There are, however, details of Boon's personality and life in the early sections of the book which do suggest that Wells may have been burlesquing Bennett as well as himself in the portrait of the dead writer. Having described Boon's utterly tasteless manner of dress —orange tie, faded corduroy trousers, claret-colored socks— he said that Boon "liked his game; he liked his success and the opulent stateliness it gave to the absurdities of Mrs. Boon. . . ." [19] The tasteless dress may well have been a spoofing of Bennett's sartorial elegance, and there is a hint of Marguerite in that judgment on Mrs. Boon.

Wells gave Boon a secretary named Miss Bathwick, who also served as his literary judge. Boon was very dependent on her and quite at her mercy in questions of taste in his writing. The point of introducing Miss Bathwick into the story becomes clear if the passage is read as a burlesque of Bennett's relationship with Miss Nerney. Wells then went on to talk about Boon's published work, which was so different from the things he was writing in his own hand and free from Miss Bathwick's censorship. The published books were

> planned and announced, developed, written, boomed, applauded. . . . The work upon which his present fame is founded is methodical, punctual, and careful, and it progressed with a sort of inevitable precision from beginning to end, and so on to another beginning. . . . His hundred thousand words of good, healthy, straightforward story came out in five months with a precision almost astronomical. In that sense he took his public very seriously. To have missed his morning exercise

the pseudonym Reginald Bliss, who was supposedly George Boon's literary executor. The sketches included in *Boon* were a selection of Boon's unpublished writings. The hoax failed. Wells was readily identified as the author.

[18] Lovat Dickson, *H. G. Wells: His Turbulent Life and Times* (New York, 1969), 206.

[19] Wells, *Boon*, 29.

behind Miss Bathwick's back [Boon dictated his stories to Miss Bathwick] would have seemed to him the most immoral . . . proceedings.[20]

It is impossible to believe that Wells did not have Bennett in mind when he wrote those lines.

Bennett never commented on the possibility of his having been a model for Boon. Neither did he show any rancor over Wells's rather acid evaluation of his position in English letters. If he was aware of any cooling of Wells's regard for him, he made no mention of it; and he continued to interest himself in Wells's life. In a rather puzzling letter to Mrs. Wells on October 11, Bennett, being either facetious or acting to head off some undisclosed trouble between Mrs. Wells and her husband, wrote: "I leapt on the *Sunday Times*. All the indiscretions were in it, including the worst, so I suppose all is over now between you and H. G. I suggest you both come here [to Comarques] to make it up again."[21]

At the time of his visit to the Wellses, Bennett was struggling to resume work on *The Lion's Share*. His long separation from the book was making it extremely difficult for him to get it moving again; and there is no doubt that his efforts to breathe life into the novel were only partially successful. In its second half the story slumps. The verve with which he wrote the opening chapters was lost in the excitement of his trip to the Fronts, in the distresses of his illness, and in his efforts to complete the Front articles.

His contract obligations and his need for money, however, made it imperative that the book be written, and with dogged determination he set himself to work. But the task was to prove difficult. On September 22 he noted in his journal that ideas for the last half of *The Lion's Share* were "coming very slowly." The following day he added that he had, "after great efforts," collected "sufficient ideas" to allow him to proceed with the

---

[20] *Ibid.*, 31–32.
[21] In a note to this letter, Harris Wilson has written that "A careful perusal of the *Sunday Times* of 10 October 1915 yielded no explanation for this allusion." Since the Wellses did, in fact, visit Comarques a short time later, it can be assumed that the trouble was not serious.

writing. But whatever enthusiasm he had been able to muster was given a blow by the final word from Whigham that *The Strand* would not publish *The Lion's Share*. Bennett was disappointed. He had been confident that he would, in the end, be able to persuade the magazine's board of directors to take the novel. However, Pinker succeeded in selling the serial rights to the book to the *Grand Magazine*, thereby delivering Bennett from the threat of a severe financial loss. Once under way, he went bleakly forward with the writing, until he finished the final chapter on December 1.

Whatever judgments are made about the novel's excellence or lack of it, it suffered from having been written in two parts. When one reflects on the speed and the enthusiasm with which Bennett wrote the first part of the novel and on the resulting liveliness of the writing and compares that first half with the concluding section, begun some four months later, the conclusion is inescapable that the book was a war casualty. *The Lion's Share* had not from its inception possessed the ingredients of a great novel, but in its early chapters it had the promise of being a very good book of its kind. But Bennett's inspiration failed, and the novel lost its drive.

Whigham, not always easy to please, was delighted with *The Lion's Share*, but his enthusiasm was not great enough to make him keep his payments to Bennett up-to-date. Half of the purchase price had been due in June, but in October, Bennett was still waiting for his money. Finally, on the 12th, Bennett wrote in exasperation to Pinker that he would not give the magazine any more copy until the first instalment was paid for. "I have already lost more than a quarter's interest on £1,500," he complained, "and I could have invested the money very advantageously on August last." Pinker bestirred himself. The money came and Bennett went on working. It is puzzling that Pinker had allowed so much time to elapse without giving Whigham a prod. It is even more puzzling that Bennett had not asked for the money sooner, considering the pressure he had been exerting on Pinker to produce cash for him.

There was only one other minor difficulty connected with the serial publication of *The Lion's Share*. In early October, Bennett asked Pinker to have the name of Moze Hall changed to Flank Hall in the *Grand Magazine*, because he had learned that there was a Moze Hall in Essex. The name was changed in the serial and in the book that was published by Methuen the following year.

Although Bennett had completed his Front articles in September, he continued to be occupied with details of their publication in book form. Doran was handling the American publication and Methuen, the English. By September 13 he had decided to call the collection "Scenes of War," and he told Pinker to instruct Doran to use that title. He had reluctantly given the *Illustrated London News* the choice of calling the series "Scenes at the Front" or "Scenes of War" after protesting in vain that he did not want a general title for the series.

Methuen went ahead with plans to call the collection "Scenes of War;" but when Pinker sent an advance copy to Wilfred Whitten, editor of *John O' London*, who was intending to mention the book in his magazine, Whitten said that the title was poor and sent Pinker a list of alternatives. Pinker chose "Over There" as being the best of those titles suggested and sent it to Bennett, who agreed to accept the new title, with the qualification that "War Scenes on the Western Front" be made the subtitle. Methuen thought "Over There" an improvement on the old title as did Doran, who wrote from New York asking permission to use it.

On November 15 Doran sent copies of both *These Twain* and *Over There* to Bennett. Bennett was pleased with the appearance of his war book but unhappy with the jacket of *These Twain*, which, he informed Doran, bore no resemblance to anything in the novel: "It seems much more like a scene in some small, sleepy and clean old English country town. If you had ever been in the Potteries, you would understand at once." [22] At the same time he wrote to Pinker that the idea of putting

[22] *Letters,* II, 371.

*The Twain* into colors and keeping *Over There* "like an economic treatise seems to me rather odd." [23] His concern was justified. A week and a half later he called Pinker's attention to the fact that *Over There* had sold only 4,500 copies in England. He shrewdly added that if the book were to have a chance, it should be put into colored covers and marked "New Edition." His suggestion was not taken. No publisher ever seems to have taken advantage of Bennett's very keen sense of how books should be promoted. As a result of that failure both Bennett and the publishers lost money which could have been theirs.

Before finishing with his Front articles he had the pleasant and self-justifying experience of seeing "The Life of Nash Nicklin" appear in the September issue of *Metropolitan*. With remarkable restraint he noted its publication and remarked that there was also a "eulogistic" article about him in the same issue. The article, signed J. E. H., was a piece of unqualified praise of Bennett's success in rendering life through the people and the setting of the Five Towns. In the Five Towns, according to the writer, Bennett had "tasted the true salt and savor of life itself." [24] Praise was also given to Bennett's ability to draw for his readers the lighter side of life, but the writer concluded that Bennett's greatest strength was his awareness of the drama of existence and that it was his powerful rendering of it which "takes us by the throat and makes us gasp." Bennett must have been struck by the irony of the praise, which took as its base the material and the attitudes toward it which he had now so completely rejected.

He was also attracting attention in England, although not for his fiction. In the course of the fall and the early winter, he was interviewed on film for a newspaper syndicate. His interviewer was Percy Allen, M.P., with whom he had a long conversation about Allen's speech-making tour around the world. Bennett was particularly interested in Allen's account of the terrible conditions under which Japanese women were forced to work in a factory he had visited.

[23] Ogden Collection, November 11, 1915.
[24] *Ibid.*, September 11, 1915.

Bennett was attracting popular attention in a way which he had never done before the war. His name was blazoned across the sides of London busses in *Daily News* ads, in company with those of H. G. Wells and Horatio Bottomley, who were, respectively, the stars of the *Morning Post* and *John Bull.* Increasingly he was becoming a public figure; and although he said very little about his new role, it is clear from his willingness, even eagerness, to step into the spotlight of public attention that he enjoyed it.

If his work with the defense committees tended to make him look slightly ridiculous, his efforts in connection with his *Daily News* series did not. The articles gave expression to something profound in his nature which the war had wakened. His attention in the articles was increasingly focused on social issues, which he sensed were fundamental to the nation's well-being. He never feared a military defeat of the Allies, but what did frighten him was the possibility that reactionary forces in the country would seize the excuse of the war to entrench themselves in positions of power and to undermine the gains made in the country in the area of political and social democracy. A year of war had produced in him deep-seated anxieties about the state of English democracy and of social justice.

By the fall of 1915 he had centered on three or four topics which went deeply enough into the contest of the national life to allow him while dealing with them to comment on the entire fabric of government and the processes of the English social system. The need to democratize the civil services, the folly of conscription, the conservatism of the War Office, and the state of labor relations were the subjects which held his attention. In writing about them he was able, at the same time, to defend the laboring classes against social as well as economic exploitation and to castigate the moneyed classes for their reactionary principles and for their failure to understand the danger of their position.

Having already denied Wells's assertion that political debate was wasteful and a threat to the nation's security as well, he came out on August 26 in "The Situation" even more strongly in defense of democracy. He opened the article with an attack on conscription and moved from that to an attack on class prejudice in the War Office and in the officer ranks of the services. In a maneuver which had become typical of his method in the articles, he then expanded his criticism until it embraced all of the "upper classes." He warned them of the danger of being blind to the "possibilities of the early future;" and he called their blindness a "most frightening, bloodcurdling, and nationally humiliating phenomenon," hinting that if they did not bend to democratic demands, they might well be broken. It was a remarkably outspoken attack and one which he would continue to make in the strongest terms.

Two weeks later in "The Regiment," an article describing life in a typical army unit, he made a special point of praising the enlisted men serving at the Front, pointing out that they were brave and full of fortitude. As for their relations with the officers, he said simply that the officers did not understand them. Almost as a footnote to his praise of the men, he deplored the fact that Army red tape often prevented their being properly cared for. As an example of what he was condemning, he pointed out that in order for a soldier to have two teeth drawn he must fill in twenty-four forms before he could get to the dentist. If only one tooth needed drawing, the soldier could not get that done at all, unless he were willing to pay for the extraction out of his own pocket. It is instructive, however, that while he was able to give a full description of an officer's day, he could say next to nothing about the daily routine of the common soldier. He sympathized with the enlisted men, but he knew as little about them as did their officers.

However little he knew about the lives of soldiers, he had a solid understanding of the danger inherent in forcing men to fight. In the fall he wrote two articles attacking the proposed conscription bill—"Clatter and Racket," published on September 24, and "Last Words on Conscription," which appeared on October 5. In the first he reviewed his arguments in favor of retaining a voluntary recruiting system and condemned Lloyd George for his support of conscription. In the second he came to the heart of his objections. Convinced that conscription would divide a hitherto united country, he warned his readers that "the industrial class objects to conscription because it is contrary to common sense . . . and because the industrial class has a deep and very well-founded class suspicion of the whole business." [25]

He was equally dogmatic about the right of labor to protect itself in disputes with capital. On September 18 in "The Briton of the Trade Unionists" he defended the Trade Unions and their members against the threat of repressive legislation aimed at curtailing their power and hindering the working man's efforts to improve his position. Working conditions in munitions factories were, he insisted, very bad and could be greatly improved. He implied that the industrial class was not convinced that others were being asked to make sacrifices in proportion to those being asked of it. To counter this feeling, Bennett suggested imposing a heavy taxation on wealth in order to show the worker that burdens were being shared.

On December 7 he went north for the purpose of looking at the munitions factories. Labor difficulties had been increasing in that area but whether or not his trip was one of those taken at "official suggestion" is not known. "On the Clyde," published in the *Daily News* on December 22, was based on his observations. The tone of the article was subdued and reassuring. He reported that he had found the trouble had been exaggerated by those who had written about it. Since it cannot be proved to be otherwise, it must be assumed that he was writing honestly about what he had seen, although the article's lack of thrust is perplexing. Perhaps he gave a more accurate picture of what he saw in the factories along the Clyde in *The Pretty Lady*, which he wrote two years later. Conception, one of the characters in the novel, described her experiences in the muni-

[25] Bennett's efforts to stem the tide of support for the conscription bill were futile. In the fall of 1915 Conservative pressure to pass such a bill forced Asquith into a dodge designed to save the voluntary system. His plan was to allow men of military age to "attest" their willingness to serve if called upon. The plan failed of passage in the House, and conscription became inevitable. Asquith gave in, and in January, 1916, the first Military Service act became law.

tions plants, painting scenes of suffering and danger that Bennett did not even hint at in the article. His failure to give his readers a detailed account of what he had seen was probably a result of his conviction that in the face of strikes and of wild rumors about the possibility of a working-class revolution, it was his responsibility to speak calmly. Whatever his motives were and however one judges his decision to suppress unpleasant information, "On the Clyde" remains oddly out of place among his earlier and more sharply critical pieces; and there is nothing in it of his usually uncompromising demand for social justice.

His public stance regarding the major issues of the day were becoming increasingly fixed. He was solidly on the side of the liberal forces on all questions of social legislation and in regard to broad national aims. His partisanship, however, was never shrill and was never served at the expense of his belief in the value of open and honest criticism. It may, of course, be argued that he declined from this practice whenever he wrote under the direction of the Ministry of Information; but his free-swinging criticism of men in government and of government policies with which he disagreed more than counterbalanced his "official" publications. In "The Antidote," published on August 18, he came out strongly in favor of public criticism of all official action at all levels and expressed his conviction that an educated people would choose wisely when given enough information. His belief in the essential wisdom of Englishmen and in their desire to act in the best interests of the country was a faith which lay behind his political attitudes. England, he believed, was great because of its people; and he was convinced that if leaders would act on the assumption that the judgment of the people was fundamentally sound, the nation would have little to fear.

He intended his articles to be a contribution to the war effort, but he felt the need to involve himself more directly with events. He satisfied this need by serving on the defense committee for Frinton and by giving his time and energies to the WARC. As chairman of the WARC he was saddled with the task, undertaken in the fall, of arranging a benefit concert. The concert was to be held in February in the Haymarket Theatre; and as the fall advanced, he found himself giving more and more time to its preparation.[26] His journal and his letters contain frequent references to the event without revealing very much about his feelings. It was not until the concert was over that he hinted at the trouble it had caused him. On the day following the concert he wrote in his journal that the affair "had gone off without a hitch, and I was very glad when it was over. I had no particular trouble, but I will never organize another." [27]

The war continued to bring his way an odd assortment of people. Officers came and went at Comarques, remaining or going for the most part without his comment. Occasionally he gleaned from them material for the *Daily News* articles, but more often what they told him was only mess rumor, which he occasionally recorded in his journal and then dismissed as worthless. For the most part these chance encounters with people gave him little pleasure. A Mrs. T. Stuart, however, whom he met at one of Marguerite's London dinners, interested him. She was an author and illustrator of a book on gardens, and he put a note about her in the journal to the effect that she would be a good character for his next novel.[28]

He continued to lunch at various clubs with friends and business acquaintances. Now and then new men to whom he responded warmly were introduced into his group. Two such men were J. M. Bullock, editor of *The Graphic,* and another man whom Bennett identified only as a "wealthy manufacturer." The manufacturer shared Bennett's views on the importance of rehabilitating wounded soldiers, and they spent a happy hour proposing schemes to one another. Bennett called Bullock "a fierce little Aberdorian [*sic*]," who had excellent ideas. He found satisfaction in the fact that Bullock disapproved of Lloyd George and was convinced that England should never have

[26] He wrote to Max Beerbohm in December to ask for his help: "I am getting up a *high-class* concert at the Haymarket Theatre," he wrote. "Will you design me a cartoonish-sort-of-cover for the programme?" Beerbohm obliged. (*Letters,* II, 372.)

[27] *Journal,* 581.

[28] Bennett did not use her in *The Roll Call,* which followed *The Lion's Share.*

had to send a single man to France. "I heartily agreed with him," Bennett wrote later. Did his quick agreement mean that he had changed his views about the justification of England's entrance into the war? Since he did not elaborate on the remark, it is difficult to determine his precise meaning. From the time of the publication of *Liberty* he had continued to insist that England's participation in the war was essential if democracy were not to be destroyed in Europe and eventually in England.

His journal is rich in comment about people; but of the person who was most deeply involved in his life, he said little. He made only three important references to Marguerite during all the months from July to December. The first was on September 15 when he described having met her at the station on her return from a trip to London. There had been almost nightly warnings of Zeppelin raids, and an attack was expected on the night of Marguerite's return. Her train was late, and Bennett made some rather nervous inquiries as to its whereabouts. A porter told him that the line had been opened and that the train would soon be in.

Standing on the dark platform, Bennett stared into the surrounding gloom trying to pick out the light which would signal the train's approach. "This mysteriousness of unseen things known to be coming—such as Zeppelins and the trains," he wrote, "was rather impressive. Then suddenly a red light changes to green in the air. Two engines attached to each other rumble through the station. Then M.'s train. After a long delay Marguerite's silhouette very darkly far down the platform." [29] Was it concern for Marguerite's safety that prompted him to record the experience, or was he simply moved by the drama of the moment? A case could probably be made either way.

The two other references to Marguerite, however, carry overtones of irritation with her behavior. The West Somerset Yeomanry were being moved out of Essex; and because a number of the unit's officers had been billetted at Comarques, Marguerite decided to give them a farewell concert. Bennett did not describe

29 *Journal*, 569.

the affair beyond saying that Rickards came down from London to attend it and that Marguerite "danced . . . and made a speech."

One of the officers attending the concert was a Captain Wicksteed. On Sunday evening on the day following the concert, Marguerite and one of her women friends had gone to Wicksteed's room to help him pack. Bennett took note of their solicitude and recorded that the young man took great pleasure in their company and that they "spent some time in the moonlit garden." A sentence in the Tuesday journal entry reported that Wicksteed was still in the house. The packing, obviously, had been premature. If the incident was without emotional content, why did he record it at all? If not, was he embarrassed by Marguerite's behavior toward Wicksteed?

Another event involving a person very close to him was the marriage in late November of his friend Rickards to Mina Parker. The two men had been extremely intimate for many years; and although Bennett had become somewhat critical of Rickards' slowness in doing anything in support of the war effort, he continued to admire the architect's genius and to prize his company. But there is no hint of personal loss in his reference to Rickards' marriage. His only comment was that Rickards had been forced to take a considerable amount of ribbing from his fellow clubmen on the subject of his approaching marriage. Bennett thought the most amusing comment made was by a man who said to Rickards, "I'm married myself and *never regretted a day of it.*"

Bennett's overriding interest, however, continued to be his writing and the business interests stemming from it. During 1915 he published two books, *These Twain* and *Over There*, and wrote *The Lion's Share*. But it was a thin year in other ways. Only two of his short stories were published, "The Muscovy Ducks" and "The Life of Nash Nicklin," both of which are excellent in their particular ways. Aware of the difficulty he had been experiencing with his stories, Bennett lavished considerable care on the writing of these two; and his anger at Whigham's rejection of "Nash Nicklin" and his insistence on its superiority to "Muscovy Ducks," which he thought was a good story and which Whigham had accepted, is indicative of the degree to which he felt committed to them as standards of his work.

None of his plays was being produced in London, although *Milestones* was under stock rights in the United States and drawing $250 a week, half of which was lost in agents' fees, and the remaining portion had to be divided with Knoblock. In November he sold the film rights to *The Grand Babylon Hotel*, and in December he sent a hopeful letter to Pinker asking what money was to come to him from the English sale of *The Great Adventure* film. His *Daily News* articles were bringing him a steady forty pounds a month, and royalties on his books in print remained at a stable but relatively low level.

His income from these combined sources, however, was, due to his heavy expenses at Comarques and in London, distressingly small. What actually saved him in 1915 from a serious financial crisis was the sale of *These Twain*. George Doran paid Bennett over five thousand dollars for the American rights to the novel; and Munsey, as part of a bargain which he was later to regret because of complications over *The Roll Call*, paid Bennett fifteen thousand dollars for the right of first publication in his *Munsey's Magazine*.[30] Sale of the English and of the American rights of *These Twain* brought Bennett more money than he had ever before received for a novel. Despite this success his financial position was far from secure, as his repeated requests for early monthly statements from Pinker testify. He was spending up to the limits and perhaps beyond the limits of his income. A hint of his predicament appears in a letter to Pinker in December which asks his agent "to pay in one hundred pounds to Cooks at Ludgate Circus at once," and qualifies his request with "if there is a balance in your books in my favor." [31]

Disturbed by his failure to produce a play and by the producers' lack of interest in those he had already written, he attempted to cheer himself up with hopes for the new war play he had in mind. That he was not really getting ahead with the

[30] Gordan, *Arnold Bennett*, 34.
[31] Ogden Collection, December 27, 1915.

play, however, is demonstrated by the alacrity with which he turned his attentions in December to writing a play for Doris Keane, a somewhat desperate decision.

In early December Miss Keane once again asked Bennett to do an adaptation of *Sacred and Profane Love* for her. She had been after him for two years to do the play, and he had consistently refused. He was still extremely reluctant to commit himself. The reasons for his reluctance were complex and deep-seated. At its deepest level, his reluctance was a result of uncertainty about his ability to write a successful play. He buried this anxiety under bravado about the ease with which plays were turned out and produced, but he had no inner convictions about his ability to produce a hit. Neither did he want to run the risk of writing a play that would flop. He had a reputation to maintain. But he couldn't leave playwriting alone. He was as fascinated by the prospect of turning out a smashingly successful play as the sparrow by the serpent's eye and frequently with as disastrous consequences, as he knew to his sorrow. He had written only one really successful play, *The Great Adventure*. *Milestones* was a collaboration, and in the three years since *The Great Adventure*, he had done nothing for the stage except *Don Juan*, which was a failure by every standard. However, he needed money, and it was his need for money which drove him to take up seriously Doris Keane's request for a play.[32]

His first move was to write Pinker for two tickets to *Romance*, taking care to protect his escape route by saying, "I should want to hear her views on the sort of play she has in mind," adding that he had "no notion of writing the play" unless he was "much startled by her powers or she agreed to my notion of a play."

Five days later he sent Pinker a note from Glasgow to the effect that he would write the play for her, having decided that

[32] Doris Keane was an American actress. In the winter of 1915 she was appearing in Edward Sheldon's very successful play *Romance* (which Vedrenne described to Bennett as "*Milestones* and muck, and more muck than milestones"). Bennett saw the play twice, becoming increasingly enthusiastic about Miss Keane's performance. He said that she had a "most powerful personality." See *Letters*, I, 233n, and *Journal*, 576.

her ideas were "all right." "I shall write that play" were his words. It is doubtful that he actually felt that confident, but he was now fully committed, and he notified Doris Keane that he would go ahead with plans for the play if contract agreements could be arranged.

Bennett was deeply affected by Doris Keane in her role of Madame Cavallini, but his response to her was certainly not limited solely to her acting ability. While it would be rash to suggest that he fell in love with her, there is a hint of romantic interest in the personal praise and attention which he gave her after having watched her performance. He seems to have been attracted to actresses, and it is probably more than chance that both Marguerite and Dorothy Cheston were associated with the theater when he came under their spells. If it is true that *The Lion's Share* expresses, in fictional terms, Bennett's desire to reach out to new and exciting experiences, his response to Doris Keane may well have been an example of that desire in a personal and more significant context.

His enthusiasm for the actress, however, did not make him careless about contract arrangements. He rejected her proposal that he accept a flat five hundred pound advance on delivery of the manuscript, the payment being a full settlement for the English rights to the play with the American rights remaining in her hands. That sort of arrangement, he wrote Pinker, placed him in danger of having a play on his hands which he had done for a particular actress and for the writing of which he would get only five hundred pounds.

He did not spell it out, but he was protecting himself against the possibility of failure, an eventuality which he must have had in the back of his mind when he wrote Pinker a further disclaimer to the effect that the play he was writing would have "only a small chance of being sold to an ordinary management either here or in America." It was the same sort of defense he had raised regarding *Don Juan*. Doubt about his ability to produce a successful play was deeply fixed in his mind. The closing sentence of his letter to Pinker gave away the full extent of it: "I am only agreeing to write the play because I was deeply impressed by Miss Keane's acting." [33] The year closed with contract negotiations between Pinker and Doris Keane's agent still under way.

In his final journal entry for 1915, Bennett recorded that he had written 272,000 words during the year, "not counting Journals." The first full year of the war had been, he wrote, "the best book and serial year" he had ever had, although he had not issued a single new novel. His contracts with Munsey, Doran, Methuen, *The Metropolitan,* and *The Grand* for *These Twain* and *The Lion's Share* and *Over There* account for the success of the year. He also admitted somewhat ruefully that it had been his "worst theatrical year since before *The Honeymoon,*" which had gone into production in 1911.

The breakdown in his health following the trips to the Fronts effectively slowed the rush of creative energy which had been released by the opening chapters of *The Lion's Share.* But bad health alone cannot account for the falling off of his creative powers in the closing months of 1915. Bennett was standing between two worlds. He had rejected the Five Towns and had turned toward the glamour of London and Paris. His efforts, however, to work out the intellectual and the emotional problems posed by this shift of focus were being hampered by his inability, because of the war, to give himself utterly to solving those problems. At a time when he should have been giving his creative energies to the task of exploring his new materials and working out new methods of expressing them, his energies were being drained away in journalism and committee work.

Of equal importance to his state of mind but less easy to measure accurately was the impact on his writing of his dissatisfaction with his life at Comarques. Marguerite was neither a comfort nor an inspiration to him. Increasingly they were living separate and expensive lives, travelling independently between Thorpe-le-Soken and London, where Marguerite was cultivating a new and war-bred circle of friends from which Bennett was either excluded or forced into against his real wishes; and it is a reasonable guess that for the greater part of the time he was

[33] *Letters,* I, 233–34.

alternately bored and irritated by Marguerite's company. Increasingly life had become for him a dull routine of work, broken only by the diversion of his club lunches. He was no longer going to plays or concerts or galleries, and over everything hung the dark cloud of financial worries.

# VI

## CRISIS OF INFELICITIES

Reginald Pound, looking back over the long history of trouble that led to Bennett's separation from Marguerite in 1921, concluded, perhaps in perplexity, that the break-up was the result of "a slowly gathering crisis of infelicities." Pound's statement suggests that the marriage gradually sagged and finally collapsed under the accumulated weight of their incompatibilities. In one sense, of course, that is precisely what did happen. But to imagine that the movement toward separation was a steady one, progressing with a kind of tidal gravity, is to be misled.

It would be equally wrong to assume that the strains on their marriage were all internal, all stemming from differences in temperament. Such was not the case. The changes in the world around them and the changes in Bennett's attitude toward that shifting world contributed to his unhappiness at Comarques; and the serious disruption of his creative life, which was brought on by the war, divided Bennett from Marguerite and drove her to increasingly desperate measures to secure what she considered to be her rights as a wife.

The year 1916 was critical for Bennett's marriage. His relationship with Marguerite moved onto a new footing mainly because of the collapse of Bennett's health, the quasi-legal adoption of his nephew Richard, and Bennett's decision to establish a permanent residence for himself in London. These developments were, in part, attributable to what Pound called "infelicities" in the marriage, but they soon became causes as well as effects of Bennett's growing estrangement from Marguerite.

At least in the beginning the search for a London location appears to have been a joint undertaking. Marguerite wanted a place in the city which she and her husband could share. Bennett was spending a considerable part of his time in London; and his neglect of Marguerite, which she had always resented, was increased by his frequent absences from Comarques. By 1916 Comarques had, in almost every sense, ceased to be a real home for Bennett. Crowded with billetted officers and guests, separated as it was from the center of intellectual life with which Bennett found so much pleasure and stimulation, and located in a rural setting which Bennett found depressing, the house had become a burden and a prison to him.

There was an amusing obliqueness in his method of house hunting. In the early months of the year, he never admitted that he was interested in finding a place in London for Marguerite and himself, but his sudden concern with his friends' London quarters is testimony of that interest. The first hint that his thoughts were turning in that direction is given in the journal entry for January 1. He had been visiting Harris Brown in Brown's bachelor quarters and came away very favorably impressed. He gave a detailed description of Brown's flat and expressed admiration for what he had seen there. A week later he and Marguerite dined with the Alfred Scotts in their home on Westbourne Terrace, and Bennett was delighted with the house, concluding that a house was much superior to a flat.

There were many reasons for his wanting London accommodations. In addition to the fact that his work on the WARC concert was taking two or three days a week of his time, the long trips to and from London were tiring him. Exhaustion and the nervous strain of committee work, among other things, were undermining his health. In addition to his neuralgia and the recurrent insomnia, from which he had always suffered, he was now plagued by dyspepsia. His first reference to it in the journal occurred on January 8, when he recorded that he had dined at the Rickards and had been too dyspeptic to eat much. His afterthought "The beef was tough" summed up his general mood.

By the last week of January, he was seriously ill. He became so sick in London that he could make no notes and even forgot what he did. Having gotten back to Comarques, he found himself so enfeebled that resuming the London trips was out of the question; and his work was reduced to getting out a *Daily News* article and continuing with "the cursed and tedious organization of the Haymarket concert for WARC."

He was scarcely recovered from that attack when he foolishly allowed himself to be persuaded to ride twenty miles on horseback with a group of officers from Comarques to Frinton and back. He had not ridden a horse since 1902. An officer by the name of Corfield, who was billetted at Comarques, apparently suggested the ride in such a way that Bennett's pride was challenged. Bennett rode at the head of the group of officers, coldly ignoring Marguerite's car creeping along behind them and the number of people in Frinton who recognized him and greeted him with military salutes. Reaching the sea, Bennett turned his horse on the beach and rode straight back to Comarques.

"Why did you follow me with the car?" he demanded of Marguerite when they were alone. "I knew nothing would happen. It was rather ridiculous, you know." He did say that he had found the experience "very fatiguing," but when he returned he was able to enjoy an evening of piano playing with Frank Swinnerton as an audience. The following day he complained of lumbago but went to London anyway, denying to Marguerite that he did not feel well enough to go. Marguerite was to insist later that she had attempted to dissuade her husband from making the horseback ride, but she did not take the trouble to conceal an almost malicious amusement in the consequences which that ride had for Bennett. "My favorite officer," she reported, had "asked him on his return when he would ride again." He said that he would not ride again; he was too busy. "Of course not, sir," the officer replied." [1] By Tuesday, Bennett could no longer hide his condition; still, in spite of dyspepsia and a "fearful lumbago," he insisted on taking Rickards and his wife to dinner at the Ambassador. Two days later he recorded in his journal that he had been suffering from acute lumbago and that he "walked like an old man, arousing compassion in all beholders." [2]

[1] M. Bennett, *My Arnold Bennett*, 122.
[2] Unpublished Journal, February 3, 1916.

The handwriting in which he recorded the progress of his illness, which continued for a week, was extremely small and cramped, a certain sign in Bennett of emotional stress. The change in handwriting was not due solely to physical pain. Throughout the spring it continued to be small and cramped, growing so bad in June that some of the journal entries are nearly illegible. Exactly what happened at Comarques immediately before and immediately after that ride is largely a matter of conjecture. It is almost certain, however, that the entire affair was emotionally upsetting to him. His insistence on leaving for London on the day following the ride, when he should have been resting, Marguerite's amusement shared with Corfield over her husband's discomfort, and Bennett's later reference to himself as a pitiable old man are all indicative of the direction the trouble had taken.

He had upheld his manhood and successfully defended his pride, but he had paid a high price for the triumph, certainly physically and perhaps emotionally as well. Throughout the month he continued to complain of ailments, adding headaches to the already long list. His resentment toward Marguerite, which may or may not have been increased by events connected with the ride to Frinton, came to the surface in the entry for February 27, in which he recorded somewhat testily that Marguerite had been out "theatering and suppering and came home late and woke me up; hence [a] bad night." He rose the following morning, he complained, "much enfeebled." It appeared again in his account of Marguerite's all night excursion to Colchester on a dancing party with Evelyn Hill and two officers. A severe late March snowstorm developed during the night, and on the way home Bennett's car was smashed into a tree which had fallen across the road.

For a period of several months after the end of March, he gave up searching actively for a London flat. His health grew worse, and by early July he was suffering so acutely from neuralgia and dyspepsia that the doctor forbade him to do any more organizing work. Pinker took over his functions on the WARC for two weeks while Bennett remained at Comarques attempting to recover his strength. Finding that rest alone was not working the hoped for results, he wrote on July 17 to notify Pinker that he was going north with Marguerite for a short holiday and that Pinker should not communicate with him unless something very critical arose.[3]

His writing between January 1 and the middle of July had been limited to some pocket philosophy essays for the *Cosmopolitan;* one piece for the *Saturday Evening Post,* which seems not to have been published; *Daily News* articles; and the "Carlotta play," adapted from his novel *Sacred and Profane Love.* The play was put together in a three-week period and is devoid of any evidence of imaginative power. During the spring and early summer, he made no progress on his "war novel." He wrote no short stories and planned no new fiction during the months from January to July. Of this startling reduction in his writing, he said nothing. He must have been thoroughly aware, however, of what was happening to him; and that source of acute concern must have had an adverse effect on his health.

Bennett and Marguerite travelled north by train in easy stages. At Glasgow they took side trips to Loch Lomond and to a new munitions works. They set up temporary quarters at Blanefield where Bennett played golf with the local parson, found fault with the man's library, and said that his weakness was "the small joke." He also did some watercolors at Blanefield but thought they were mostly "very bad." From Blanefield they went to Airemore in the Highlands and stayed at a hotel with a fine view of the Cairgorm mountains. Their next stop was Edinburgh where they were driven around the city by an old driver who was "a shade drunk" but most helpful. At York, Bennett got some ideas for his next novel but made no further reference to the city, closing his account of the holiday with some practical advice for travellers staying at railway hotels: "As regards food," he wrote, "the thing to do is to stick to the grill and the sideboard, which railway companies understand, for dinner and lunch." He would have been in his element writing a *Scotland on 5 Shillings a Day.*

[3] Ogden Collection, July 17, 1916.

The holiday, his first since the summer of 1914, accomplished its purpose. His health improved throughout August, and in September he took up flat hunting again, this time going to estate agents and setting about seriously to locate a place. Marguerite joined him, and the search went on in earnest until the end of September, when Marguerite suddenly decided that she didn't want a flat after all. It was a critical decision as far as their marriage was concerned. Bennett had, apparently, made up his mind by this time to have a place in London. In the second week of October he "negotiated" for a permanent place at the RTYC. On November 3 he wrote in the journal that he had come to London two days before and taken "possession of Apartment C at the RTYC. . . . Rather like celibate life in Paris again . . . extraordinary sensation of having resumed a closed chapter of existence." [4]

By moving into the RTYC, Bennett had not so much resumed a chapter of existence as closed one. Although he may have been able to point to the pressure of WARC committee work, his delicate health, and the uncertainty of the train service between London and Comarques as reasons for taking rooms at the club, the principal reason for his having done so was to get away from Comarques and Marguerite. Faced with his decision, Marguerite then demanded a London location for herself; and sometime between November and the following January, he rented a small flat for her at 53 Oxford Street. Marguerite kept this flat until, much later and at her insistence, Bennett rented a maisonette at 128 George Street, Hanover Square, which, although Bennett spent little time in it, became their common home away from Comarques.

The apartment at the RTYC and the one on Oxford Street had, of course, increased Bennett's expenses. Since Comarques continued to be fully maintained, by the close of 1916 he had three residences to support in addition to the continued journeying between London and Thorpe-le-Soken by both Bennett and Marguerite. Miss Nerney continued to live at Comarques, a situation that forced Bennett to make many trips out from

4 *Journal*, November 3, 1916.

London simply to attend to business affairs connected with his writing. There were also frequent weekend parties at Comarques with open-handed entertaining for their many guests.

Nor were these the only problems created by the new living arrangements. Marguerite, smarting under an increasing sense of abandonment, came to the conclusion that her husband was keeping a French mistress—it is interesting that the mistress had to be French. Acting on her conviction, she bribed the doorman at the RTYC to allow her to go into her husband's rooms in his absence to look for evidence of his infidelity. She found none, but her act reveals the state of their marriage.

What Marguerite suffered chiefly was a sense of neglect, of being unloved. That her own dominating personality made it almost impossible for Bennett or anyone else to give her warmth and tenderness did not make her need any less real. A child of her own was an obvious answer to that need, but she must long since have given up hope of bearing a child by Bennett. Adopting a child was, therefore, her only alternative.

At about this time the family law firm of Bennett and Baddely, of which Bennett's brother Frank was a partner, was entering the last stage of its existence. Business had declined seriously, and Frank was in deep financial difficulty. Marguerite remembered, and apparently took seriously, Florence Bennett's joking remark, made some years earlier, that if Arnold and Marguerite ever wanted a child they could have one of her numerous brood. In the summer of 1916 the idea took hold of Marguerite; and trading on Frank's difficulties, she dragooned Bennett into offering to take over the care and education of his brother's oldest son Richard if the boy were allowed to come to Comarques as his and Marguerite's child.

Dudley Barker has given an excellent account of the negotiations and misunderstandings that led up to and followed Richard's move to Comarques in August.[5] The story makes painful reading. Richard's feelings about being uprooted from his family and sent to live with his uncle and *Tante* Marguerite were never properly taken into consideration. The proposition

[5] Barker, 194–201.

put forward by Marguerite that Richard was, at the age of sixteen, to transfer his affections from his mother to his aunt was absurd and gives a nightmare quality to the entire business.

It is most easy to understand Frank Bennett's compliance in the matter. Distracted by money worries, he was bound to see the removal of his son from the house as a lifting of one burden from his shoulders and as an unequalled opportunity for Richard to move up in the world. Bennett had promised to place Richard in Oundle school, an excellent private school where two of H. G. Wells's sons were already enrolled, and later to pay for the boy's education at Cambridge as well. It was an offer that no father in Frank's position could have dismissed lightly.

It is more difficult to understand Bennett's willingness to have Richard come to Comarques under Marguerite's terms. Richard had vacationed with his uncle and aunt in the past, and Bennett could not have been ignorant of the boy's personality. He must also have known that Marguerite was expecting a degree of affection and emotional dependence from Richard that his nephew could not possibly give. He was apparently willing to act against his better judgment in the hopes that by doing so he could free himself from at least some of Marguerite's emotional demands. That he was willing to deliver Richard into her hands is proof of his own desperation. Undoubtedly, he justified his action to himself by keeping in mind the fact that he was doing both Frank and Richard a favor by providing Richard with such good prospects. In one sense he was quite right; and that Richard Bennett can recall his life at Comarques without bitterness is, perhaps, the ultimate vindication of his uncle's decision.

For Marguerite the undertaking was a total failure. Richard was unable to reciprocate the love she gave. Marguerite resented his continued attachment to his parents and quarrelled with them over the frequency and the length of the boy's visits home. What Richard, caught between his mother and Marguerite, went through in terms of emotional stress can easily be imagined.

Naturally reticent by nature and by his upbringing in the North, he was constitutionally incapable of giving Marguerite even those outward gestures of affectionate response which she claimed as her due and which would have been such a balm to her sensibilities. Still, Richard stayed with Bennett and Marguerite until 1918 when the last of a series of flare-ups resulted in Richard's leaving Comarques for good. Bennett, however, gave Richard the education he had promised him and maintained a warm correspondence with him which lasted the rest of Bennett's life. Marguerite closed her heart to Richard, after having written to Frank, following Richard's departure, that she had suffered a hurt from which she could never recover.

Richard's coming to Comarques was, at least potentially, one more drain on Bennett's dangerously depleted store of energy. But because the strains to come did not make themselves felt with much if any force in the first months of Richard's stay, Bennett was able to profit from the temporary lessening of Marguerite's unhappiness. There was, however, no simultaneous burst of writing during the late summer to suggest that any of his creative forces had been released.

By fall the year was clearly becoming one of the least productive of his writing career. In January, Pinker had referred to "the London novel" (which Bennett had told Doran was going to be his greatest novel) as though it were about to be started; but Bennett did not actually begin writing *The Roll Call* for another ten months. Bad health was one reason for the delay; and, at least in the early spring, he was absorbed in his plans for writing Doris Keane's play.

After a considerable amount of dickering over such matters as who would choose the cast for the play, Bennett signed a binding contract with Miss Keane on February 2. He insisted on and got full veto rights in cast selection as well as inclusion of a clause guaranteeing that the play would be played "absolutely" as he wrote it. He was not, however, in any great hurry to get started on the actual writing. He began construction of the play on April 1 and finished the final scene on the 24th. Considering the fact that he continued his regular visits to London, missing only the one during the final week of composition, the play was written in an astonishingly short time. He chose not to tell

Pinker until July 17 that the play was finished, at which time he sent a copy of the play to Doris Keane and left for his holiday in Scotland.[6] He may have been reworking the play between the end of April and July; but if he was making extensive changes during those weeks, it was a radical departure from his usual writing practices. Indeed, it was almost a point of honor with him not to rewrite anything. A more convincing explanation is that he did not wish to give Doris Keane the play in advance of the contract date for delivery of the manuscript. What he actually thought about the quality of the play and whether that judgment was part of his decision to hold onto it until July is not known.

*Sacred and Profane Love*, as the play was eventually called, is not one of Bennett's happiest achievements. A. B. Walkley, play reviewer for the *Times*, dealt with the play as an example of the contemporary treatment being given to love as a theme. After concluding that it was not in the traditional sense a good play, he praised it as an attempt to deal with modern love as experienced by a modern woman "made for love" but found little else to praise in it.[7] Written in four acts, it follows the plot of the novel in general outline but substitutes a happy ending for the book's tragic conclusion. Essentially melodramatic, the action of the play is built around Carlotta Peel, a young girl of the Five Towns who falls in love with and for one night gives herself to Emilio Diaz, a famous pianist.

Carlotta's motivation for giving herself to Diaz is not compelling. Neither is her return to Diaz seven years later, although she explains her action as being a reaffirmation of faith, presumably a faith in the virtue of love. There is only one memorable speech in the play, and it is so clearly Bennett himself speaking out of the Five Towns that it acquires a life of its own. After lying to her aunt in order to get to London to hear Diaz play and then going with him to his rooms, Carlotta tells Diaz that she will tell her aunt the truth about what she has done.

[6] *Letters*, I, 239.
[7] A. B. Walkley, "Theatrical Amorism," *Pastiche and Prejudice* (London, 1921), 160–65.

"But must you?" Diaz asks. "Must I!" she responds. "I always pay the price—cash! And I always will. There's something in me that makes me. And I like to." [8]

Doris Keane was disappointed with the play. On the first of September she wrote Bennett asking him either to make changes in it or to allow her to withdraw from the contract for half of the fee previously agreed upon. Bennett refused. In a long letter written on the 4th, he declined to make any changes. "I have never altered a play save to cut it," he declared. "I have never got a play produced except after extreme difficulty and amid prophecies of disaster.[9] As for reducing the fee, he refused to do that also, making as his excuse the point that he had already lost £4,500 in taking the time to write the play. He reasoned that had he not been working on the play, which would produce an advance of £1,000 he would have contracted in the same period for a novel and immediately received an advance of £5,500.

The letter is uniformly kind but firm. He expressed regret that she had not found the character of Carlotta to her liking—she had written Bennett that anyone could play the part. His own feelings were expressed in the closing lines of the letter: "I hope you sympathize with my personal disappointment. These disappointments have to be faced." [10] It was a restrained statement; and although Bennett was once more facing the fact that he may have written an unsuccessful play, he had the comfort of knowing that his advance was secure.[11] As events were to show, he had been right in saying that the play would not be easy to place. Despite repeated efforts on his part and on Pinker's, it was not until 1919 that Basil Dean produced *Sacred and Profane Love* at the Aldwych in November of that year.

He did not, however, allow his temporary failure with "Instinct," as he called the Carlotta play in 1916, to discourage him from attempting to write another play for a particular performer. In December he had an outline in mind and was

8 Arnold Bennett, *Sacred and Profane Love* (London, 1919), 43.
9 *Letters*, I, 242.
10 *Ibid.*, I, 244.
11 He finally settled with Miss Keane for the sum of £750.

enthusiastic about its possibilities.[12] It was not to be an adaptation this time but an entirely new play. Vedrenne heard of it through Pinker and wanted to get the promise of it from Bennett, but he wanted to look at a synopsis before committing himself. Bennett declined to provide one, insisting that before anything was done in that line, Vedrenne would have to sign a contract. Vedrenne hesitated, and Bennett relented to the extent of saying that the play would be "witty and light" and specially adapted for Dennis Eadie, an actor and manager.[13]

Bennett had not been entirely honest with Doris Keane when he computed the extent of his losses in agreeing to write her play. No doubt he wished to put the best possible face on his refusal to let her out of their contract, but the only writing he was actually doing in January of 1916 was his *Daily News* articles. He had already contracted for his "London novel" but was doing nothing on it. The *Daily News* articles were coming out weekly; but his relationship with Gardiner, which had always been prickly, was about to grow worse. The newspaper had originally taken a stand against a conscription bill, and Bennett had supported their policy in his articles. By January, however, the paper was hedging on its stand at a time when Bennett's attacks were becoming increasingly vitriolic. In the second week of January, he submitted an article, which may have been called "The Rat Trap," devoted to a denunciation of the proposed conscription bill, and ran into Gardiner's strong objections.[14]

The *Daily News* refused to publish the piece but was forced to pay for it when Bennett insisted on the letter of their original agreement being observed. Bennett wrote to Pinker to the effect that the newspaper could do as it wished about publishing the article; but if they did not pay him for it, he would stop writing for them. He had, he continued, notified them twenty-four

---

[12] The play was called *The Title*, and Vedrenne began seriously to negotiate for it in late December.

[13] Ogden Collection, December 18, 1916.

[14] If, as Hepburn suggests in a note on page 235 of the *Letters*, I, the article was "The Rat Trap," it was probably a rewrite of a piece originally written in the fall of 1914, for which Bennett had been unable to find a publisher.

hours in advance of starting to write the article what in general it would be about. They had offered no objections.

Gardiner apparently resented Bennett's ultimatum, which was passed on to him by way of Pinker, and may at that time have made up his mind to drop Bennett from the pages of the *Daily News*. If Gardiner was waiting for an opportunity to cut Bennett's connection with the paper, the chance came in April. There was new trouble over an article, and Gardiner immediately wrote to Bennett, telling him that his material was no longer wanted. The financial loss amounted to one hundred dollars a week, a reduction which Bennett must have felt keenly; but his response to the news was characteristically low keyed. In the journal entry for April 26 in which he recorded in quick succession the birth of Betty Sharpe's daughter, the Dublin revolt, the capture of Roger Casement, and news of a naval engagement off Lowestoft, he noted that he had received a letter from A. G. Gardiner "practically putting an end" to his connection with the *Daily News*. He sent Gardiner's letter to Pinker with an attached note which read, "I need offer no remark on it." [15]

Over a dozen of his articles had appeared in the *Daily News* between January and May. About half of them were dull and repetitive, but the remaining pieces were lively and effective journalism. One of the most interesting was "Our Very Existence as an Empire," which appeared on Wednesday, February 2. The article was written in response to the decision made by the Government Committee on Public Retrenchment to close the public Museums and Galleries as an economy measure and as a visible sign that the nation was at war.

The Committee's action gave Bennett the opportunity not only to attack the decision itself but also to air some related complaints as well. "As a fact," he began, "museums and galleries are rather like moral soap and water" and as such served a very useful function in preserving morale. If they were closed, he asked, what would people do for diversion? "Apparently," he continued with increasing scorn, "the contrast between the classical and splendid theatrical fare of Berlin and the dreadful desolating rubbish now offered to playgoers in the West End is not enough for our authorities."

He went on to point out that the Committee's action was part of a national failure to see the vital connection between effective education, which museums and galleries, in part, provided, and the welfare of the country and its empire. He said that an improvement in education was imperative and that the nation's indifference to that need was at once "comic" and "tragic." Having dismissed the kind of education offered by Cambridge and Oxford as mostly useless, he praised the great universities of the North—Manchester, Leeds, Liverpool, and Sheffield—calling them the nation's "hope."

In the article for February 16, "Mr. Shaw v. The Prime Minister," he locked horns with Shaw over Shaw's NS article of February 12, in which, among other things, Shaw attacked Asquith and deplored the failure of the country to utilize the available brain power in the task of running the government. In the same article he challenged Bennett to say why he supported Asquith. Bennett gave his reasons in the *Daily News* piece, concentrating his attention on Asquith's political realism and his capacity for keeping his head in a crisis. But the center of interest in the article is Bennett's attack on Shaw's proposal that a sort of coalition of intelligence be formed in the country for the purpose of putting that aggregate intelligence to work for the nation's good.

With sly malice Bennett wrote that one could imagine the results of putting Shaw into the Prime Minister's post or of staffing the government with inexperienced men drawn from Shaw's so-called "intelligencia." "The notion of teaching these grandmothers [members of the Cabinet] to suck eggs," he pointed out, "is rather a comic notion." As for the general level of intelligence among the men in government, he thought that it was probably at least as high as in those men outside it. He concluded that Shaw was naive if he believed that the formation of a group of "intelligent outside critics" could have much influence on the government in power or that the group could expect to be asked to replace men already in power. "To put such a scheme forward," Bennett concluded, "implies an almost sensational lack of the sense of reality." In the journal he dismissed Shaw's plan as "idiotic."

The need for intelligence in government remained acute, nevertheless; and its absence was nowhere more evident than in the failure of those in power to see that England was headed for serious trouble with Ireland. Parliament had passed a Home Rule Bill in May of 1914; but along with many other measures it was set aside at the outbreak of the war. Given the militant hostility of Ulster toward the bill, Asquith was probably glad of the opportunity of postponing its implementation. But the Prime Minister made the mistake of assuming that his complacency was shared by Catholic Ireland. It was not.

Had the British government taken the elementary precautions of seeing to it that the pride of the Irish Nationalists was preserved it might have avoided trouble. Kitchener, however, did not trust the Irish, and he helped to block the formation of an Irish volunteer division to fight in France. When it was finally formed, the flags and regimental insignias, sewn and contributed by Irish women, were rejected. As a further humiliation only one officer in five in the division was a Catholic, the rest being chiefly Protestant Ulstermen. As a final insult the commanding officer of the Ulster Volunteers announced, without receiving a rebuke from the British government, that after the war he would use his Volunteers to smash Home Rule.[16]

These conditions were exactly those most calculated to foster the growth of the radical Sinn Fein [literally, "we ourselves"], which by 1916 was demanding full self-government for Ireland. By the spring of 1916 it had increased its strength enough to plan an armed uprising for Easter Sunday. Germany had been approached by Roger Casement, a one-time English diplomat, trying to gain support for the rebellion. On Good Friday, Casement landed on the Irish coast from a German submarine and was immediately captured. He had returned to warn the

[16] W. P. Hall and R. G. Albion, *A History of England and the British Empire* (New York, 1946), 876.

Irish that significant German support could not be expected and that the revolt should be called off. A German ship, disguised as a neutral merchantman, carrying arms and ammunition from Germany, was stopped by a British gunboat near Tralee and told to prepare for inspection. The German captain immediately hoisted his nation's colors and scuttled the ship.

Easter Sunday passed without incident, but on Monday rebels in Dublin, acting independently, captured the Government Post Office Building and declared the Irish Republic. British forces in Dublin responded and broke the rebellion after a week of fighting. A hundred British soldiers and 450 Irish were killed, forcing the surviving members of the Provisional Government of the Irish Republic to surrender. Casement and the seven signers of the proclamation of independence were tried and executed. Of the commanding officers of the rebel force, only Eamonn de Valera escaped the death penalty.[17]

Asquith went to Dublin in hopes of redeeming the situation by granting immediate Home Rule, but at the last moment he lost courage. Lloyd George, seeing an opportunity to increase his political stock at Asquith's expense, set to work to hammer out an agreement on Ireland. His proposal was that Ulster be kept a part of the United Kingdom until after the war and that Home Rule be granted at once to the remaining twenty-six counties of southern Ireland. Asquith, however, frightened by conservative opposition, did not carry the plan through. Dublin Castle was left to rule Ireland, and the blood of the martyrs of the Easter rebellion was left to be avenged by more blood.

Meanwhile, the English government, anxious to mitigate the bad publicity of the Irish revolt, recruited writers to go to Dublin and then to write in support of British policy in Ireland. Masterman's office asked Bennett to put his pen to work in the cause, and Bennett consented to go to Dublin. The result of his trip was an article which appeared in the *New York Times* on May 28. It was the second piece he had written for Masterman on the Irish question. The earlier article was done in late February or early March, but all that is known of it is that

[17] A. J. P. Taylor, *English History, 1914–1945* (New York, 1965), 56.

Masterman had been pleased with it and that Bennett called it "propaganda stuff for the U.S.A."

Bennett's evaluation of the Irish revolt in the *New York Times* article for May 28 is an irritating mixture of cynical misrepresentation and honest commentary. Bennett deliberately set out to discredit the men who led the revolt and their motives. He wrote that the uprising was the work of an irreconcilable minority of Irishmen representing insurgent labor; of apostles of vengeance against British authority, who were themselves guilty of every political crime including homicide; and of "unadulterated Sinn Fein." He stressed repeatedly in the article that support for the revolt came principally from outside Ireland, from Germany and the American based Clan-na-Gael. As a final criticism he attempted to convince his readers that the rank and file of those who took part in the fighting had not known what their leaders had planned until it was too late for them to extricate themselves from the trouble. He also said that those who fought were very young, implying that their leaders had exploited their youthful ignorance for a base end.

When he came to deal with the responsibility of the British government in the crisis, he said that it was "neither more nor less than the historic responsibility inherited from hundreds of years of Anglo-Saxon unimaginativeness." He went on to say that the real source of the trouble was not bad government practices but a basic difference in temperament between the two peoples. That assessment of the situation is an evasion, and the evasion must have been deliberate.

On the other hand, it is not possible to quarrel with his assertion that Anglo-Irish troubles were of long standing and were exacerbated by the related problem of Ulster. He was probably also right in saying that many with no interest in the political or social aspects of the conflict had joined in the fray for the purpose of looting or simply indulging in violence. But Bennett's technique in the article is to dodge those issues which, if confronted, would have forced him to find fault with British rule in Ireland. It was all very well for him to insist that both the Sinn Fein and the Clan-na-Gael were undemocratic and probably corrupt in their leadership; but it remains a fact that the Irish uprising was the only revolt of its kind to occur in Europe during the entire war, a fact embarrassing to England's claim that she was fighting to preserve democracy.

It is difficult to judge Bennett's true attitude toward the Irish revolt because he did not put his opinions into writing in other pieces. Incredible though it may be, he may have been expressing his true convictions in the *Times* article. What is more likely, however, is that he was writing propaganda calculated to show the British government in the best possible light and to discredit as much as possible any suggestion that the Easter Rebellion was a genuine expression of Catholic Ireland's desire for self-government.

In January, Bennett was asked to do quite another sort of article, one with which he was thoroughly familiar. The *Woman's Home Companion* offered him thirty cents a word for four articles of not more than 1,500 words each, to be written along the line of "How to Live on Twenty-Four Hours a Day." He refused, insisting that he would not settle for less than one hundred pounds for any commissioned article sold in the United States. There was a two months' silence; and then the *Woman's Home Companion* capitulated, offering Bennett five hundred dollars each for four articles. The magazine sent along some suggested titles—"Living with Your Wife," "Who is the Poor Man?," "Getting Acquainted with Yourself," "The Only Cure for Nerves," and "The Sense of Humor (How to Tell if You Have One)." George Doran urged Bennett to do the series because, in his opinion, the articles would have excellent possibilities as a book. Bennett instructed Pinker to draw up a contract with the *Woman's Home Companion* and to tell the editors that he would use their suggested titles, adding that he knew exactly what was wanted, "which happens to be just the sort of thing I am prepared to do." [18]

On March 8 he completed an unidentified article for the *Saturday Evening Post*, which the magazine may have decided not to publish, and then turned to the *Woman's Home Compan-*

[18] Butler Collection, January 12, 1916; March 3, 1916.

*ion* series. Pinker received the first of the four pieces on May 31. It was "Living with Your Wife—or Your Husband," a subject on which Bennett had reason to consider himself competent to write, at least as far as experience went. It is less certain that he was fitted by that experience to write optimistically on the subject. By the end of August he had finished the last article. The series appeared in England in *The Strand*, Greenhough Smith having bought it in June, demonstrating that editorial policy in *The Strand* was not to exclude Bennett because of the trouble over *The Lion's Share*.

With the material for the *Companion* finished, he went through September with no contracts for articles and with no stated interest in writing any. But in October, over lunch at the Reform Club, Clifford Sharp asked him to do a weekly article for the *NS*. Bennett described what Sharp wanted as "so-called inside group" articles. Bennett did not make it altogether clear what "group" Sharp had in mind; but it was probably a reference to those branches of government, such as the Ministry of Information, which Bennett had special knowledge through his contacts with Masterman, Mair, and others.

Sharp was undoubtedly feeling a new sense of freedom and probably relief as well when he asked Bennett to become a regular contributor to the *NS*.[19] Shaw had finally made up his mind to resign from the journal's directorate, a decision which Bennett called a "good thing." Shaw had been out of sympathy with the *NS*'s editorial policy for some time, and he was at odds with the Webbs as well. In the preceding February, Bennett had discussed with the Webbs his own and Shaw's articles on Asquith. Bennett wrote in his journal that the Webbs blamed Shaw for "being 'common' (which he is) and 'slack' (which he apparently is), but they admitted his incomparable skill." [20] The parenthetic comments are Bennett's, but it is difficult to judge how strong a criticism of Shaw they are because despite their

[19] Bennett had been writing intermittently for the *NS* since at least as early as April, 1913, when he wrote "Phenomena at Covent Garden" for the journal as a gift to the Webbs, having been persuaded to do it by the "skillful fascinations of Beatrice Webb."

[20] Unpublished Journal, February 19, 1916.

disagreements Bennett liked and admired Shaw and thought of
him as a basically decent and kindly man.

On Monday, October 23, he wrote the first of his "causeries"
for the NS. It was published under the title "Observations" and
signed Sardonyx, a name which Bennett signed to all his NS
articles, although the real identity of Sardonyx did not long
remain a mystery. Bennett's presence in the NS was, in Edward
Hyams's view, something of an anomaly. Hyams has written
that Bennett's articles stuck out of the pages of the NS "like a
sore thumb" and read like a "gossip column." He has also
pointed out that they quickly dwindled in size and had to be
filled out either by Squire, who was literary editor, or by Robert
Ensor, who was a political and foreign news commentator for
the NS. Hyams thought that a lack of anything to say caused
the shrinkage rather than a shortage of space.[21]

Bennett made no mention of any difficulty in finding material
for his NS articles, and throughout the final weeks of 1916 the
pieces appear to be his own and usually ran the better part of
two full columns. His first article was on a favorite subject, the
reactionary character of the War Office. In it he held up for
ridicule the conservative opposition within the department to the
development and the use of tanks, mentioning in particular one
officer who told Bennett that he did "not believe in tanks one
little bit." "Doubtless," Bennett remarked, "he was dreaming of
a future in which cavalry should come galloping and sabring into
its own again."

The November and December articles for 1916 are an interesting record of what Bennett found worth writing about and what
he thought would interest the NS readers. They are a peculiar
mix of political commentary, judgments on the state of civilian
morale, the inefficiency of government departments, and idio-
syncratic observations on such diverse subjects as the Lord
Mayor's Banquet and women's suffrage.

In one of his best pieces, published on December 23, he took
up arms against those permanent fixtures of all bureaucracies,
"departmental servants," laying on them the charge of lengthen-

[21] Edward Hyams, New Statesman (London, 1963), 69–70.

ing the war or at least reducing the effectiveness of the country's efforts by their obstructionism and maddening insistence on following routines, however absurd those routines might be. As a group, he wrote, they were "obstinate, blind," and possessed of "appalling prejudice and jealousy."

Aside from its liveliness, the article is interesting for the presence in it of a description of the trouble and frustration in store for a new director when he takes control of a government department. Later in *Lord Raingo* Bennett reproduced in dramatic form the paragraphs dealing with a director's problems. In the scene in which Lord Raingo takes over the directorship of the Ministry of Records, his problems are precisely those described by Bennett in the *NS* article. The conversion is an excellent example of the care Bennett took to conserve his material and illustrates how he worked up background material for his fiction.

One of the weakest of the pieces was the November 18 article on the Lord Mayor's Banquet. Bennett had attended the banquet on the 9th and had written up the event in a long journal entry, giving such details as "Soup tepid. Fish cold. Pheasant good. Cold meat good. No veg. Sweets excellent. . . . Awful dowdiness of women, including nobs." [22] Despite some attempt on Bennett's part to talk about the quality of the various speakers, among whom was Asquith, the article was a failure. It was an inferior working over of the journal entry, unenlivened by what Hyams called the "gossip column" anecdotes that gave vitality to most of his articles.

When he chose to make them so, Bennett's judgments on people and events could be extremely trenchant, but he had no gift for subtlety. His comments always were more the Viking axe blow than the rapier thrust. Referring to a series of meetings that had been held in the city to determine the business community's reaction to the submarine crisis, he wrote that the meeting called together by Lord Beresford was "a circus overstaffed with clowns." In another article he defended women against the charge that they would be unprincipled in politics,

[22] *Journal*, 604.

concluding that they would need "a little more practice" before they could "seriously hope to rival men in the domain of political turpitude." In a more serious vein he observed that while there was not in England "one law for the rich and another for the poor," it was regrettably obvious that the application of the law was "in inverse ratio to the wealth and position of the person who defies it."

Since Bennett was paid nothing for his *NS* articles, his motive for writing them was not financial. He probably missed the satisfaction of addressing a national audience, which his column in the *Daily News* had given him; and he may also have felt that his articles in the *NS* were making a contribution to the war effort. It was Bennett's conviction that the war was being fought, in part at least, to preserve democracy. His articles were generally in defense of democratic principles and in support of civilian morale; and to the extent that he felt he was countering the reactionary influences at work in society, he was contributing to the national effort.

Between January 1916 and the following October, Bennett did no novel writing. The pause between books was one of the longest in his career. He had a novel in mind during the period; and as indicated by what he had said to Doran in December of the previous year, he intended it to be a major work. The long fallow period leading up to October could have been a time of careful planning and preparation; but whatever Bennett originally intended, the months between January and October did not produce much systematic planning. He had a general outline for the novel in mind as early as 1915, but there is no evidence that he began elaborating on it before the summer of 1916. In July he recorded in his journal that he had been walking to Pinker's by way of Gracechurch Street and had found material there for his next novel. The area gave him, he said, "a tremendous impression of wealth and common sense." [23]

[23] *Journal*, July 22, 1916. Gracechurch Street lies to the south and east of the Bank of England and runs north from the Monument into Bishopsgate. It is within the City, which probably accounts for the impression of "wealth and common sense" Bennett got from walking there. The principal setting for *The Roll Call*, however, is Chelsea.

The first indication that he was making any progress at all with the book came in August when Doran asked for and was given an outline of the novel. With more grace than he usually displayed on such occasions, Bennett sent Pinker a synopsis to be passed along to Doran. In the synopsis Bennett outlined a plot that was close to the one he eventually built into *The Roll Call*. There is one important difference between the two plots, however; and the difference is, in all likelihood, the difference between what Bennett would like to have written and what he felt the public would demand.

In the synopsis George Cannon leaves his wife Lois, returns to Marguerite, his first love, and finds happiness with her. When he wrote the synopsis, Bennett made George's separation from his family permanent. But in the novel George remains married to Lois, making his escape from an unsatisfactory marriage by way of the army. George's deliverance from his marriage is a compromise, and at the end of the war he will still have to face the fact of his dissatisfaction with Lois. Why did Bennett make this change in the actual novel? His commercial instincts probably warned him that public sentiment would be against a man who walked out on his responsibilities. After all, a war was going on and men were being called upon to serve a cause higher than their physical passions.

Another explanation is that Bennett scaled down his intentions for the book between the time of writing the synopsis and beginning the novel. He appears to have abandoned his scheme for writing a major serious work in favor of bringing out a popular novel, his first with a war setting, suited to the hour. Once that decision was made the form the novel was to take was determined. In the reading public's view George's enlisting would be seen as a commendable response to the call of duty rather than what it actually was, a running away. It was an ingenious compromise, but it is doubtful that Bennett was happy with it.

Assuming the second explanation to be the correct one, another and very important question is raised. Why did he decide against trying to write a major work? Perhaps his awareness that his powers were not equal to the task wisely made him settle for something less grand in design that he could hope to do successfully. Despite the lowered aims he did not find the writing easy. In September he recorded hopefully that he had found some good material in two promenade concerts which he attended; but by October he had fallen back on some very old writing in order to bolster his sagging imagination. On October 9 Bennett asked Pinker to dig out some *Academy* articles which had been put together years before and which Bennett had once hoped to publish in book form. Two or three of the pieces were titled "The Fallow Fields of Fiction," and one of them contained a description of Westminster Cathedral which Bennett particularly wanted to use in his novel.

In considering the gap between Bennett's original intention and his eventual achievement in *The Roll Call*, it must be concluded that his imaginative powers were so seriously impaired by ill health, exhaustion, and the distractions of his crumbling marriage and of his social life that he was unable to find either material or inspiration to support his effort. By October he had abandoned all hope of writing a really first-class novel and had given himself to the task of grinding out a book with some hope of commercial success. Had it not been for his August holiday, he might not have mustered strength enough even for that. Throughout the fall and winter he struggled to get words down on paper; his efforts are recorded in word counts and an almost desperate search for copy.

By the second week of November he had written 16,000 words of the novel; and by the end of December he had done 35,000. But the writing had gone very unevenly. Sickness had begun to dog him again. On November 30 he decided to stop working on the book entirely and put it aside for a week.[24] Then he took it up again on December 7 and read through what he had written. "Not so bad," he decided, adding that he had been much "refreshed and reinvigorated" by reading Dreiser's *The Financier*, which "absolutely held" him, and *The Titan*,

[24] Unpublished Journal, November 30, 1916.

which was "not so good." He was clearly having trouble thinking of anything to write.

A temporary exhaustion of creative powers may have been common to many writers during the war. Hall Caine, for instance, recorded such an interruption. The shock effect of the war must have been great and undoubtedly raised in the minds of fiction writers doubts about the validity of what they were doing. Bennett never admitted to having such doubts or, for that matter, to being upset by the war at all. But it is unlikely that he entirely escaped its emotionally debilitating effects. The terrible loss of life being reported in the press and the rapid disintegration of the familiar and comforting orderliness of existence could not have left him unscathed.

Bennett did escape the pain of having one of his immediate family involved in the war. He and his brothers were too old for active service, and none of his nephews were old enough. He did, however, have friends whose sons were serving. James Pinker's son Eric was commissioned and in France with the army. Occasionally, Bennett in his business notes questioned Pinker about Eric's whereabouts and how he was getting along. Another friend, Frank Rosher, an East India merchant, had a son in the Royal Naval Air Service. Harold Rosher was twenty years old when the war broke out. He enlisted immediately and had reached the rank of Flight-Lieutenant when he was killed in 1916 in a landing accident. Frank Rosher published his son's letters to the family in November, 1916, and Bennett wrote an introduction to the book.[25] The Introduction is stiffly conventional. Bennett praised Harold Rosher's courage, integrity, and patriotism, but there is nothing to suggest how he felt personally about the young man's death. There is the same cold detachment that appeared in his account of his mother's death.

If he was unable or unwilling to comment directly on his own responses to the war and the changes it was bringing to his

[25] The volume was published in England under the title *In the Royal Naval Air Service* (London, 1916). In the United States the title was changed to *With The Flying Squadron* (New York, 1916).

pattern of living, his reactions to them found indirect expression through what he wrote. An example was his response to the theatrical fare being offered in the West End. In January he went to see *Bauldy* at the Royalty Theatre and called it "absolutely dreadful." The following month he saw Sir Charles Villiers Stanford's new opera *The Critic* with no more pleasure than he had expressed over *Bauldy*. He said that Stanford's opera was "thoroughly rotten." Webster's *Daddy-Long-Legs*, which he saw in September, distressed him even more. He denounced it as being "an absolutely putrid play." [26]

What exactly he objected to in these plays is expressed in the opening pages of *The Pretty Lady*, which although written later, is set in the 1915–1916 period of the war. He describes an unnamed play, clearly meant to stand for the typical West End hit, and then damns it for being crude, vulgar, and cheap. "It was," Bennett wrote, "licensed to say that which in private could not be said where men and women meet, and that which could not be printed. It gave voice to the silent appeal of pictures and posters and illustrated weeklies all over town. . . ." [27]

Although Bennett often regarded himself as a herald of change, he was not altogether comfortable with the process of change itself. When he encountered evidence of the new sexual freedoms being hastened by the war, he was often troubled. On May 8 he wrote in the journal that a dispatch rider had stopped in the village to have a long talk with a girl who came out of her house to meet him. "She is the schoolmistress," Bennett recorded with poorly concealed disapproval, "but still little more than a flapper, with a vast ribbonbow in her too fluffy hair." At about the same time he fired his maid for refusing to wash the insides of the downstairs windows. The apostle of the right of labor to defend itself against exploitation found that he could not negotiate the question of whether or not maids should wash windows. The theory of change was one thing; the reality, something else.

On the other hand, he was no champion of the old order,

[26] *Journal*, February 11, 1916; September 2, 1916.
[27] Arnold Bennett, *The Pretty Lady* (London, 1918), 1.

which was being ground up by the pressures of war. He had attacked the dull respectability of Frinton in *The Lion's Share* and the rigidity of the nation's social structure in innumerable articles. He had come to despise provincialism in all its forms and grasped every opportunity to ridicule it. He found, for instance, a woman in Frinton who made her living boarding dogs in heat and nursing pregnant dogs. "It is marvelously characteristic of Frinton," he wrote with withering sarcasm.[28] His conflicting attitudes forced him into a dilemma, and that dilemma undoubtedly contributed to the immobilizing of his creative powers.

He found some comfort, however, in painting and began taking lessons in the summer with an artist by the name of Bright, to whom he had been introduced by Rickards. He was also cheered enormously by the fact, discovered after he had taken permanent rooms at the RTYC, that he could have fresh sole for breakfast in the Club dining room for only two shillings and fourpence. The world had not entirely gone mad. Pockets of sanity remained.

Looking back over the year, however, Bennett could not have found much cause for rejoicing. The war, bad health, and troubles with Marguerite had helped to reduce his output to 127,600 words, less than half of his output for 1915. He attempted to gloss over the decline by saying that totals of later years could not be compared with totals of earlier years because recently he had not been counting his journal. No rationalization, however, altered the fact that his productivity had fallen off enormously, and that his creative powers were seriously in ebb.

In many ways *The Roll Call* suggests the nature of his difficulty. It was to have been his first great "London novel," but its leading character was from the Five Towns and intimately connected with that district. In fact Bennett expressed in his synopsis of the novel his intention to shift the focus of the book away from the Five Towns but, at the same time, to carry their spirit to London. He was on a fence.

[28] Unpublished Journal, May 21, 1916.

When it came to the test of attempting a serious book, he was still not ready to give up the security which the Five Towns material offered him. He appears to have been trying desperately to hold onto the certainties of a past which were no longer certainties to him and simultaneously to grasp present realities, which he did not more than partially understand. The consequences of his confusion in *The Roll Call* will be discussed later; the immediate results for Bennett of having moved into a kind of half-way world of the imagination was creative stagnation.

# VII

## REVIVAL AND DECLINE

"I went to my new flat at 52 Oxford Street last night," Bennett wrote in his first journal entry for the new year. It was a misleading entry. From the very beginning the flat was Marguerite's; although Bennett paid the rent, he entered it only as a visitor. There was no indication that he wanted any other arrangement. He was very happy with his own rooms at the RTYC, where he was comfortably settled among his books. As far as the Oxford Street flat was concerned, Bennett went up from Picadilly at fairly regular intervals to dine with Marguerite or to take her out for dinner and the theater, but it was a rare occasion when he spent the night there.

Bennett and Marguerite continued to use Comarques for weekend entertaining, although they were not always there together or with the same group of friends. There is nothing, however, in the journal or in his correspondence for this period that suggests any agreement upon a separation or even an understanding that each would go his own way. It appears that by taking separate lodgings in London and devoting themselves to their own affairs they effected a separation, planned or not. Bennett filled his hours in town with committee meetings and business and social engagements from which Marguerite was excluded. A typical London day for Bennett began at the RTYC with a morning of writing, then lunch at the Reform Club with Wells, Mair, Swinnerton, Masterman, or another of his many friends. After lunch was finished he spent the remainder of the afternoon in writing or attending meetings. In the evening he dined out, occasionally with Marguerite, and then either went to the theater or returned to the Reform Club for a night of talking, smoking, and drinking.

At intervals, to break the London routine and to live up to his role of owner of a country house, he took friends down to

Comarques for a long weekend. During the second week of January he took Hugh Walpole and Frank Swinnerton with him to Essex for a few days of relaxation. Finding that they had the house to themselves, Bennett recorded that they had "two uproarious evenings, too long and too smoky." It was the first time for months that Bennett admitted to thoroughly enjoying himself.

At some point in the weekend, the subject of Bennett's Jacob Tonson articles came up for discussion; and on Sunday Walpole made Bennett dig out the manuscript copies of the pieces. Once started on them, Walpole became so engrossed in the articles that he spent all of Sunday afternoon reading them. When he was finished, he insisted that they should be brought out in volume form. Swinnerton concurred; and Bennett, delighted with the prospects of getting out a book without having to make a significant effort, gave Swinnerton permission to speak to Spaulding at Chatto and Windus about publishing the articles.

The Jacob Tonson series had come into being in 1908 while Bennett was living in Fontainbleau. Having sold A. R. Orage, editor of the *New Age*, the pocket philosophy *How to Live on Twenty-four Hours a Day* and, among other things, an article on H. G. Wells, he conceived the idea of writing a regular series for the *New Age* to be called "Books and Persons." Orage accepted Bennett's suggestion; and the "Books and Persons" column, which was an immediate success, ran for about three years. Bennett signed the articles Jacob Tonson, but the real identity of the author was no mystery. For the first eighteen months he wrote the series gratis. After that he was paid one guinea a week for his labors. When his connection with the magazine was finally severed, the articles went into Bennett's files to be more or less forgotten until Walpole asked to see them.

By January 14 Bennett had definitely made up his mind to go ahead with the collection. He had read through most of the material and had found it "enormously vivacious." Chatto and Windus were eager to have the book; and Bennett agreed to give it to them, with one practical stipulation that the book have an index, despite the additional cost involved in its preparation. On January 22 Pinker notified Bennett that contract arrangements had been settled with Spaulding and that publication could proceed.

Unfortunately, no one had thought to consult A. R. Orage about the material; and Orage, whose connection with the *New Age* had ended in financial disaster for him, threatened to bring suit against Chatto and Windus over the question of ownership of the "Books and Person" copyright. At the same time Orage notified Spaulding that if Bennett would ask permission to publish the articles, Orage would readily grant it. For the moment Bennett kept out of the controversy, leaving Pinker to carry on negotiations. Pinker finally came to the conclusion that Orage's claim to the material had no legal basis and advised Bennett that Orage could be told to "go to the deuce" if Bennett chose not to ask permission.

Bennett, however, had no intention of adding to the unpleasantness of the situation. He sent Orage a letter, which brought an immediate and pleasant response from his one-time editor. "Ten years of struggle," Orage wrote with touching frankness, "with nothing but bankruptcy to show for it have probably made me rather touchy upon matters affecting the *New Age*." [1] There was no litigation and no further bad feelings. Bennett's letter had smoothed the way for publication. A few months later *Books and Persons* came out in England, and George Doran brought out the book in the fall in the United States. The collection had a very satisfactory sale—so satisfactory in fact that in October, Pinker asked Swinnerton about the chances for a second volume. Swinnerton said that Chatto and Windus would be delighted to have a second volume; but Bennett, for unknown reasons, refused to consider the proposal.

Shortly after the appearance of *Books and Persons*, Rebecca West wrote to Bennett congratulating him on the collection and recalling the circumstances under which she had originally read the Jacob Tonson articles: "I was for two years forced by a benevolent government to attend cookery class every Friday

[1] Ogden Collection, March 22, 1917.

afternoon, and it was my habit to make these hours that would otherwise have been unprofitable more valuable than the rest of my education put together by reading Jacob Tonson. It seems strange to reread them without the accompaniment of remarks on the proper way of stuffing a cod. . . ." [2]

*Books and Persons* was a windfall to the suddenly infertile Bennett. It cost him little effort and brought him welcome money at a time when he had no creative energy to spare. He was still working desperately to complete *The Roll Call* and was writing six journalism articles a month in addition to meeting his committee obligations with the WARC. He was doing a weekly *NS* piece; and in the first week of January, Gardiner had asked him to resume writing his *Daily News* series. Bennett agreed to write a semi-weekly article for a period of six months at the rate of twenty-one pounds per article, the same rate of payment he had received for the earlier series which had terminated the previous spring. Whatever troubles had existed between him and Gardiner were now over, and he and the *Daily News* editor formed a congenial working partnership.

Bennett signed another contract in January, this one with Vedrenne for an option on a new play. There was no play in existence, of course; it was once more only an idea in Bennett's mind. His eagerness to sign a contract for the play is a bit puzzling, since under the terms of the agreement he would receive no money until the script was actually in Vedrenne's hands; and Bennett insisted that a clause be entered in the contract stating that the delivery date was to be June, 1918, "or within six months of the signing of the peace treaty if peace is not signed in 1917." [3] He had no intention of settling down to write the play in the near future, and a year was to pass before he even prepared an outline.[4] What probably accounts for his determination to be under contract for a play was the desire to have a settled plan and to feel that he was indeed a writer of

[2] *Ibid.*, July 4, 1917.
[3] Butler Collection, January 9, 1917.
[4] *Journal*, 647.

plays. His confidence in his ability to write plays undoubtedly needed bolstering.

Bennett entered the new year with his health suddenly improving, and the increase in vitality continued into the middle of February. For a month and a half he stopped complaining of dyspepsia, neuralgia, and headaches. Even his insomnia ceased being a burden to him. His spirits improved with his health and on the 28th of January in a rare burst of enthusiasm, he wrote that he was in "unusually good form for work." [5] He found ideas for *The Roll Call* coming more easily, a condition which greatly relieved him. He visited Westminster Cathedral and discovered new ways of using it in his novel. The new year had brought Bennett a new and necessary burst of creative energy, but his euphoria was short-lived.

In the last week of February he was stricken with a "chill" on the stomach, which was so severe that he stopped keeping his journal, although he managed to get out a short, single-column article for the *NS*. Unlike the headaches, neuralgia, dyspepsia, and insomnia, the illness appears to have been of the strictly physical sort; but it heralded the return of his old complaints. With their return his ability to find ideas for *The Roll Call* faded, and he was once more forced to make great efforts to stimulate his imagination. On March 1 he recorded that he "seemed to be wandering around all day in search of ideas" for the novel. His search took him back to Westminster Cathedral, Lanchester's Bond Street shop—he had dealt at length with Bond Street years before in *The Glimpse*—and several clubs. These wanderings produced 1,200 words of copy the next day and left enough material over for a full week of work, a situation that was less encouraging than it appeared to be. The writing was coming very hard, and he seems to have found it necessary to scrape material for every page.

In the same week that his health failed, he added to his responsibilities by contracting with the *Cosmopolitan* to do six articles in the vein of his popular pocket-philosophy books. The

[5] *Ibid.*, 614.

articles were to be two to three thousand words in length, and Pinker had persuaded *Cosmopolitan* to pay six hundred dollars for each piece. In early March, Pinker sold the series to *Nash's Magazine* for six hundred and fifty pounds.

Ever since his early association with *Woman* before the turn of the century, for which he had written articles giving advice on everything from clothes to romance, he had siezed every opportunity that came his way to write "how-to-live" articles. He enjoyed giving advice and felt that he was good at it. More important, he found that when he put his advice into essay form, people read what he wrote with great pleasure; and the money came rolling in.

But the new series meant new deadlines, and he was not strong enough to take on the additional work without further endangering his health. It is possible that the dread alone of having to do yet more work affected his health adversely. It certainly affected his state of mind. By the end of the second week of March he was complaining of sleeping ill "day after day." On the 15th he wrote that he had completed 1,100 words of his novel the previous day after having had a very bad night and was so exhausted in the afternoon that he "could scarcely even walk." Then his neuralgia came back to plague him.

The brief return of his health was probably due to his having settled down in London and the accompanying sense of freedom associated with having taken up a slightly new and more independent way of life. But the change was not great enough to free him for long from those inner tensions and conflicts which during the past three years had been finding expression in his chronic ailments.

It is interesting to note that editor Newman Flower, beginning with the 1917 journal entries, chose to reduce the number of Bennett's references to his health and finally to exclude them almost altogether from the published journal. As 1917 advanced, those references became a litany of his suffering. Week after week he recorded aches and agonies until it is impossible to avoid the conclusion that they were, for the most part, only the symptom of some deeper and nonphysical malady. Flower may have come to the same conclusion and made his decision to cut the entries on the basis of it; but whatever his motives were in removing Bennett's references to his health, the effect was to give in the published journal an entirely different picture of Bennett from the real one. The image of the calm man, at ease and in command of his emotions, is basically false; the real Bennett in the opening months of 1917 was on the verge of emotional and physical collapse.

One of the very marked characteristics of Bennett's work habits had been the regularity with which he sat down to his writing day after day and produced his 1,200 to 1,600 words. With *The Roll Call*, however, he changed his method. The last half of the novel was written in bursts of work which, more often than not, left him physically exhausted and drained of creative energy. To prepare for these marathon efforts, he spent a great deal of time collecting ideas. Then in a rush he would pour out the story in a frenzy of effort. For some reason he had lost that capacity for powerful and steady writing which in years past had produced such staggering quantities of material.

For a man of Bennett's regular habits and for whom a regular stint of writing was a duty, the breakdown of his writing routine suggests a serious dislocation of his emotional life. Rushing to complete work that should have been done the week before or wandering about desperately seeking ideas were forms of behavior totally foreign to Bennett's accustomed pattern of work. What seems to have given way—although he never admitted to such a failure—was his confidence that he would be able to go on successfully with *The Roll Call*. Added to that sense of insecurity was the awareness that the book he was writing was not what he wanted it to be, that it was a compromise with popular taste and his own waning powers. There is an underlying note of desperation in most of the journal entries dealing with *The Roll Call*, and his bravado does not conceal that anxiety.

On March 23 he noted that he had spent the day at the barber's and in the library of the Reform Club "in meditation," collecting ideas for the second half of *The Roll Call*. Then he neglected the novel altogether for several days before going down to Comarques for a week of writing. During that week he managed to get 5,000 words down on paper, 2,500 of which he wrote in a single day. Bennett called it an "immense burst of work," which indeed it was; but since he had done little or no writing the week before, he had only managed by his herculean effort to keep himself up to schedule.

Forcing his muse had the double disadvantage not only of tiring him excessively but also of loosening his control over what he was writing. In a remarkable departure from his usual custom, he decided that he was going to have to change a part of what he had written. The tone of the novel had gone wrong, he concluded; it had become "too sarcastic against the Army." [6] The consequence of the admission was immediate exhaustion and the loss of a day's work. But he forced himself to decide on the necessary changes, and four days later he threw himself again into the writing. In what he called "a great creative weekend," he wrote another 3,000 words, decided on the title *The Roll Call*, and fell back from his labors in exhaustion. On April 30 he brought the novel to a close "in accordance" with his timetable.

His troubles with the novel, however, were not yet over. He sent the manuscript to Pinker, who forwarded it to Munsey. Temporarily at least Bennett must have felt a great sense of relief. He had signed a contract with Munsey for the book three years before at a price of $17,500. The novel had cost him dearly in terms of nervous energy expended, but now he hoped to claim the rewards for his efforts. On May 22, however, Davis wrote to Pinker to say that Munsey was not taking the novel. The reasons Davis gave were that *The Roll Call* was a fourth Clayhanger novel and not at all the sort of novel that had been called for in the original agreement. What had been promised, according to Davis, was a light book with plenty of plot in the style of *Buried Alive*.[7] Pinker, probably guessing that serious trouble was ahead and not wanting Bennett to act precipitately, delayed sending Davis's letter to Bennett until June 8.

[6] Unpublished Journal, April 20, 1917.
[7] *Letters*, I, 251.

The Munsey contract, for which *The Roll Call* was the first of three novels promised, was financially the largest that Bennett had ever signed. It had been an outgrowth of the Clayhanger books and is a fair measure of Bennett's commercial success at the time he put his name to it. What Munsey's refusal meant to Bennett was not only that the most important book contract he had ever signed was suddenly in jeopardy but also that his ability to deliver acceptable material was called into question. Considering the struggles through which he had passed and his own painful compromises in the book, Munsey's refusal must have appeared as a confirmation of his worst fears. But, as always, he covered his anxiety with bluster.

He immediately got off a long letter to Pinker, expressing outrage at this new example of the duplicity of editors, and insisting that none of Davis's criticisms of the novel were sound. "The assertion that there is no plot in *The Roll Call* is ridiculous," he wrote, going on to point out the nature and the complexity of the plot. He found even more fault with the statement that *The Roll Call* was a Clayhanger novel. "It is wholly a London and Paris novel," he insisted and accused Davis of being "disingenuous." Having stated the difficulties which authors face with editors who buy material in advance and then kick at the material when it is delivered because it is not what they expected, Bennett pointed out that a contract was binding and that Pinker should prepare to take action to insure that the contract was honored.[8]

For a period of two months cables went back and forth across the Atlantic bearing charges and counter charges. Pinker, anxious to avoid becoming involved in litigation, appealed to George Doran to act as mediator in the struggle. Doran agreed to do what he could, and toward the end of June he cabled Pinker to say that he had seen a letter from Bennett to the Munsey Syndicate saying that the novel of Hilda's son was not for sale but that a humorous novel "in the vein of *Buried Alive*" was. He added that he knew the dangers run by a man who steps in to stop a fight and in this case he intended to remain strictly neutral,

[8] *Ibid.*, 252–54.

rendering what help he could to both parties in their efforts to patch up the quarrel.[9]

Bennett had been insisting that he had no recollection of any statement on his part giving the precise nature of the novel that Munsey was to receive. The appearance of the letter, however, convinced Pinker that Munsey had strong legal grounds for rejecting *The Roll Call*, especially since Davis and Munsey were wisely insisting, whether or not it was true, that it was on the basis of Bennett's letter that the original contract had been drawn up. Tempers on both sides of the ocean gradually cooled, and in the last week of July, Munsey offered Pinker the sum of £3,668 for *The Roll Call* with the rider that the contract for two more Bennett novels be cancelled. Pinker accepted, and Bennett responded to the news with a single sentence: "This affair is well over and I am much relieved." [10]

He may have been relieved, but he could hardly have been pleased. The book had been a problem to him from the moment he sat down to write the synopsis, and he seems never to have known exactly what sort of book he was writing. Originally, it was to have been a major effort, but he drew back from that intention as he found himself increasingly incapable of bringing the writing up to his own critical standards. In one of the letters which Bennett wrote to Pinker in reference to Munsey's objections to the novel, he insisted that *The Roll Call* was a "serious" novel.[11] By using the term "serious" he was distinguishing the book from such light efforts as *Buried Alive*, but he was fully aware that he had not written a work of the caliber of *Clayhanger* or even *These Twain*. Where then does *The Roll Call* stand among Bennett's novels?

Georges Lafourcade called it "a very inferior piece of work" in which Bennett went back to the "atmosphere and characters of his early Chelsea novels." [12] The return, according to Lafourcade, was probably due to an "exhaustion of the creative faculty." On the positive side Lafourcade found the style of the

[9] *Ibid.*, 256.
[10] Butler Collection, July 30, 1917.
[11] *Letters*, I, 252.
[12] Lafourcade, *Arnold Bennett*, 145.

book vivid and arresting. Other writers have been less generous. Dudley Barker has called it only slightly better than *The Lion's Share;* Reginald Pound lumped it with Bennett's "rent paying novels;" and Geoffrey West referred to its "weariness." [13]

Lafourcade was right in asserting that Bennett had fallen back on old material. Not only are Lois and Marguerite close approximations of Janet Orgreaves and Hilda Lessways, as the latter two characters appeared in the immediately preceding novels, there are other resemblances to characters and events from earlier books. Mr. Turnbull, for example, a tea merchant and a minor character in *The Roll Call,* is Mr. Bittenger, who appeared originally in the short story "Vera's Second Christmas Adventure." He is reproduced exactly, even down to his chestnut colored wig. Some years later, when he came to write "The Woman Who Stole Everything," Bennett reversed the process and borrowed from *The Roll Call.*

It is less than fair, however, to dismiss *The Roll Call* as a tired book written by a tired man. To give Bennett full credit, it is necessary to keep in mind that in *The Roll Call* he was attempting a new kind of writing, a fact that only Lafourcade among Bennett's biographers seems to have noted. The book is Bennett's first war novel, the first of three, the other two being *The Pretty Lady* and *Lord Raingo,* which were to be published in 1918 and 1926 respectively.

*The Roll Call* is further distinguished from his earlier novels by an atmosphere quite different from the one to be found in the Clayhanger books or even *The Price of Love,* in which it is possible to see Bennett's tendency to move in a new direction with his fiction. There is a new freedom of the spirit blowing through *The Roll Call* as there had been in *The Lion's Share.* George Cannon in *The Roll Call* and Audrey Moze in *The Lion's Share* both inhabit a world where opportunity is limited by the individual's capacities, not by the cultural and physical environment. Both novels are set in the cosmopolitan worlds of London and Paris. The narrow world of the Five Towns is gone. George Cannon's world is London, the great city in which

[13] Geoffrey West, *The Problem of Arnold Bennett* (London, 1932), 79.

he passes his apprenticeship as an architect and from which he draws inspiration.

The consequences of this shift of location for character development are illustrated by an episode mid-way through *The Roll Call* in which George accompanies Lois to a West End theater to see a new play, *The Gay Spark*. The play, according to the narrator, "pivoted unendingly on the same twin centers of alcohol and concupiscence," settling down in the second and third acts to a total preoccupation with sex. George was shocked and astonished by the play's "poorness" and "cheapness," and "dullness." [14] But he was even more astonished to discover that no one else seemed to object to the play. He was also shaken by the discovery that the young women in the audience were not embarrassed by what was unfolding before them on the stage. George Cannon is forced by the circumstances in which he finds himself to expand his consciousness, to enlarge his thinking in order to come to terms with the play and with what it's reception told him about the nature of the people around him. In London, George has to grow up to his world. In the Five Towns he would have to fight to free himself from their limiting influences.

As for the physical setting, London inspired George in a way which the pottery banks with their smoke and fire could not have done. Probably the dominating physical image in *The Roll Call* is Westminster Cathedral. From the Cathedral and from the man who designed it, George derives a sense of purpose. The shift in setting produced a new focus in Bennett's writing. His characters were no longer reacting against their environment or being stifled by it. It was giving them the strength and the opportunity to grow.

It was probably this new experience of life on which Bennett had hoped to build in *The Roll Call*, endowing it with the same power that he had given to time in *The Old Wives' Tale*. If that were his intention, the novel was to be an affirmation of life's potentials rather than a jeremiad on its limitations. The synopsis of the novel, which he sent to Doran in the late summer of

[14] Bennett, *The Roll Call*, 183.

1916, showed George achieving professional success as an architect and eventually gaining personal happiness by leaving Lois and going back to Marguerite.

The novel, however, must be judged by what Bennett did with it rather than what he might have done. What he actually did was to reshape his original intentions to meet what he thought to be the popular taste of the moment. By introducing the war, which is never more than a peripheral interest in the book and a shaky machine for getting George out of his marital dilemma, Bennett divided the center of interest in the novel and provided himself with a weak alternative to having George face up to and deal with the problem of his unhappy marriage. But Bennett retreated from that affirmation of faith in the individual's ability to achieve happiness, an affirmation he was anxious to give expression to in the early months of the book's evolution. For that affirmation he substituted a pseudo-mystical experience in which George, through a dream, is called to the colors. The device is wholly ineffective and as a motivating force for George's later behavior is painfully unconvincing.

Lafourcade called *The Roll Call* a transitional novel, but it is more of an abortion than a transition. It is not possible to say exactly what went wrong in the writing, beyond suggesting that as Bennett's creative energies waned his capacity for making an imaginative response to the material also weakened, driving him back into formula writing with all of its paraphernalia of cliché and predictability.

Bennett seems to have put very little of himself into the novel, although George's weariness and his dissatisfaction with his accumulated possessions and the elaborate structure of his life may have been Bennett's own disillusionment finding expression. For the most part, Bennett appears only as a commentator, speaking through the narrative. There is nothing in the commentary as intrusive as Bennett's entry into the death scene of John Baines, but his entrance is sometimes unmistakable. George is introduced to the phenomenon of Latin women, and the narrative speaker stops the action to describe them as being possessed by "a ruthless egotism" and completely lacking in a sense of shame for their unscrupulous behavior toward men, "their cherished enemies." [15] The bitter criticism is almost certainly an authorial comment on Marguerite.

Publication of *The Roll Call* was held up for many months because Munsey would neither publish the novel himself nor release it to Doran or Methuen. Much bad feeling had been stirred up by the quarrel between writer and publisher, and Munsey's delay in issuing the novel in his magazine appears to be vindictive. Munsey was a man with a terrible temper, as his letter to Pinker testifies—a letter brought on by Pinker's refusal to resell *The Roll Call* for Munsey without commission. Fortunately, Bennett did not have time to brood over Munsey's behavior. By the end of July, Bennett was fully occupied with new work and had been busy almost from the moment that he sent the manuscript of *The Roll Call* to Pinker in late April.

Not all of the new distractions were pleasant. His health continued to trouble him, and he seemed unable to find time to get the rest that he needed. If there were any period during the war in which Bennett was a driven man, it was between March and August of 1917. He was in these months almost at the end of his physical strength. Money troubles were dogging him. He was sick much of the time, but he worked relentlessly at his journalism, at the articles for *Cosmopolitan,* and at *The Roll Call.* Within a month of having finished that novel, he began on *The Pretty Lady.*

On May 4 he went down to London to take several days' holiday. He was exhausted from the efforts of completing *The Roll Call* and was suffering a "reaction" to having finished the book. The "reaction" to which he referred was a fall in spirits, which was probably not only one of the effects of his weariness but also a consequence of knowing that the novel had fallen far short of his original hopes for it. In his exhausted state he must have felt intensely the failure of his creative powers.

Not since setting out for France on his tour of the Fronts had he acknowledged feeling depressed, but after May of 1917 he was to record frequent attacks of gloom. He had no sooner

15 *Ibid.*, 193.

reached the RTYC when he received word from Pinker that the *Strand* would consider taking the war savings article Bennett had in mind if he could produce it in three days. The article was an "officially inspired piece" and was to be designed as a device for getting people to invest their money in the War Loan. Wearily, Bennett set to work, not realizing that Pinker had not made it clear to Greenhough Smith that the article was to be propaganda material.

By the 6th he had sent the article to Pinker with a tardy injunction to his agent to make sure that Smith would not be dissatisfied with it. He told Pinker not to worry Smith about the price. He would, he wrote, have offered to do the article for nothing "only it is bad for editors to get things for nothing." [16] Smith glanced through the article and sent it straight back to Pinker. Bennett became angry with Pinker and accused the agent of not having followed instructions in regard to preparing Smith for what was coming. In one of his rare expressions of irritation with his client, Pinker retorted that he had no idea that "Are We a Thrifty Race" was to be "just a straight tribute to the National War Savings Committee." [17] Bennett let the matter drop, and Pinker placed the article with the *Fortnightly Review* the following December. It appeared at the same time in the United States in *Fortune*.

Another negotiation that went sour was his attempts to work out a scheme with T. B. Wells of *Harper's* for publishing a series of articles based on his yachting cruise up the Tiber in the summer of 1914. Wells had asked Bennett the previous January about some travel articles, and there had been an exchange of views but nothing more. In March, Wells wrote again, asking Bennett what had happened to their negotiations. Bennett replied rather curtly that while he would rather write for *Harper's* than for any other magazine, Wells would have to offer him a price for his material that bore some relationship to the prices he was being offered for it elsewhere. He then added that perhaps Wells would like to reconsider the yachting

16 *Letters*, I, 249.
17 Butler Collection, May 11, 1917.

articles; but Wells chose not to do so, and Bennett did not write the articles.

His articles for *Cosmopolitan*, on the other hand, were being accepted with pleasure. The first of the six, "The Meaning of Frocks," went to Pinker on April 19, and the remaining five followed at regular intervals. On June 21 Bennett signed a contract with Hodder and Stoughton for a volume edition of the articles but could not suggest a title for them. Weeks passed and at the end of August he was still without a title when Pinker pressed him to suggest something because Hodder and Stoughton were about to begin printing. But Bennett continued to delay until he was delivered from his difficulty by his friend Wheeler, who gave him a "first-class idea" for a comic novel and two "first-class titles" for essay collections. He sent one of the titles, "Self and Self-Management," to Hodder and Stoughton. The publishers were satisfied with it and the following year both Hodder and Stoughton and Doran published the collection under that title.[18]

For the most part the six essays making up *Self and Self-Management* are routine exercises in "how-to" writing, but trivial as they are Bennett put into them more of himself than was going into his uninspired fiction; and because he did draw directly on his own experience in writing them, they are worth examining in some detail. The style in which the pieces are written is lucid and the pace fast, not unlike, in some respects, the pattern of a skilled vendor of vegetable slicers. The pace exerts a fascination of its own, quite apart from the quality of the ideas being presented. But there are places in the essays that are genuinely arresting, making one regret that Bennett could not have held all of the essays up to the level achieved in those occasional sentences.

The first essay in the collection, "Running Away from Life," is the most serious of the pieces and the most interesting. In the opening paragraphs Bennett appears to be doing an inferior imitation of Addison's dissection of the Coquette's heart, but he

[18] Arnold Bennett, *Self and Self-Management: Essays About Existing* (New York, 1918).

quickly left that unrewarding subject to ask what exactly it was in life that so many people fled from. His answer to the question is at once intriguing and dissatisfying. What people run away from, according to Bennett, is something "mysterious and sinister." One holds one's breath for the rest—until it comes: "That [mysterious and sinister] something is neither more nor less than life itself in its every essence." [19]

But what in life is mysterious and sinister? Bennett did not answer that question. With those two adjectives, *mysterious* and *sinister*, he reached the limits to which he was willing to go in revealing his own subjective response to life. Whether he could not say more or whether he would not cannot, at this distance, be determined. In his fiction the mystery is posed most strikingly in the scene in *The Old Wives' Tale* in which Sophia gazes on the dead body of Gerald Scales.

Whatever that terrible something was that Bennett glimpsed in life he left it hidden; and since he had no religious faith in the conventional Christian sense, he appears to have defended himself against despair by glorifying duty. In "Running Away from Life" he stated very specifically that "there can be no happiness where duty has been left undone." [20] The monk in *Don Juan* said much the same thing: Wisdom is seeing one's next duty and doing it.

It can be argued that "Running Away from Life" is too slight a piece of writing to be burdened with such significance; but here as in Bennett's best fiction the reader is led up to the iron doors of ultimate understanding and left waiting, hat in hand. The reader is left in much the same situation as Sophia, who stands gazing on the shrunken face of Gerald Scales and feels the riddle of life killing her. Bennett cannot be blamed for not having answered the ultimate questions about the meaning of life, but he can be held responsible for having posed the questions and then dodged them; and Bennett's reader is not so much in danger of being killed by life's riddle as by his curiosity about what Bennett found "mysterious and sinister" in that riddle.

[19] *Ibid.*, 14.
[20] *Ibid.*, 12.

Probably more than any other characteristic of his writing, Bennett's unwillingness to allow the reader into the dark and innermost chambers of his heart defines his limitations as an artist.[21]

"Some Axioms about War Work" is a much lighter piece of writing, but it contains some references to Bennett's own experiences with the WARC and the Essex Defense Committee which are more personal than almost anything in his journals referring to his committee work. One of the points he made in the article was that there were many disappointments in store for the person who takes up war work. "Probably no sight is more depressing," he wrote, "than the cordon of faces around a Committeeroom table." There is a certain bleakness of tone throughout the essay, and it is not countered by any suggestion from Bennett that war work might be exhilarating or rewarding. It is an unpleasant task to be done. The people with whom one is forced to work are depressing and irritating, but also one will be equally depressing and irritating to them. As a final warning he pointed out that one has "to get away from the illusion that you can live a new life and still keep on living the old." [22] He meant that in accommodating one's life to the demands of war work one inevitably changed one's life. Considering the pattern of his own life over the preceding three years, it was an observation rich in personal significance and perhaps in irony as well.

The third essay, "The Diary Habit," urged those who felt the need to keep a diary to begin it at once and not be embarrassed by any fear that they will have nothing to say or that what they do have to say will be of no interest. He then dealt with the difficulty of being truthful in a diary, concluding that there was no more challenging task than that of putting down on paper something personally compromising. Half ruefully he admitted

[21] In *The Glimpse* (London, 1909) Bennett gave Morrice Loring a "glimpse" of life's ultimate meaning. The meaning was essentially that every man is incurably alone and that individuals are strangers to one another, even those in love. But Bennett did not call that solitary condition "mysterious" or "sinister," and it was not from that that people were said to be fleeing in "Running Away from Life."

[22] Bennett, *Self and Self-Management*, 32, 29.

that "you may keep a diary, but beyond question it will not be absolutely true." He summed up his arguments in favor of keeping a diary by saying that self-gratification was the only legitimate reason for beginning and for continuing a diary. As for the possibility of profit, he wrote, taking thought of his origins, that "is not the main point—though it is a point." He was somewhat clearer on one's hopes of achieving immortality through the pages of a diary. The possibility did not interest him. The thought of posterity "left him stone cold." [23]

It is doubtful, of course, that Bennett was entirely "cold" to thoughts about his future reputation. He had always written his books with a distinction in mind between those which he thought "serious" and those which were light and therefore ephemeral. The serious books were clearly written to last, *The Old Wives' Tale* especially. It had been his hope at one point in the construction of the novel that *The Roll Call* would take its place beside the Clayhanger trilogy. That it did not was due to the collapse of his creative energies and not to his indifference toward posterity and its judgment.

Very little importance should be given to his remark about posterity in "The Diary Habit." He was simply building his image of the bluff, down-to-earth, commonsensical man of affairs who was too busy getting along in the world to concern himself with worries about what posterity might think of him. There is, however, the possibility that his own sense of failure over *The Roll Call* prompted him to make the disclaimer in advance of publication of the novel. As for his own journals, they were certainly kept with an eye to the future and their preservation in that future.

The remaining three essays—"The Complete Fusser," "A Dangerous Lecture to a Young Woman," and "The Meaning of Frocks"—are rather flat. Only "A Dangerous Lecture to a Young Woman," built around a frame within a frame, is sufficiently interesting to warrant comment. In the essay Bennett describes an encounter with a young woman who asked him to explain how to put into practice the advice he had given in his

[23] *Ibid.*, 43, 46–47.

earlier articles on how to improve one's self. He told her that
everything depended upon one's own capacity to release inner
energies, but he was not precise in saying how that was to be
accomplished. Having told the young woman that she did and,
at the same time, did not have unlimited energy, he paused over
the contradiction to reflect that, after all, one "cannot be sure
of anything—this is not a perfect world." The young woman
must have gone away more puzzled than ever, but the series
did not suffer from her perplexity. The general reader seems to
have been satisfied, and in November he contracted with *Cosmopolitan* for six more articles of the same sort.

In addition to his writing and his committee work, Bennett
managed to lead an active social life, most of which centered
around lunches and evenings at the Reform Club with frequent
nights out for dinner and the theater. He lunched or dined with
Wells several times in the first half of the year and on two occasions "tossed" with Wells for the bill and won, much to his
satisfaction. In May he met Siegfried Sassoon and liked him
very much. Sassoon lunched with Bennett twice in the following month and on the second occasion told Bennett in some detail about his experiences at the Front. Bennett recorded that
Sassoon was expecting to be decorated for "bombing work,"
and that the young man thought it would be exciting to go back
to the Front once again and then come home for good, having
given the Germans another chance to kill him. Bennett made
no comment on the bravado in Sassoon's remarks; but he did
quote him on one aspect of the fighting man's life, recording
that war was, for the most part, "a tedious nuisance," with
great moments and that he "would like them again." [24]

He occasionally saw Shaw and delighted in arguing with him,
making a careful record of those rare times in which he managed
to "shift" G.B.S. a little in the course of their conversation. He
met Barrie again and liked the way he talked about his sons,
who were in the army.[25] Mair, Massingham, Masterman, Gar-

[24] *Journal*, 629.
[25] Three of Barrie's five unofficially adopted sons were in the services. George
was killed in action in 1915. Peter was wounded but survived, and John came

diner, Ross, and Swinnerton were more or less regular companions at lunch or for an evening of "jollification" in the large upstairs smoking room of the Reform Club, where Bennett sat on the green leather sofa, a cigarette between his fingers, enjoying the easy flow of conversation and the sometimes bawdy wit.

On one such occasion he had the pleasure of renewing an old friendship with T. P. O'Connor, M.P. and editor of *T. P.'s Weekly*, to which Bennett had been a contributor in the early days of his career. O'Connor was soon amusing Bennett with an account of his youth and of his extreme gullibility as a young man, particularly in regard to women. "It was all very well," he told Bennett, "but the connections of a simple man with women were apt to have pecuniary endings." It was a comment exactly designed to amuse Bennett.

Rebecca West has said that Bennett in his later years became rather insensitive to the relationships of other people, even blind to them. That may have been because he was too busy and too preoccupied to notice things which did not absolutely demand his attention. It was certainly not due to the fact that his ability to see the dramatic content of human relationships had been deadened. In late July he dined with James Barrie at Barrie's flat, at the river end of Robert Street, in company with Thomas Hardy and his wife. Bennett was pleased to find Hardy still very alert and lively in conversation.

During dinner Hardy took up the subject of Chekhov's short stories, arguing in support of the point that some of the stories were not "justifiable" because they "told nothing unusual." Bennett listened politely and recorded later that on the whole Hardy had carried the discussion off rather well, although the realist in Bennett was slightly ruffled by Hardy's assumption that the *unusual* was the basis of all "justifiable" stories.

After dinner Barrie telephoned Shaw and the Wellses and

through the war without injury. The boys were the sons of Arthur Davies, who died in 1907, and Sylvia Jocelyn de Busson du Maurier Davies, who died three years later. Barrie, who had loved Sylvia Davies for years, assumed responsibility for the boys after their father's death. Following their mother's death, he took over their complete care.

invited them to join the group. As soon as the new company arrived, Barrie insisted that everyone go out onto the balcony to watch the searchlights playing over the city and making white trails across the dark sky. Bennett acknowledged that Barrie had one of the finest views of London to be found, but his pleasure in the view was seriously reduced by his concern over the fact that he was out in the night air without a hat. He noted that Hardy put a handkerchief over his head for protection. "I sneezed," he recorded in the journal.

Once they had regained the shelter of the flat, Shaw and Wells began talking about the war. Hardy grew increasingly quiet, and Bennett thought that he looked fatigued. "I then departed," Bennett wrote, "and told Barrie that Hardy ought to go to bed." Barrie tactfully agreed. The evening made a deep impression on Bennett. Reflecting on it later, he remarked that "the spectacle of Wells and G.B.S. talking firmly and strongly about the war, in their comparative youth, in front of this aged, fatigued, and silent man—incomparably their superior as a creative artist—was very striking." [26] He got out of bed the following morning with a headache which he attributed to "Hardy and cigarettes."

In the spring an old friend, Pauline Smith, came to London to stay with Marguerite at the Oxford Street flat. Bennett immediately took her and Marguerite out to dinner. His friendship with Pauline Smith, that silent and retiring woman, was a remarkable relationship. There were powerful ties holding them together, although following the outbreak of the war, their principal contact was by correspondence, all of which they eventually destroyed, in keeping with a mutual promise made years before.

Another woman with whom he established the beginnings of a friendship that later faded was Rebecca West. He had first met her in November, 1915. She became an occasional visitor at Comarques, and he saw her periodically in London at the theater or in restaurants. In February he had dinner with her

[26] Journal, 633.

and H. G. Wells, and it may have been on this occasion that he asked West to send him her books to read.

In July she wrote to congratulate him on *Books and Persons* and four months later sent him her new book, *Henry James*, which Nesbit was publishing. In the accompanying letter she wrote that she had a serial, *The Return of the Soldier*, appearing in January in *The Century* and that she would send him that too. "You'll regret," she added, "ever having suggested that I should send you my books." [27] Over the next few years they exchanged infrequent notes and occasionally lunched or dined together. They talked about literary figures of the day and about her books. In an undated letter she confessed to having been won over to Bennett's view of Dreiser, although in an earlier letter she had put up a spirited defense of her view that Dreiser was a much flawed novelist. But their friendship did not, apparently, flourish; and Miss West's admiration for Bennett as a man declined sharply.

As for his family relationships at this time, he found that he was forced to concern himself with his brother Frank's affairs. Finances and not Richard were the issue. Richard was safely enrolled at Oundle school, and Marguerite's problems with her adopted son had not yet reached the critical stage. In fact Richard was spending much of his free time with Marguerite at the London flat. But Frank Bennett was in deep water financially. His business was slipping toward bankruptcy, and on January 24 Bennett recorded that Frank had travelled down from Burslem to consult with him. Two weeks later he noted that his brother's affairs seemed "darker than ever." [28] Shortly afterward the business failed entirely, but Bennett made no reference to its ultimate collapse.

Aside from the amusement and distraction that he derived from the people with whom he surrounded himself, one of Bennett's chief interests was the theater, although his opinion of the plays being performed in the West End sank lower and

[27] Ogden Collection, November 10, 1917.
[28] Unpublished Journal, Februry 3, 1917.

lower as the war progressed. He had said in *The Roll Call*, clearly speaking both for and about himself, that George Cannon did not object to the salaciousness of *The Gay Spark* but rather to its dullness. But the disclaimer is not entirely convincing. Bennett was clearly distressed by the freedom with which sex was being treated both in and out of the theater, as the opening pages of *The Pretty Lady* make clear. He was almost certainly sexually repressed himself, perhaps very seriously so; and sexuality in any guise appears to have repelled him.

Bennett was not alone in deploring the fate that had overtaken the theater since 1914. In the prefatory comments to *Heartbreak House*, especially the sections titled "How the Theater Fared" and "The Soldier at the Theater Front," Shaw explained why he had withheld his play from production and, at the same time, made a sharp criticism of the direction plays had taken during the war. It was his opinion that the sudden appearance of great numbers of soldiers in the theatergoing audience had led producers to cater to the lowest common denominator in the tastes of that audience. What the theaters settled on were ancient gag routines and sex. Since all such offerings were happily received by the swarms of soldiers on leave and their flapper friends, the theaters responded by giving what was wanted. The hour for serious drama had passed. Managements would not handle it, and the audiences did not want it. Shaw felt that it was a mistake not to have attempted to educate the new audience by presenting them with plays of some merit; but he also acknowledged that since a theater was first and last, in the view of its owners, a business, there was no real chance that such an attempt could have been made.[29]

One of the first plays Bennett went to see in the new year was Knoblock's *Home on Leave*. Oddly enough it was the first play of Knoblock's that he had ever seen, and his sole comment on it was that the play was "excessively ingenuous." In early March he went to see the film version of *Milestones* and judged it to be "good as films go, but very tedious in the end."[30] He

---

[29] George Bernard Shaw, *Heartbreak House* (New York, 1928), xli–xlv.
[30] Unpublished Journal, February 3, 1917; March 18, 1917.

might well have been talking about a film story with which he had not the slightest connection.[31] His reticence is almost comic. Some months later he went to another film, *Intolerance*, and called it a "stupendous affair—I mean the Babylonian scenes." But he found the story very "crude," especially in such details as "an auto racing a train!" He added that it was a "most fatiguing 3-hour affair." [32]

There was only one really bright spot in his theater-going during the first half of 1917, and that was a evening at the end of March spent with Marguerite at the Ambassador Theatre. The bill was made up of a ballet, *Pomme d'Or*, which they arrived too late to see, and three short plays—Anatole France's *The Man Who Married a Dumb Wife;* Pierre Veber's *Gonzague;* and Vansittart's French Revolution play, *Class*. He liked *Gonzague* best, calling it a "most ingeniously constructed affair." In his judgment there was no writer in England "who could construct a little farce so well." The evening was, he said, the best he had had in the theater for a very long time, perhaps since the beginning of the war.[33] Clearly, what appealed to him in the theater was neither English nor contemporary. But foreignness alone in a playwright did not win Bennett's automatic approval.

In May, Bennett saw Ibsen's *Ghosts* at the Kingsway Theatre and was not very impressed with the play. He thought the first two acts held up well enough but the third seemed "childish." At about the same time, he went to Galsworthy's *The Foundations* at the Royalty and said only that it was "interesting in parts." [34] He was less restrained in his response to Brieux's *Les Trois Filles de M. Dupont*. It was "extremely crude throughout," he wrote, "and so false sometimes that I could not look at the stage." He admitted, however, that it was "a good tract for those who need such things."

His dislike of the plays being performed in the West End

31 Bennett made about £100 in royalties in 1916 and 1917 from the film. The film first appeared in December, 1916.
32 *Journal*, June 1, 1917.
33 *Ibid.*, 622.
34 Unpublished Journal, May 25, 1917; July 18, 1917.

and his almost total neglect of novels being published were a bad sign in a writer who was trying to give a new direction to his own work. He was in fact reading very little in comparison with previous years and expressing admiration only for Balzac and occasionally Rabelais. During all of 1917 he expressed interest in only two new English novels. One was Alec Waugh's *Loom of Youth;* [35] the other, Conrad's *The Shadow-Line*, which Bennett called "a short story disguised as a novel." He judged it to be "very good, but a certain anti-climax where the climax ought to be." [36] He dismissed Chesterton's *History of England* as "a capricious exercize," and labored through a "lot of Saintsbury's *History of the French Novel*. He reread Hardy's *A Pair of Blue Eyes* and admired its irony, but there is no evidence that he was making any effort to follow the shifting mood of the novel as it was emerging. And yet he defended James Joyce, writing ten years later that Joyce was an important figure in the evolution of the novel. And he knew something of the work of Lawrence, Forster, Ford, and other Georgians.

He responded to the war with consistent detachment. Though he continued to serve on the WARC, his move to London effectively severed his connection with the defense committees in Essex. The breaking away from the military-civilian muddle of the East coast defense program was a blessing for Bennett because he invariably lost his sense of proportion whenever he became involved with its follies. The closest he came during this period to a direct official participation in the national war effort was his rejection of the suggestion by Geoffrey Howard, an acquaintance from the North, that Bennett should stand for Parliament as the Staffordshire representative. If for no other reason, Bennett's stammer would have forced him to decline such an undertaking.

[35] The book was called to Bennett's attention by a friend who told him that a "most extraordinary crowd" of pupils had been brought together at the Royal Military College. There were poets and novelists among the students and perhaps "one or two geniuses" in the lot. In particular, the friend reported, Arthur Waugh's son Alec was there and had written a novel about his life as a student at Sherborne. Bennett kept the name in mind and the following fall read *Loom of Youth* with "great interest."
[36] *Journal*, 619.

The journal references to the war during the first half of 1917 are relatively few and do not reflect a deep concern over such problems as German submarine attacks on British shipping or the worsening labor troubles, particularly in the North. He reported on a dinner engagement with Sir William Weir, Director of Air Supply, with John R. Richmond, an engineer friend, and with a Major Weir of the Air Corps and was convinced that the men had deliberately tried to startle him with dark tales about submarines, strikes, lack of air power, and so on. Bennett wrote with satisfaction that he refused to be seriously upset by their recital.

The war did make itself felt directly at Comarques in the late spring, however. In response to the generally admitted shortage of wheat, Bennett decided that bread would no longer be put on the table when dinner was served. It would hereafter be kept on the sideboard and anyone who wanted bread with his meal would have to ask for it specifically. Bennett was very proud of his "dodge" for saving bread and said that the value of such restraints was "mainly disciplinary." He got the idea, he recorded, from Wells and went on to say that if all of the "well-to-do classes" practiced such self-control "the wheat problem would be trifling." [37]

The war came somewhat closer to him in early June when Marguerite was caught in the London air raid of June 13, in which 157 people were killed and 432 injured.[38] Marguerite and a companion were just getting down from a train in Liverpool Street Station when the bombs began falling. The train they had been on was struck, people began running for cover, and in the confusion Marguerite was separated from her friend. But the two women found one another again later in a crowd of people who were trying to get into an underground lavatory. Bennett gave a careful account of what had happened to Marguerite's friend and what her reactions were, including her feeling of having "found herself" near the lavatory with no recollection of having gotten there. He was later to use her ex-

[37] *Ibid.*, 625.
[38] *Ibid.*, 630n.

perience in *The Pretty Lady*. But what Marguerite's sensations were during the raid he did not record, even in the journal. Apparently, he was not interested in her reactions.

It is difficult to judge the degree of intimacy existing between Bennett and Marguerite at this point in their marriage. Although the journal carefully notes the occasions at which he called at her flat or took her out for an evening, his only reported discussion with her was a reference to the unjustness of her attitude toward the United States and the fact that the entry of the United States into the war was forcing her to change that attitude.

They were together at Comarques quite frequently, but his staying overnight at her flat was an event rare enough to warrant a reference to it in the journal. The overnight visit took place in May when he "went to M.'s flat to live for three days." It is noteworthy that in January he had called the flat *his*, but here it is *M.'s*. The visit was cut short by Marguerite's departure for Comarques on the 18th. He then returned to the RTYC, and on the 19th he reported that he had been sick all day from having drunk too much sparkling Moselle the night before. There may well have been a connection between his over-imbibing and Marguerite's abandoning him at the flat.

The best indicators of Bennett's reaction to the war, at least on the level of his public response, are the articles which he wrote for the *Daily News* and the *NS*. In both series he avoided, for the most part, talking about the military aspects of the conflict and concentrated on the operation of various government departments and on the social stresses being generated by the war. He undoubtedly realized that Hilaire Belloc in *Land and Water*, as well as other writers, was doing a more than adequate job of discussing strategy, troop deployment, and the significance of the German military responses. He had, in any case, committed himself in the *NS* to taking a political line in his articles, but he had a free hand in choosing topics for the *Daily News* series.

When he took up the *Daily News* series for the second time, however, he returned at once to those topics which had held his attention the preceding year. His first article, written on January 15 and published two days later, was chiefly a protest against making peace with Germany before subjecting her to a thorough military defeat. It was a repetition of the original line he had taken soon after the outbreak of hostilities, and two and one-half years of war had not changed his mind. He did not often change his mind about anything. Once he had determined what the "commonsense" aproach or attitude should be to a given subject, he stuck like a burr to his position.

In "Submarines and the War Office," published on January 31, he demanded a statement from the government on the specific nature of the submarine threat to which official government spokesmen had been referring in general terms. Once again he was insisting that the British people be given the truth about their position, confident, as always, that Englishmen would fight hardest and most effectively when they were treated as free men. His argument rested on an unstated assumption that a free people would always act to preserve their freedom, but that in order to act wisely they had to be put in command of the facts which, taken together, described their condition.

What Bennett feared above all else in political-social matters was an erosion of democratic freedoms. He was particularly sensitive to the government's tendency to mask its real actions with misleading statements or to refuse to comment at all on what it was doing. His concern led him to make repeated and virulent attacks on the War Office, whose operations were not only secret but almost wholly free from those checks which rendered the government the servant and not the master of the people it governed.

The War Office, he wrote, "is the last stronghold of the surviving caste. . . . It understands neither history, nor sociology, nor economics, nor the mechanism of politics, nor the meaning of democracy." He went on to describe it as a survival that had to be replaced by a more democratic organization. In specific terms his stated objections to the War Office were what he called its determination to subordinate efficiency to privilege; but what rankled in the center of his being was the exclusiveness of outlook held by the upper-ranking officers in the services and the tenacity with which they held to the principle that only men of a certain class were fit to be officers.

H. G. Wells also hated the arbitrariness of dividing the world by class lines into those who counted and those who did not. But whereas Wells proposed sweeping away the old measures of men and building a world where supermen would rule—one is reminded of D. H. Lawrence's natural aristocracy as another alternative to the class and money structured society—Bennett asked only for a political democracy in which one would be rewarded with position according to one's excellence. And he called the process by which that ideal democracy would be achieved social evolution.

However, it was not evolution but German machine guns which destroyed the English military caste system. By the time Bennett was writing, the British Army had already lost so many of its field officers that promotion from the ranks became an inescapable necessity. Whatever feelings of exclusiveness the members of the War Office may have continued to share, in practice the wall of privilege had been blown to bits on the Somme in that long agony of the previous summer.

Bennett hammered away at his theme throughout the spring. In "Against Secret Misgivings" he acknowledged the existence of only two classes and only one struggle. The basic conflict, as he saw it, was between those with the "aristocratic idea" and those with the "democratic ideal." It was a person's response to the democratic ideal that determined to which class he belonged, and there was no doubt about where Bennett stood. Planted solidly in the democratic ranks, he had fought every "pro-German" measure that a nervy government had advanced since the beginning of the war. He had denounced conscription and opposed it as long as there had been a hope of defeating it. Once that hope was dead, he turned his attacks against the tribunals and medical boards whose stupidity and incompetence put cripples, chronic invalids, and mental defectives into uniform. Now, in the spring of 1917 he couched his pen and rode against the proposal for required National Service, insisting that by making such service compulsory, hostility between the laboring class and the employing class would be exacerbated.

He renewed his attack on privilege in "The Great Educational Reform," published on April 25, which began as a congratulatory note to Herbert Fisher, the new Minister of Education, but soon became a statement of Bennett's views on English education. He wanted teachers to be paid higher salaries and a system of inspection established under which public schools would be examined. His reason for wanting public schools studied was that they were, like the War Office, "survivals." What he was aiming at was the disestablishment of the public school and its replacement by free state-supported schools. Although Richard was safely enrolled at Oundle, Bennett wrote of such schools that the "best of them are old fashioned and the worst idiotic."

Occasionally, his dislike of the public school system led him into crankiness. In "Observations" for April 14 he angrily denounced a newspaper picture of Eton boys preparing a potato field for planting. He found fault with the master's posture, the way the boys were holding their spades, their manner of addressing the row, and their obvious ineptness. When the picture appeared on the Continent, he complained, it would create a terrible impression because on the Continent "digging is understood."

His bitterness toward all evidence of a social prejudice working through a political form found further expression in his *Daily News* article for early May, "Censors, Reaction, and Inefficiency," and in "Pacifism and the Treatment of Labor," which was published later in the month. He was prompted to write by the fact that the May 9 issue of *The Nation* had been banned for foreign sale because, according to the censor, the enemy were using articles praising America's entry into the war for propaganda purposes. Bennett asked if the *Morning Post* or the *Times* would ever be banned. "Never in this world!" he answered. "Why? Because they are reactionary and the War Office oligarchy is reactionary." *The Nation* was banned, he maintained, because it was a liberal journal and rather pacifistic.

It is true that its editor Henry Massingham was a strong opponent of the war; but Bennett was probably crediting the censor with too much logic, considering the fact that the censor's efforts in general were about as purposeful as the pecking of a blind hen.

In the second piece, "Pacifism and the Treatment of Labor," he defended a strike by a group of engineers on the ground that the strike had been brought on at least in part by "the blundering class." The employers, he charged, were guilty of "bad faith, repeated injustice, quibbling, delays . . . and the exhibition of crude class-prejudice." Not satisfied with that blast against employers, he turned on the government and said that it was reactionary and did not understand labor and never would.

Not all of Bennett's articles were negative or condemnatory. In his June 3 article, "The War and the Air," he put forward a strong argument in favor of building an air fleet and making it as powerful as resources would permit. He also favored placing Winston Churchill in control of the new service. "I know that he is dangerous," Bennett wrote, defending his choice, "I admit that he smoked a cigar at the siege of Antwerp and that he has a very inconvenient quality (for others) of centering the limelight on himself wherever he may be." But Bennett was quite prepared to risk Churchill's flamboyance and confessed to being pleased with his cigar smoking at Antwerp. "I maintain," Bennett concluded, "that the limelight-attracting quality is precisely the quality needed for an air service."

There was a certain acidity, however, in one of Bennett's later comments on Churchill. In the journal entry for December 16, 1917, Bennett described a dinner he had attended with a group of M.P.s at which Churchill was one of the speakers. Following his speech, Churchill made "an amiable tour of the tables." Bennett noted that he "wore all of his medals dangling on the lapel of his dress coat." With mock innocence Bennett observed, "I suppose this is all right, but I had never seen it before except on the dress coat of the hall porter of this [RTYC] club." [39]

[39] *Journal*, 640.

In the first months of the war Bennett had periodically found himself writing in opposition to the views of H. G. Wells concerning national affairs; but by 1917 the two men had drawn much closer together in general outlook. In January the two friends found themselves writing for the *Daily News* and very much in agreement with one another. Wells was writing, at Gardiner's invitation, a short series called "How People Think About the War," which ran through the month of January. In August another of his pieces appeared in the *Daily News*. It was "A Reasonable Man's Peace" [40] and was a statement of opposition to those who wished to impose impossible terms on Germany after the war, terms which would deny her trade and reduce her population to the point of starvation. Bennett's attitude toward the terms of the peace were essentially those expressed by Wells.

They also shared the conviction that the English educational system should be overhauled, and they shared essentially the same views on the desirability of making England a more socially and politically democratic nation. In one of the "Observations" for April, Bennett took an obvious delight in praising Wells's letter of the week before to the *Times*, in which Wells expressed his support for more thoroughly republican forms of government for England and for European nations. Bennett strongly seconded him. Their differences over the war centered on the question of when peace should be made. Bennett was holding out for a military defeat of Germany while Wells favored an immediate move toward a diplomatic settlement of the conflict.

In the *NS* series Bennett dealt with essentially the same subjects as attracted his attention in the *Daily News* pieces. In the *NS*, however, he employed a lighter touch and was inclined to make the column appear to be jottings on men and events rather than careful analyses. He occasionally introduced material that was almost wholly entertainment. Writing about *Punch* in March, he said that it had "at one stroke recovered its waning reputation for humor by simultaneously decreasing its size and doubling its price." The following week he had another go at

[40] Arnold Bennett, "A Reasonable Man's Peace," *The Daily News and Leader*, August 4, 1917, p. 2.

*Punch*, more seriously this time, calling it "prim and feeble." Comparing it with its continental counterparts—*Le Rire, Jugend*, and *Simplicissimus*—he found the magazine sadly lacking in vigor.

A constant target of his journalistic wrath in the *NS* was Lord Northcliffe and the Northcliffian Press, which Bennett appears to have viewed as being just short of seditious. The "stunt press" he called the papers in Northciffe's stable, and it was rare when "Observations" did not contain at least one slashing attack on the man and his publications. On May 26, for example, he referred to the generally felt fear of food riots and the "Northcliffian funk" in the face of them. Bennett took the occasion to write that "the prophet of the standard loaf and sweet peas is in mortal fear of food riots, and apparently is not susceptible to the operations of reason." Bennett seems to have alternately hated, feared, and admired Northcliffe. His dislike of the publisher stemmed from a basic distrust of the man, a distrust of the P. T. Barnum business techniques which Northcliffe employed. Bennett's fear of him stemmed from the enormous political power which Northcliffe wielded and from the reactionary politics which Northcliffe championed. What he admired in Northcliffe was the man's business acumen and his deliberate use of his power.

Bennett was more frequently petty and cranky in the *NS* than in the *Daily News*. His attack on the Eton boys was one example of that peevishness. Another was his condemnation of the people who occupied the boxes at the opening of the grand opera season at Drury Lane. He called them "gaudy" and implied that they were rude and overbearing, giving the impression of "owning the entire enterprise." [41] There was no point to the attack beyond the fact that once again Bennett had revealed that deep hostility he felt toward the upper-class; and by attacking them in that fashion, he was still pulling his forelock in their presence.

When he was thoroughly indignant, however, over a matter worthy of his indignation, he could be impressive. For a period

[41] Arnold Bennett, "Observations," *New Statesman*, VII (June 16, 1917), 252.

of two years he had been taking verbal shots at Sir Edward Carson, who in Bennett's eyes was the very soul of Toryism. In July, Carson was appointed to the War Cabinet, and Bennett's response to the appointment was a blistering attack. "That this incompetent and reactionary Irishman, who rose to fame by preaching and glorifying treason, should be in the War Cabinet is as enormous an insult to democratic England as the presence of Lord Milner there."

Bennett wrote an article for the August 4 issue of *NS*, a short one, and made it the last piece of writing he was to do for a month. By the end of July his health had grown so bad that he was obliged to stop all work and attempt to recover with complete rest. He decided on a month's holiday at Comarques. Richard was probably there for some of the time, and Marguerite came down from London, giving the appearance of a family vacation to the event. Clifford Sharp and Frederick Marriott were also there as company for Bennett, and Marguerite had two of her women friends to complete the group.

Undoubtedly Bennett needed distraction as well as rest, and there was not much likelihood of his finding it at Comarques. There were strong reasons for not taking a holiday away from home, however. The strongest was money. Bennett's monthly income for the first half of 1917 was down by half from the previous year. And although the Munsey settlement was a substantial addition to his income, that money had been counted on for three years and was, in fact, a much smaller figure than had been originally anticipated. Other strong reasons were, of course, the war and the pressure not to spend or to travel needlessly, as well as Marguerite's desire to have Richard at home with her. Tired and sick after seven months of tremendous labor, Bennett settled into Comarques, stoically preparing to embrace his misery.

# VIII

## A PRETTY LADY AND A PEER

"I took a month's holiday, ending yesterday," Bennett wrote on September 1. "Health not very good during it, but a distinct benefit as regards the outlook on work actually in progress." [1] The tone of the entry is subdued, even depressed. The vacation, taken at the insistence of his wife and his doctor, had given his body a rest, but it had done nothing to rejuvenate his creative powers. He had done no writing, not even in the journal. What he needed and did not find was a diversion sufficiently stimulating to refresh his mind and his spirit. Dabbling at his water colors or staring bleakly at London street life from the windows of his RTYC rooms, to which he retreated at intervals during August to escape the deadly monotony of Comarques, did little to restore him.

It is not possible to sort out all the threads of Bennett's discontent, but some can be distinguished from the rest. He was bored; he was worried about his ability to write; and he was unhappy. At least part of the weariness of which he complained seems to have been a result of his boredom with journalism and the dull routine of his life. It was not Bennett's way, nor his relief, to cry out as Wells did to him in early October: "My boom is over. I've had my boom. I'm yesterday." How much better it would have been for Bennett could he have unburdened himself with equal frankness, even exaggeration. Unfortunately he could not; and it is possible that had he at this time allowed a crack to form in his outer composure, the whole facade might have crumbled. For perhaps the first time in his adult life, Bennett had lost his zest for living.

Apparently, he was not even quarrelling with Marguerite, which was in itself an ominous sign because it meant that they were no longer struggling to resolve their differences. In fact,

[1] *Journal*, 634.

he ceased to record his irritation with her. Aside from noting those occasions when they dined together or went to the theater together, his only direct comment concerning her came in December when he reported being put off work by the "distraction" of visiting her flat. They may on this occasion have quarrelled, but his comment is another of those ambiguous statements on private matters by means of which he hid the exact nature of his feelings. What is most clear is that neither in his wife's company nor away from it could he at this time find a source of inspiration that would sustain him.

The weakening thrust of his creativity was another source of concern. He could not have been mistaken about what had happened to him during those months he spent writing *The Roll Call;* and he could see the pattern repeating itself in *The Pretty Lady,* which he had begun the previous May. Although he made no comment on Wells's lament over lost power, in the preceding months Bennett must have been visited with the same kind of doubt about his own position as a serious novelist.

Wells was speaking out of disillusionment over the general state of human affairs and the conduct of the war in particular, a state of mind explored in detail in *Mr. Britling Sees It Through* (1916), a state of mind probably not fundamentally altered by the passing of a year and the writing of *God The Invisible King* (1917). It must be said to Bennett's credit that he did not "discover" God or suddenly "find religion" as a solution to his or to his nation's problems as did Wells with painful expedience. Neither did he stoop to the exploitation of personal and national frustrations as did Marie Corelli in *Is All Well With England?* (1917).

Bennett's unhappiness undoubtedly stemmed principally from the emptiness of his emotional life. The life had become sterile, like his marriage. It has been pointed out that there was a relationship between Bennett's love life and his writings, and it is demonstrably true that his best work was done when he was deeply involved emotionally with a woman. He wrote *The Old Wives' Tale* during the early excitement of his marriage to Marguerite; and the Clayhanger books, especially *These Twain,* were written when he was struggling to find a solution to problems posed by his marriage. When he fell in love with Dorothy Cheston, his powers were at least temporarily restored, as *Riceyman Steps* and *Lord Raingo* demonstrate. But in the midwar period, particularly after he had taken rooms at the RTYC, he appears to have been in an emotional desert, which produced a corresponding aridity of spirit.

It is not surprising that his unhappiness was expressed increasingly in imaginary ills. From early September through the remaining months of the year, he complained almost without pause of neuralgia, depression, insomnia, "chills," and exhaustion. In the second week of September, alarmed by the prospect of a total breakdown in health, he placed himself in the hands of Dr. Frank Shufflebotham, a physician (and poison gas expert) from Stoke-on-Trent, whom he had met the preceding February. Shufflebotham immediately put Bennett through a series of examinations, including a radiograph exploration of his digestive system, and "found nothing wrong except a common slight slowness of the work in the colon." [2]

Bennett felt the diagnosis confirmed his conviction that doctors were incapable of dealing effectively with his complaints, and he went back to prescribing for himself. In October he recorded solemnly that his "health was gradually improving, thanks, in my opinion, not to doctor but to bismuth magnesia." [3] But there was no significant improvement in his health or, more to the point, in the state of mind which was producing many of his ailments.

Something of a parallel to Bennett's state of mind in the fall of 1917 is to be found in the scene in *The Roll Call* in which George Cannon admits to himself, in effect, that his wife and children, his house, his belongings, and his success have failed to make him happy. He is bored with his possessions and out of love with his wife. But before he reaches a full conscious understanding of the implications of all this for his future, he dreams his dream, hears his name called, and escapes to the Army, a

[2] *Ibid.*, 634–35.
[3] Unpublished Journal, October 15, 1917.

running away which masquerades as a response to the call of duty.

Without insisting that Bennett had consciously or unconsciously projected his own dilemma into the representation of George's condition, there are certainly unmistakable parallels between them. In the first flush of his success, Bennett had bought Comarques, rebuilt it, furnished it, staffed it, and settled into it with a sigh of satisfaction at having joined the squirearchy. The satisfaction, however, was short-lived. What he had genuinely enjoyed as a by-product of his success was yachting, and the war had put an end to that pleasure. Comarques proved to be not only boring but also a source of disagreement between himself and Marguerite. Maintaining the place became a burden to him. He longed for London. Like George he had reached the point at which he doubted that those material evidences of success with which he had surrounded himself were worth the price he had paid for them. And, of course, there was the failure of his marriage.

Whatever affection he may still have felt for Marguerite or she for him was wrapped away under layers of mutual resentment. He was forced to resign himself to the fact that he no longer had any hope of finding tenderness, sympathy, or understanding in his marriage. Both Marguerite and Dorothy Cheston implied and others—Wells and Swinnerton among them—have stated that Bennett's sexual drive was very limited. Such may have been the case, but he was not indifferent to women. Furthermore he seems to have needed a deep emotional relationship with a woman to release his greatest powers as a writer and, perhaps, to insure his happiness.

He had been exploring the nature of such a relationship or the desire for one in his novels since *Anna of the Five Towns* (1902). One of the peaks in that long preoccupation was *These Twain*, and the second and final one was *Lord Raingo*. Bennett's interest in the special relationship of people in love with one another is examined and reexamined in his books and what is produced is almost never a love story in the conventional sense. The center of his concern is how a man and a woman find or fail to find a way to share their lives, their love for one another being but one of the factors in the relationship. In dealing with the same general problem, Wells offered a technical solution. He demanded a total sexual release for the man matched by an equally total sexual response from the woman. Given those two conditions, the relationship in Wells's opinion was bound to flourish. Lawrence called for the same thing with mystical additions, although he was inclined to portray the evolution of such relationships as conflicts. Bennett's temperament insured that he would not arrive at conclusions similar to those of Wells or Lawrence or even Forster, for that matter.

It is instructive that in general Bennett's characters fail to establish viable relationships. Anna loses her young lover before ever having him. Sophia is disillusioned by her failure to find love. Edwin and Hilda cannot make a wholly satisfactory marriage, and Sam Raingo and Delphine lose their chance at happiness. If Bennett's novels are taken as a commentary on human love, it is a depressing one. If they are taken as a reflection of his own hopes for a deep and lasting love, they give the picture of a man desperately searching for a woman with whom to share his life, but who is, at the same time, convinced that he will never find her or will find her too late. Bennett's pessimism was deep-seated, and there are no moments of transcendent hope such as Joyce creates in the wading girl scene in *A Portrait of the Artist As a Young Man.* Edwin Clayhanger may emerge from despair to declare that he will not be beaten by marriage, but the reader knows that Edwin has already been beaten and that his marriage will never be anything but an armed truce, at best, and total war, at worst.

Since *The Egoist* and *Middlemarch,* and certainly since *Jude the Obscure,* English novelists have trying to deal more frankly with the question of what constituted the surest bases upon which to build a lasting love between a man and a woman. In *Howards End* the problem tends to become confused with the issue of women's rights and with the related but still separate one of sexuality in women, which, to cite an extreme example, is presented in *Lady Chatterley's Lover* and again in Ford's *The Good Soldier,* where it is treated still differently.

Bennett's concern with sexuality was generally implicit. It is almost always Hilda, for example, who makes affectionate advances to her husband, to which Edwin sometimes responds passionately but more often with a cool detachment. Bennett's preoccupation, however, was not with sexual incompatibility but with the stresses imposed on a relationship by the contending wills of its partners. As for probing and analyzing the mystery of the man-woman relationship, Bennett never became more explicit, with one exception, than in *These Twain* when Edwin admits the maddening perplexity of his marriage but adds that Hilda has made a "romance" of his life.

The exception is *The Pretty Lady* in which Bennett makes a considerable departure from the practice of his earlier books by concentrating on the sexual aspects of Hoape's and Christine's relationship. Sexual attraction is the moving force of the novel at least in its early stages, and the result is that the relationship of Hoape and Christine is one of the most comprehensible in Bennett's novels. The reader knows precisely where the two characters stand in reference to one another, making the gradual shift in the nature of their relationship thoroughly convincing. Bennett never leaves the reader to struggle, as he does in *These Twain*, with the inexplicable.

Bennett struck on the idea for the novel in the first week of May, shortly after bringing *The Roll Call* to a close. "I had an idea for a short novel about an episode in the life of a French *cocotte*," he wrote on the 9th. "I thought I could tell practically everything about her existence without shocking the B. P."[4] He planned to set the story in Paris and make it one of his London and Paris novels dealing with "advanced" civilization.

The idea of writing such a book would hardly have occurred to him four years earlier, but the war and the swiftly altering tastes of the reading public had made it possible to deal with themes previously forbidden. Bennett was, in part, responding to public demand for sensational story material with a strong sexual interest. At the same time he was responding to his own desire to write about a man who establishes a semi-permanent relationship with a woman outside of marriage. He may also have

4 *Journal*, 626.

wanted to present a realistic picture of a prostitute's life, but that was probably not his principal motive. Bennett, somewhat tardily, was undertaking to write about the sexual appetite and about the effects of its demands on the character and the actions of a man very like himself.

Later in May he met Wells for tea at the RTYC and in the course of their conversation thought of shifting the setting of the novel from Paris to London. It was, he said, "a vastly better idea, full of possibilities." Wells agreed that the shift in setting would be an improvement and was enthusiastic about the possibilities offered by the story. Newman Flower at Cassell wrote to Bennett expressing a strong interest in having the book. Bennett sent Flower's letter to Pinker with a copy of his reply, in which he gave an estimate of 70,000 words for the novel.[5] The reduction from 100,000 words, the standard length for the prewar novels, represents both a taste for shorter novels by the reading public and an adjustment forced on the publishing trade by a paper shortage brought on by the war.

On May 25 he began writing his "*cocotte*" novel, as he called the book, "with gusto" and with his usual high hopes for its being excellent in every way. Then, except for a single journal reference in June to the effect that he had spent an afternoon searching for ideas for the story, he fell silent about the progress of the work. By the end of June he appears to have completed the final section of the first part of the novel, but in July the writing fell off and in August stopped altogether while he was attempting to recover his health again.

Flower continued to be interested in the novel and by late June was pressing Bennett for a contract. Bennett was unhappy with the way in which Methuen had been promoting his books, although he never pursued his case against the publisher with the fervor shown by Wells toward Macmillan. His dissatisfaction made him decide to give the novel to Cassell in hopes that they would be more businesslike. But he felt compelled to tell Flower that the lending libraries might well "kick" at the story, and he wanted Flower to be sure he understood the exact nature

<hr>

[5] Ogden Collection, May 21, 1917.

of the novel before accepting it.[6] Flower replied to the warning
that he was prepared to take the risk and again pressed for a
contract. Pinker worked out an agreement with Cassell in the
last week of June, and Bennett signed it.

Pinker's correspondence during the summer concerning the
novel suggests that the agent was nervous about its progress.
In August he asked what the title was to be, and Bennett was
forced to reply that he did not have a title or any hopes of finding one in the immediate future. Toward the end of August,
Pinker wrote again, implying that Bennett would soon be sending him the completed manuscript. Bennett responded with a
sharp note in which he asked where Pinker had gotten "the unhappy idea" that the novel was finished. "It is only begun," he
wrote, going on to point out that it would not be done before
Christmas at the earliest.[7] Bennett may have been irritated that
Pinker had forgotten when the book was begun, but the sharp-
ness of his reply suggests that he had become very anxious and
sensitive about matters relating to the book's composition.

After a relatively good beginning, the writing had flagged. He
began to have trouble finding ideas and appeared to be unable
to write. The pattern of difficulties which had characterized the
writing of *The Roll Call* was emerging again. If Bennett felt any
panic over his condition, he kept it carefully hidden behind his
deceptively confident exterior. But his bridling at Pinker's letter
was an indication of his anxiety. His hope, expressed as fact in
the first journal entry for September, that the outlook for the
novel had improved, was a false hope. The work, when he took
it up again, went even more slowly than before.

He had told Pinker in June that the book would be finished
in December, but by December 11 he had written only 40,000
of the promised 75,000 words.[8] Throughout September and
October the writing dragged along, and he managed to get only
three or four chapters finished. He was working in the erratic
way that had characterized the composition of *The Roll Call*,

[6] *Ibid.*, June 28, 1917.
[7] *Ibid.*, August 31, 1917.
[8] Butler Collection, December 11, 1917.

which meant that there were stretches of days in which he put
nothing down on paper followed by sudden bursts of effort
during which he would occasionally turn out an entire chapter
in a single morning. The method was not suited to either his
physical condition or to his state of mind. What he needed to
do and could not do was to write a set number of words every
day, enabling him to say to himself or to his friends, "Another
1200 words today . . . All of the best." Illness, exhaustion, depression, and a failure of inspiration combined to deny him that
security. He was also still pressed for money. His income during
1917 had been barely adequate to meet his expenses, and the
constant financial need was a continuous strain.

During September and October he made some effort to regain
enthusiasm for the novel. He reread what he had already written
—a standard device with him for reassuring himself that what
he had written was good—and retabulated all of his notes. The
retabulating was not characteristic of his working methods, and
the fact that he wasted time in such a task confirms the suspicion
one gains from his journal entries that he was not satisfied with
the book. The novel was being put together like a patchwork
quilt. The episodes involving war superstitions were stuffed into
the story to fill up space. He used them to give a feeble topical
interest to the novel and because George Whale had given
Bennett access to his extensive collection of war superstitions.[9]
The air raids described in the book fit more convincingly into
the story; but they too are fillers, put in to create atmosphere
and a sense of immediacy rather than to provide an intrinsic
background to the action of the novel or to the development of
character.

On October 25 he went off to Dublin on a government assignment to gather material for more war propaganda articles of
the sort he had done in the spring. The trip effectively stopped
all work on the novel. Returning exhausted a week later, he
made no effort to pick up the writing; and during November he
appears not to have set down so much as a word. In fact, during
November he experienced a general slump in work and in spirits.
Only in his *Daily News* and *NS* articles was there any evidence

9 *Journal*, 636.

of his old spirit and power. Even here the "bounce" was artificial, a kind of mechanical maintaining of his public pose. Continuing bad health and increased exhaustion brought on by his Dublin trip, as well as a suppressed anxiety about the submarine menace and his inability to find inspiration for the novel, threw him completely off his writing stride. Not even the knowledge that he had a December deadline to meet held him to his desk.

Toward the middle of November, Pinker began pressing him again to finish the novel or at least to send Cassell a note about it for their spring list. The request for a note to the publishers was prompted by the fact that Bennett had been unable to find a title for the novel. On December 3 he wrote a late response to Pinker's letter in which he told his agent that "the novel has been considerably delayed through pressure of other work, and illness." [10] (The "other work" presumably was the Dublin trip.) He added that he expected to have the book finished by the end of January but that the only title he had been able to think of was "The Pretty Lady." A week later he wrote again to Pinker to say that "The Pretty Lady" would definitely be the title. Newman Flower was satisfied with the choice, and his fears about delivery were allayed by Bennett's promise to have the book finished by the end of January.

By an effort of will he began in December to work on the novel in earnest. Turkish baths and "a little dissipation" improved his health somewhat, and he was once again able to find ideas to turn into copy. But his confidence in himself was not restored, and his state of mind was revealed by his comments on a lunch with Robert Ross,[11] at which he met Robert Graves and another young man whose identity is lost. Graves's collection of

[10] Butler Collection, November 26, 1917; December 3, 1917.
[11] Robert Baldwin Ross (1869–1918) was a Canadian by birth but raised and educated in England. Although chiefly remembered as the friend of Oscar Wilde, he had a distinguished career as an art critic and as a literary journalist. He was associated with such publications as the *Scots Observer*, for which he wrote art criticism and book reviews while that journal was under the editorship of W. E. Henley, and the *Morning Post*, where he served as art critic. Following the death of Oscar Wilde, Ross administered the estate. By 1908 Ross had succeeded in placing Wilde's books back on the bookstands and in having his plays revived. It had been Ross's courageous decision in 1905 to bring out Wilde's *De Profundis* that led to the renewed interest in Wilde and to the ultimate clearing of Wilde's debts.

poems *Fairies and Fusiliers* appeared in 1917, but Bennett did not comment on Graves's poetry and may not have been familiar with it. He was, he wrote, "very much pleased" with the two youths and went on to say that he was "more and more struck by the certainty, strength, and unconscious self-confidence of young men, so different from my middle-aged uncertainty and also my lack of physical confidence in my own body." Whatever he lacked in confidence, however, he more than made up for in grit. After the lunch he went back to the RTYC and wrote 1,200 words on the novel. But he couldn't crush the anxiety about the quality of what he was writing. A week later he read *Georgian Poetry 1916–17* and recorded that the reading "seemed to buck me up to raise the damn thing [*The Pretty Lady*] to a higher plane than it has reached save in odd places here and there." [12]

Between September and January he frequently reread what he had written but was never wholly satisfied with his work, finding dull stretches in the novel which he appeared to be unable to remedy. But on January 28 he brought the book to a close with some feeling of satisfaction, at least with the ending, which he thought was "rather ingenious, well executed, and effective." He immediately qualified that feeling of confidence, however, with the observation that he no longer tried to judge the value of one of his novels until it had been in print for at least two years. He added by way of justification for the disclaimer that he had thought *The Old Wives' Tale* "dull" when he had finished writing it and that his sister Tertia had thought the same thing.

Whatever its defects as a novel, *The Pretty Lady* was to become the most immediately successful book which he had written since the outbreak of the war, perhaps since *The Card* (1911). Bennett's evaluation of what the public wanted proved, once again, to be sound. Others, as Georges Lafourcade pointed out, had written about prostitutes; and Bennett probably knew such works as Goncourt's *La Fille Eliza*, Balzac's *Grandeur et Misère des Courtesanes*, and Zola's *Nana*—or even Gissing's *The*

*Unclassed.* But no one had attempted to do exactly what Bennett set out to do in *The Pretty Lady*.

It was Bennett's intention to present in sympathetic but not in the least sentimental terms a prostitute who was content with her life and who was capable of maintaining her dignity in the pursuit of her trade. Christine does not regard herself as a "fallen woman." She has few illusions, on the other hand, about the nature of her calling and is fully aware of the dangers which she runs in following her chosen way of life. She is, however, eminently sensible and gifted with a Gallic practicality which compels her to keep constantly in mind that she must accumulate money enough before her looks fail in order to insure herself a financially secure future. Her dream, a reasonably modest one, is that Hoape will establish her in a flat as his mistress. In every respect, except for her desire to become Hoape's mistress and in her superstitions, she remains coldly professional.

Bennett's task in drawing such a character was, of course, complicated by the prudishness of one segment of his reading public and by the threat posed to a successful promotion of the novel by the various groups and individuals who perched like harpies above the publishing world, ready to pounce screaming on any book that could be called pornographic or a threat to the security of the state, established religion, or the family. With the example of Wells's *Ann Veronica* (1909) and Lawrence's *The Rainbow* (1915) to remind him of what could happen when a writer presumed too far on the British public's tolerance or counted too heavily on its willingness to be understanding, Bennett knew that he would have to judge every word and every scene in the book in terms of how it would be received not only by those liberated citizens who no longer blanched when they saw adultery treated lightly on the London stage but also by those who frequented the fiercely respectable lending libraries where Mrs. Grundy and not Priapus was the reigning deity.

Of course, to propose to tell a forthright story about a prostitute without condemning her for her choice of life and, at the same time, to tell that story in such a way that no one would be offended was a contradiction in terms. It could not have been done, and Bennett did not really believe that it could. He knew well enough that the libraries would "kick." But he came as close to bringing off the trick as, perhaps, any writer could have done in that time and in that place. *The Pretty Lady* stands as a tribute to Bennett's skill in sailing close to the reefs of public outrage without losing his ship. It may be granted that tastes were changing and that the majority of readers were gradually becoming more tolerant of sex in their novels, but the uproars that had surrounded the publication of *Jude The Obscure*, to name an early *cause célèbre* created by the frank treatment of sex in a novel, were still echoing in the corridors of the publishing houses, amplified by other and later troubles stemming from the appearance of similarly controversial books.

English publishers of the first decades of the present century could hardly be characterized as fearless defenders of the freedom of writers to write as they chose. It was, therefore, a mark in favor of Cassell that the company agreed to take Bennett's *"cocotte"* novel. During the week of January 23, Bennett delivered the completed manuscript to Pinker.[13] Flower was happy with the book and, displaying a remarkable sense of urgency, set the last week of April or the first week of May as the date of publication. By February 20 Bennett had finished correcting the proofs of the novel and returned them to Flower. In the course of his rereading he had the satisfaction of finding that the story held his interest well, "a good test," he thought, of the novel. On the whole he was satisfied with his effort, but he admitted that he had left things out of the book which would have improved it.[14]

Only one difficulty connected with the publication of *The Pretty Lady* continued to trouble him, and that was Munsey's refusal to sell the serial rights to *The Roll Call* and to allow Doran and Methuen to bring out the novel in book form. Bennett was very anxious to have *The Roll Call* appear in advance of *The Pretty Lady* because if publication occurred in

[13] Ogden Collection, January 23, 1918.
[14] *Journal*, 653.

reverse, the time sequence of the novels would be inverted, *The Roll Call* having been set at the outbreak of the war and *The Pretty Lady* placed in the midwar period. Bennett asked Pinker as well as Doran to intercede with Munsey, but Munsey withheld the rights until after *The Pretty Lady* was issued. Bennett did not get the corrected proofs of *The Roll Call* into Methuen's hands until the middle of June. Hutchinson was to have the English serial rights to the novel, and contracts were signed in July. But Methuen was slow in getting *The Roll Call* through the printer's, and the book was not issued in England until early winter. Hutchinson began serializing the novel in England in the middle of January, 1919.[15]

*The Pretty Lady* made its appearance in early April and was an immediate success. The reviewers, as might be expected, were divided over the book; but its sales increased steadily. By the 23rd of April, Cassell had brought out a second edition, and by May 19 the book had sold 17,500 copies.[16] Problems concerning the book, however, began within a week of its publication. The booksellers of Bath and of Cambridge combined to boycott the novel, and by the end of May, Cassell was under attack by two Catholic organizations which were objecting strenuously to the subject matter in the novel and to its treatment of the Catholic religion. On April 14 *The Sunday Chronicle,* published a bitter attack, charging Bennett with having written pornography.

H. M. Richardson's review in *The Sunday Chronicle* quivers with outraged morality and is probably a fairly representative example of objections raised against the book by its detractors. Having called *The Pretty Lady* "unsavory," Richardson comes to his real target, which is Bennett himself; and although he quotes from the book and comments on it, he never abandons his personal attack on the author. Richardson became so angered by what he found in the novel that he abandoned any attempt to deal with the book as literature, falling back on such words as "damnable," "decadent," "ignoble," and "corrupting" to ease

---

15 Butler Collection, July 10, 1918; September 18, 1918.
16 *Ibid.,* May 19, 1918.

his indignation. What enraged Richardson was Bennett's failure to treat "the seamy side of sex" with either cynical wit or "moral passion," in other words, to treat it as a vice and condemn it. In a conclusion scarcely short of hysteria, Richardson summarizes his charges against Bennett by comparing him to German soldiers who commit acts of barbarism while "blinded by blood." His final paragraph demands that the book be banned under the Defense of the Realm Act "as a work calculated to destroy the moral [*sic*] of the people. It is a book which will degrade any decent book stall." [17] In May, Smith's banned the book from its bookstalls and libraries.

The two Catholic organizations to take exception to *The Pretty Lady* were the Catholic Federation and the Catholic Truth Society. Both groups took the line that the book contained material offensive to Catholics and that the subject matter of the book was repulsive. W. P. Mara, honorary lay secretary of the Catholic Federation, wrote to Cassell in early May threatening to take action against the publishing house unless the book were withdrawn. [18] It was the kind of letter that made publishers very nervous, and Bennett was sufficiently disturbed by the letter to send a copy of *The Pretty Lady* to Attorney General F. E. Smith, and later Lord Birkenhead to forestall any police action against the book. [19] He also wrote a letter to Cassell refusing to suppress any portion of the novel.

On May 28 James Britten, Honorary Secretary for the Catholic Truth Society, wrote to Cassell, taking a similar line to that adopted by Mara.

> I am directed by my Committee to call your attention to a novel—"The Pretty Lady" by Mr. Arnold Bennett—recently published by your firm. They desire me to point out what must be obvious to every reader, though it seems to have escaped

[17] H. M. Richardson, "An Ignoble New Novel," *The Sunday Chronicle*, April 14, 1918.
[18] Pound, *Arnold Bennett*, 271.
[19] Bennett and Smith were casual friends. In December, 1917, Smith had asked Bennett to accompany him on a two-month tour of the U.S.; but Bennett had refused, adding in the journal entry in which he recorded the invitation that he liked Smith as a companion but that he had no desire to spend two months with him in the U.S.A.

your notice that the book deals in the crudest way with subjects which it is not usual to present in a story intended for
general circulation, and further that the numerous references
to matters connected with Catholicism are couched in terms
which are offensive to Catholics.[20]

Bennett asked Pinker to reply to Britten in exactly the same
terms in which he had replied to Mara. He also asked his agent
to tell Flower to assume that a similar letter had been sent to
him. The protest from the Catholic Truth Society appears to
have been the last serious objection to *The Pretty Lady* on the
grounds that it was immoral or irreligious. Presumably Smith's
continued its ban on the book; but because Cassell refused to be
intimidated by threats of legal action and boycott while the
book and its author were under fire, the company outfaced the
opposition and kept the novel before the public, with the result
that by September 19 it had sold 30,000 copies.[21]

In spite of the excellent sale, Bennett was dissatisfied with
Cassell's promotion of the novel. He expressed an initial pleasure
at the book's reception, but he soon became disgusted with Cassell's unwillingness to spend money advertising it. On May 31 he
asked Flower why the book was not being advertised more
thoroughly and got the reply that the book was doing so well
that it did not need promotion. Bennett reported Flower's response to Pinker and added indignantly that Swinnerton said it
was just the time to advertise. For several weeks he continued to
protest against Cassell's indifference and then gave up the fight
with the lament that if the novel "had been adequately advertised, it would have had an appreciably higher sale." [22]

Bennett enjoyed a double triumph with *The Pretty Lady*.
Not only were the sales of the novel unusually high for one of
his books but also critical response to the work was, on the
whole, good. Those who enjoyed the book tended to be enthusiastic, and those who objected to it did so violently. Among
Bennett's biographers though, only Georges Lafourcade—that

[20] Ogden Collection, May 28, 1918.
[21] Butler Collection, September 19, 1918.
[22] Ogden Collection, May 31, 1918; June 8, 1918.

he was French may be significant—thought the book anything more than a potboiler. What Lafourcade found particularly admirable in the novel was the painstaking development of Christine's character and the careful construction of the novel itself.

Others who admired the work were people as markedly different in character, background, and taste as Hugh Walpole, Lord Beaverbrook, George Moore, the novelist and poet James Stevens, and Dame Rebecca West. Perhaps to some extent they were praising the idea behind the novel—the idea that a prostitute's life was as deserving of objective and artistic handling as the life of any other person and that the behavior of a man who sought her services was equally deserving of dispassionate treatment. Considering the limitations under which a popular writer was forced to work in that period, Bennett managed to be exceedingly frank in his treatment of Christine and Hoape. He was marvelously successful in suggesting where he could not specify, and the suggesting is never coy. Its purpose is always to make clear by implication what the law and public taste would not allow him to say outright.

In terms of what Bennett did with Christine, his achievement in the novel is quite remarkable. She is rendered with such clarity and conviction that George Moore was certain that Bennett must have lived with her. In Moore's judgment, given to Bennett in conversation, she was the most perfectly achieved *cocotte* in literature.[23] And she manages to be convincing despite the almost ludicrous manner of speaking which Bennett imposed on her. By rendering her French literally in English, Bennett made her speak like a cross between a primitive Quaker and a French maid in a skit.

Unfortunately, he was less successful with his other characters. Hoape, the middle-aged, wealthy bachelor hero of the novel, is a more or less unsympathetic character. His sophistication has a repelling hardness about it that makes one doubt that he is capable of any real warmth of feeling, and there is such a high degree of calculation in his actions that he is almost sinister. He is not without emotion, but it is emotion under such iron control

[23] *Journal*, 731.

that it is scarcely emotion at all. When, for example, Conception tells Hoape that she intends to commit suicide, she does so in the perfect confidence that he will receive the news calmly and dispassionately. And so he does. Then he diverts her attention away from death by deliberately reawakening the woman in her with a few carefully chosen words which imply that he may be in love with her. But he remains so thoroughly in control of himself and of the situation that the scene is ultimately unconvincing.

Conception Smith is also a failure. She is not really a character at all but rather a composite portrait of the "New Woman," a kind of literary suitcase into which Bennett has stuffed all of his notes on the type. Through her, Bennett comments on women in war work, the agony of women who lose their husbands in the war, and the risks of emotional disintegration and loss of happiness run by the almost anchorless "emancipated" woman. She also serves as a third romantic interest in Hoape's life. As a result of this crowded material, Conception never really comes to life.

Queenie Paulle, Conception's aristocratic equivalent, is even less alive than Conception. The spoiled and willfull daughter of wealth and title, she remains from her first appearance to her last little more than a caricature. Bennett makes cruel fun of her war work and by the manner of her death suggests that she and her kind are futile and self-destructive. She is killed by a scrap of antiaircraft shell which penetrates her brain while she foolishly exposes herself to danger by standing on the roof of her London house during an air raid. Without carrying the implications too far, it is worth pointing out that an English rather than a German shell fragment kills Queenie.

Far more direct social comment appears in *The Pretty Lady* than in any other of Bennett's novels. The entire representation of Queenie as a flashy leech living off the nation's blood is only one instance of his satiric thrusts at the inequalities and injustices of contemporary English life. In chapter six Hoape discovers that he is going to make a great deal of money out of the war and is positively delighted by the prospect, although later he decides to give away all of his extra profits. And yet still later

when his man Braiding enlists and Mrs. Braiding apologized to
Hoape for the inconvenience Hoape will be caused by her husband's enlisting, Hoape is flabbergasted and angry:

> She had apologized to him because Braiding had departed to
> save the Empire without first asking his permission. It was not
> merely astounding—it flabbergasted. He had always felt that
> there was something fundamentally wrong in the social fabric,
> and he had long had a preoccupation to the effect that it was
> his business, his, to take a share in finding out what was wrong
> and in discovering and applying a cure. . . . There must be
> something wrong when a member of one class would behave to
> a member of another class as Mrs. Braiding behaved to him—
> without protest from him.[24]

But Hoape is by no means all of a piece. His concern for Mrs.
Braiding did not make him sensitive to another and more striking
example of the inequity in the "social fabric" with which he
was brought into contact. Shortly after his interview with his
housekeeper, Hoape stopped at his bootmaker's to complain that
one of his new boots pained his toes. Bennett describes the shop
and notes in passing that its name was known from "Peru to
Hong Kong." The manager promises Hoape that all would be
attended to; and then noticing that his customer's boots are not
properly polished, he goes to a speaking tube and snaps, "Polisher!"

What follows that abrupt command is one of the strangest
and, in some respects, the most disturbing passages in Bennett's
writing. No paraphrase can do it justice, and it follows in its
entirety:

> A trap door opened in the floor of the shop and a horrible,
> pallid, weak, cringing man came out of the earth of St. James's,
> and knelt before God far more submissively than even the
> manager had knelt. He had brushes and blacking, and he
> blacked and he brushed and he breathed alternately, undoing
> with his breath or his filthy hand what he had done with his
> brush. He never looked up, never spoke. When he had made
> the boots like mirrors he gathered together his implements and
> vanished, silent and dutifully bent, through the trap door back

24 Bennett, *The Pretty Lady*, 34.

into the earth of St. James's. And because the trap door had not shut properly the manager stamped on it and stamped down the pale man definitely into the darkness underneath. And then G. J. was wafted out of the shop with smiles and bows.[25]

There is something of Dickens in the passage but more of Wells, and the Polisher is closer kin to the dim underground creatures of *The Time Machine* than the suffering hosts of Dicken's downtrodden. But Hoape was untouched by the incident, did not even notice the Polisher; and because of that and because Bennett left the incident unconnected to any other event in the novel, its effect is stillborn. He might have chosen to tie the event to Mrs. Braiding's humility or to the terrifying conditions under which women worked in the munitions factories in the North, conditions which Conception describes in chapter twenty-seven.

Conception's account of the accident in which a young woman has her hair and scalp ripped from her head by one of the machines is an example of what Bennett was presenting as typical of the dangers to which women who worked in those factories were exposed. But Bennett did not connect the incidents and may not have felt that there was any connection. The result for the reader is a confusing jumble of seemingly related material, the significance of which is left unstated. He must make of it what he can without any indication of what Bennett intended.

The greatest weakness in the novel is precisely this lack of coherence. It makes itself felt again in the attention which Bennett gives to Christine's superstitious corruptions of her religion and in the superstition of the soldier Edgar W., who showed Christine his "mascot," a picture of Christ surrounded by flames and thorns stamped on an oval piece of red cloth. Edgar was convinced that the piece of cloth had the power to turn back bullets. Bennett undoubtedly got the mascot idea from George Whale's collection of war superstitions, and what he took from Whale he simply put into the novel in the crudest clip and paste fashion. Christine's superstitions do in a general if rather unsatisfactory way explain her preoccupation with Edgar, a preoccupa-

[25] *Ibid.*, 39.

tion which leads to the incident which drives Hoape from her; but there is no vital relationship between her superstition and the development of her character.

Lafourcade admitted that the book was not a "masterpiece" and summarized its failures by concluding that the style was uneven, the minor characters artificial, the coincidences too numerous, and the ill-assorted incidents making up the story unsatisfactory.[26] No one is likely to contradict Lafourcade's judgment. But that is not to say that there are not good things in it or that those who praised it were merely being perverse.

The most distressing fact about *The Pretty Lady* is that it should have been a much better novel than it turned out to be. It might even have been a great one. But Bennett wrote it at a time when his powers of concentration were at an ebb as were his creative faculties. He had a good idea, he had interesting materials, but he was unable to bring them together into an organic whole. The slow and fragmented process of composition proved to be fatal to the book's unity. It was put together in bits and pieces with one section having a functional relationship with the other sections only to the extent that the relationships of Christine, Hoape, and Conception are continued throughout the novel. For the rest, Bennett seems to have filled out the chapters with whatever material he had at hand when he sat down to write. He obviously meant what he said when he spoke of collecting ideas for the book. *The Pretty Lady* is a record of those collecting expeditions with each set of specimens staring out separately from the pages.

Although the book is titled *The Pretty Lady*, the central character is really Gilbert Hoape. A middle-aged bachelor of fixed habits and opinions, Hoape is, in certain ways, a projection of Bennett himself. The directly autobiographical details which Bennett employed in drawing Hoape are numerous and interesting. Hoape is Bennett's age and the son of a lawyer. He is a member of the Reform Club. He likes music, good clothes, tastefully decorated rooms, and the company of attractive and intelligent women. He is chairman of a war committee very like the WARC, and his punctuality is "absolute."

26 Lafourcade, *Arnold Bennett,* 183.

Hoape is a bachelor "whose habits had the value of inestimable jewels and whose perfect independence was the most precious thing in the world." Gilman, who is Hoape's equivalent in *The Lion's Share*, is anxious to marry one of the young women whose company he seeks, but throughout most of the story Gilbert Hoape feels differently. He sets his mind against marrying Conception because he sees very clearly that she would turn his existence into an "endless drama." He hardens himself against temptation with a stern warning: "No; he must not mistake affectionate sympathy for tenderness, nor tolerate the sexual exploitation of his pity." [27]

Hoape prizes Christine, whom he has not the slightest idea of marrying, for her acquiescence and her responsiveness and her passivity. He is quite a different character from Gilman; or if he is not wholly different, he is remarkably changed. There is a greater degree of hardness in Hoape than in Gilman; and he is a world removed from Edwin Clayhanger. Hoape would never say that Conception's "devilish talent for the sensational" had made a "romance" of his life as Edwin Clayhanger says of Hilda's similar talent. Hoape knows that Conception would make a hell of his life, and his idea of "romance" is to put Christine "among her own things" where she belongs and keep her to himself.

*The Pretty Lady*, unlike his other novels for the preceding seven years, does not deal with marriage. The subject matter of the book made marriage an awkward difficulty that Bennett may have thought best to avoid. For one thing, Hoape's bachelorhood makes his relationship with Christine far less open to criticism than would have been the case had he been a married man. The moralists could not charge Bennett with corrupting the integrity of marriage; and, at the same time, he could appeal to the reading public's desire for experimental and exciting presentation of sexual relationships. It is also possible that Bennett had exhausted his own interest in the married state.

His marriage was all but dead. He had reverted, in part at least, to a bachelor life; and in his presentation of Hoape's relationship with Christine, he may have been exploring his own

[27] Bennett, *The Pretty Lady*, 321.

unfulfilled desire for a satisfying sexual arrangement that would not expose him to the dangers which he had encountered in his own marriage. The fictional wives which he had created from Rachel in *The Price of Love* through Hilda in *These Twain* to Lois in *The Roll Call* were all more or less unsatisfactory mates.

It would be unreasonable to insist that Bennett's own experience with marriage had nothing to do with his manner of treating it in his fiction. Unless one completely disregards the way in which Bennett exploited his own interests and preoccupations in his writing, it would be equally unreasonable to assume that when he chose to explore the possibilities of a liaison, as he did in *The Pretty Lady* and later in *Lord Raingo*, his interest in the matter was wholly artistic. This is not to confuse the artist with his materials but rather to take into account Bennett's method of projecting himself in a qualified way into such characters as Edwin Clayhanger, Mr. Gilman, George Cannon, Gilbert Hoape, and Sam Raingo.

*The Pretty Lady* may well be, in part, a fantasy in which Bennett examined with considerable personal interest the possibilities of the kind of relationship Christine and Hoape have. He was living alone a considerable part of every month at the RTYC, and he was certainly aware that his wife could not or would not give him the tenderness and the affection which he craved. Although the novel ends with Hoape rejecting Christine, the ending lacks all sense of inevitability. A "happy" ending might have easily been tacked onto the story. And there is nothing of moral uplift in the ending as it stands which might have been included to make the novel more palatable to the general public. It is a weak ending, nothing more; and Bennett may have chosen it because he had concluded that no really workable relationship could have been established between Christine and Hoape.

Christine's superstitions can be taken to represent all of the inadequacies that a woman of her sort would have for a man like Hoape. Those inadequacies would lead her into folly, and her folly would ultimately divide them. That is what actually happens in the novel. Christine, imagining herself on an errand of mercy for the Virgin Mary, sets out to find Edgar; and Hoape chances to see her stopping soldiers in the street. He misunderstands what she is doing and decides never to see her again. His decision to marry Conception, however, is totally unconvincing and in no way nullifies his earlier and more believable determination to avoid marriage. The book really ends with Hoape's decision to leave Christine, but his decision to marry Conception serves to tie up certain loose threads and provide a conventional ending for the novel. Despite his comment that he thought the ending effective, Bennett probably did not believe in the marriage he was fabricating and neither does the reader.

Clearly there are all sorts of dangers surrounding the act of reading a novel as disguised autobiography. But in Bennett's case, particularly in those novels written between 1913 and 1918 and to include *Lord Raingo*, which was set in this period, there is justification for reading with Bennett's personal life in mind. And it is *Lord Raingo* which provides the strongest indication of how autobiographical Bennett could be. In that novel Bennett began with an extramarital relationship in which Raingo has taken Delphine for his mistress while at the same time maintaining the shell of his marriage. Raingo is the culmination of a discernible drift away from faith in marriage as a means of achieving happiness. That drift parallels the disintegration of Bennett's own marriage; and by the time he came to write *Lord Raingo*, he had left his wife and was living with Dorothy Cheston. He had moved to a level of personal behavior adumbrated in every novel which he wrote during the war period.

During the years between 1914 and 1921, Bennett was struggling with the collapse of his marriage, and it is not unreasonable to expect evidence of that struggle to appear regularly in his fiction. He was unhappy; he was frequently ill; and he was desperately in need of a woman to love and to love him. By 1914 he was already in need of some revitalizing experience. The Comarques experiment had largely failed. Then the war came along, and for a time at least it sparked new fire. By 1917 the inspiration was all but gone again. He had been wakened by war to a new social awareness which found expression in his journalism and a new sense of his own power to sway public opinion, but the war had done very little to strengthen his ability to write fiction. What was needed to restore that ability was a vital relationship with a woman, and his novels of that period are full of the urgency of his need. He eventually found fulfillment in Dorothy Cheston in 1922, but he may have been speaking in part of himself when he gave Raingo the joy of his Delphine and then killed Raingo to show, among other things, that his triumph had come too late.

As black as his spirits were during the last months of 1917, something happened in November which was to bear directly on his state of mind during the following months: He met William Maxwell Aitken, better known later as Lord Beaverbrook. Having made a fortune in Canada, where he was born in 1879, Aitken went to England in 1910 with the intention of making his home there. He immediately stood as a Conservative and Unionist candidate for Parliament for Ashton-under-Lyne and won, thanks largely to the support of Bonar Law. He played an important but silent role in the fall of Asquith's government in 1916, accepted a peerage, and in 1918 became Minister of Information, a post which he held until ill health forced him to resign in October of that year. After the war he devoted much of his time to the *Daily Express,* which he had bought control of in the early days of the war.

On their second meeting Beaverbrook asked Bennett to take him to the Leicester Gallery to look at an etching by Félicien Rops, the Belgian artist. Bennett had expressed admiration for the etching; and once he had seen it, Beaverbrook immediately bought the etching and gave it to Bennett. Bennett was somewhat startled by Beaverbrook's action. "This was only our second meeting," he wrote. "*Un peu brusqué.*" [28] But Beaverbrook was not a man to stick at a precipitate act if it served his end, and the end he had in mind was to impress Bennett.

Writing for the *Montreal Star* in 1962, Beaverbrook admitted that he had set out quite deliberately to court Bennett and having gained an introduction through Robert Ross, invited

[28] *Journal,* 638.

Bennett to lunch. Beaverbrook's account of that early meeting is an epitome of the essential qualities of both men. The lunch was given at Beaverbrook's house, and Bennett arrived precisely on time. "He stood up," Beaverbrook recalled. "I asked him to sit down. He said he would not sit down until he had spoken. He solemnly took a manuscript from his pocket and read out an attack on me and my politics. 'That,' said Arnold Bennett, 'is going into the newspapers tomorrow.' I asked him to sit down. He did so. We had lunch. We never referred to the newspaper attack again." [29]

That lunch was the beginning of a very long and very close friendship which both men prized. They had much in common. They both had known the rigors of hard work. They were both aware of the social limitations imposed on them because of their origins. They could, as a consequence, understand and respect one another. Some of Bennett's friends, however, regarded his association with Beaverbrook with dismay and, recalling that friendship in later years, were to refer to Beaverbrook as Bennett's "evil genius."

The double objection to Beaverbrook was that he drew Bennett into public life and away from his writing and that he became a wedge between Bennett and Marguerite, whom he despised.[30] The first charge cannot be denied. He did offer Bennett a role in government, but it was Bennett's choice whether or not to accept the offer. From Bennett's description of Gilbert Hoape's efforts to secure a job with the government and the alacrity with which Bennett accepted Beaverbrook's offer, it may be safely concluded that Beaverbrook only presented an opportunity which Bennett had been seeking for some time. As for Beaverbrook's having come between Bennett and Marguerite,

[29] Lord Beaverbrook, "A Great Novelist's Qualities," *The Montreal Star,* January 20, 1962, pp. 2–3.
[30] In the *Montreal Star* article quoted above, Beaverbrook wrote that "Arnold had a very tiresome wife—at least, she seemed to me to be tiresome. She was French. He had married her during his early days in Paris. She used to sit on top of the piano, smoke cigars, and interrupt the flow of conversation." It is not certain that Beaverbrook ever observed Marguerite behaving in the manner which he describes, but Bennett may have mentioned his wife's bizarre behavior.

one might as convincingly charge a brook with corrupting an ocean.

It would appear that at least some of the hostility toward Beaverbrook was a result of a dislike of the man on far more general grounds than that he was a baleful influence on Bennett. Hostility sprang up around Beaverbrook with tropical luxuriance. For example, when he was appointed director of the Ministry of Information in early 1918, the entire staff of the Ministry resigned in protest, refusing to work under "that ignorant man."[31] Beaverbrook was in the slang of the day something of a "bounder," a state of being suggesting social leprosy. But then, Bennett was also something of a "bounder," at least in John Galsworthy's view; and Galsworthy knew about such things. One may atone in time for almost any crime in England except that of not being a gentleman. Neither Bennett nor Beaverbrook was a gentleman, and that was something else they had in common.

Shortly after meeting Beaverbrook, Bennett was elected, without his knowledge, to the Carlton Club or the Other Club, as it was more frequently called. The membership of the Other Club was made up principally of politicians and judges. Bennett was one of the first eminent novelists asked to join, and the invitation was to him a great honor. His own account of the matter was confined to remarks about the men whom he met at his first dinner there. His table companion was F. E. Smith, whom he liked. He thought Sir Mark Sykes, author and Army officer, was the most interesting man present and was very impressed with the originality of a caricature which Sykes did of him and F. E. Smith. He noted that the Duke of Marlborough was in the Chair to give the toast to the King and that Sir Edward Lutyens, the architect and artist, "amiably played the amusing fool."[32]

He had another entertaining evening in December at a poetry recital given by Lady Sibyl Colefax. The evening was saved for him by a reading of T. S. Eliot's "Hippopotamus," which he thought excellent. "Had I been the house," he wrote, "this would

[31] *Journal*, 657.
[32] *Ibid.*, 638.

have brought the house down." He was also favorably impressed by the poet Irene Rutherford McLeod, who read two of Sassoon's poems and at least one of her own, which Bennett described as being "pretty goodish." In closing he remarked that the Sitwell family "was much in evidence, *tres cultivée*." [33] His sense of humor was still intact. The tone of the entry was the lightest for several months, but the good spirits were not lasting. By the middle of the month he was plunged in gloom again as a result, at least in part, of the trouble he was having with *The Pretty Lady*.

For reasons not wholly clear, Bennett's depression seems to have been intensified at about this time by a trip which he took in the first week of November to Dublin. The journey was undertaken under government suggestion, and its purpose was to produce journalism in support of the government's Irish policies. Bennett dutifully made the visit and kept a small journal of notes on his impressions. He returned to London on the 4th totally exhausted and suffering from neuralgia. The following day he wrote the required article, which appeared in the *Daily News* on Thursday, November 8, under the title "Dublin Castle." It was a straightforward piece of writing in support of Home Rule. His impatience with the Irish muddle, however, was expressed more frankly in *The Pretty Lady* by his dismissing the Easter Revolt with the comment that Christine, using "commonsense," would have settled the trouble in forty-eight hours.[34]

Undoubtedly he felt an increasing sense of pressure from the loss of a week's writing time; and that awareness of time lost, coupled with his flagging energies, may have caused his spirits to plummet. But the equally real and pressing need for money forced him to go on contracting for work as though he were in top writing form. On November 13 Pinker contracted with *Cosmopolitan Magazine* for six more articles in the same vein as those he had in the spring, Bennett having responded to Pinker's query about the possibility of his doing more of them

---

[33] *Ibid.*, 639.
[34] Bennett, *The Pretty Lady*, 238.

with the assurance that he could go on writing such material indefinitely.[35] English rights were bought by *Nash's Magazine*. He also accepted a contract from Douglass Doty, who had gone as editor from *Century* to *Cosmopolitan*, for two or three articles with a French setting. These articles were to be designed to catch the interest of American readers who were, in Doty's opinion, becoming very preoccupied with all things French.

He had at least one pleasant diversion, however, in November, and that was the replacing of John B. Atkins's book *A Floating Home*. Pinker had originally settled with Methuen for publication of the book, but Methuen postponed publication long past the reasonable time limit in such matters. Bennett asked Pinker to get a promised date of publication out of Methuen, but Methuen refused to set a specific time or even to say that the book would be published at all.[36] At Bennett's suggestion Pinker transferred the book to Chatto and Windus. The change of publishers brought Bennett a windfall of £30 for the watercolors he had prepared for the book, and for the next month he occupied his odd moments retouching the paintings.[37]

After an absence from the theater lasting for nearly four months, Bennett returned to his playgoing in December with the premiere of James Barrie's *Dear Brutus*, which Bennett described as "a great success and deserved. . . . I enjoyed the play nearly throughout." He followed Barrie's play with one by Granville-Barker, *Vote By Ballot*. "It contained any amount of witty and true dialogue," Bennett observed, "but it was not what I call a play." [38]

The effects of Bennett's deliberate refusal to take seriously what was being done on the London stage were making themselves felt. He was gradually getting out of touch with the spirit of the popular theater and was coming to see its differences from the theater of five years earlier as signs of inferiority and degeneracy. But his interest in the people who went to the theater

[35] Butler Collection, November 13, 1917.
[36] Ogden Collection, November 22, 1917.
[37] Butler Collection, December 20, 1917.
[38] *Journal*, 640, 641.

had not lessened. He wrote that the theater was packed with "the usual crowd," and added almost wistfully that he saw in the audience "wives and mistresses of the same men all mixed up and friendly together." [39]

Following his month's holiday in August, Bennett returned to his journalism with his biases intact. In the *Daily News* articles he attacked Lloyd George, the War Cabinet, and those who wanted peace without first crushing the German military machine. His hostility toward Lloyd George is difficult to explain. It was Lord Beaverbrook's opinion that Bennett's politics and those of the Prime Minister coincided almost exactly. According to Beaverbrook, Bennett never was able to give a satisfactory explanation of his hostility toward Lloyd George, but there is no doubt that the antipathy was deeply rooted. Even after his appointment to the Ministry of Information, he remained uniformly cool toward his ultimate superior.[40]

Bennett had been Asquith's unswerving champion, and he may well have seen Lloyd George as a usurper. The fact that the Prime Minister was Welsh was another factor in Bennett's dislike. Bennett repeatedly pointed out that one of the greatest weaknesses of the War Cabinet was the small number of Englishmen on it. He was on one occasion repeating his argument to an Army officer who immediately agreed with him and pleased Bennett enormously by asking, "Did you ever know a Celt [to] win a war?"

Bennett was a man of strong convictions. He was also much more radical in his political views than may have been generally guessed by his friends and acquaintances, but a reasonably careful sifting of his journalism will produce sufficient material to support the view that by 1918 Bennett was far more Socialist than Liberal in political outlook. Beginning in January, 1918, he included at the end of his *NS* pieces quotes from Lloyd George's early speeches to show how the Prime Minister had backslid in his liberalism from the early fire-eating days when he was building his career. Bennett saw that slippage as a traitorous abandon-

39 *Ibid.*, 641.
40 Beaverbrook, "A Great Novelist's Qualities," 3.

ment of principles. Increasingly he threw his support behind Labor and what he thought of as the forces of democracy.

On September 5 the *Daily News* carried an article of his which shows the direction in which Bennett's political sympathies were inclining by this time. "Stockholm" began with an attack on the War Cabinet and went from that well-worn topic to a statement of support for the Stockholm Conference. Bennett described the Conference as an international meeting of "democrats" prepared to take a hand in shaping the world after the war. The Conference had been called by the Second International, which had been inactive since 1914, for the purpose of bringing together socialist groups of all shadings of thought to examine the world situation.

In August the British Labor Party voted overwhelmingly to attend the Conference; but the War Cabinet, which had favored participation in May, reversed itself in August and refused to issue the necessary passports to the delegates which would allow them to leave the country.[41] It was against this choking off of political and individual liberty that Bennett was protesting. "The idea of the Stockholm Conference is not dead, far less buried," he wrote defiantly. "So far as privileged opposition in this country is concerned, democrats can count on the pleasing fact that we have a Prime Minister who has the principles of a weathercock."

Throughout the remainder of 1917, Bennett continued to slash away at the War Cabinet, which had become for him the personification of reaction and privilege. On October 17 he wrote that the operations of the Cabinet were "a scandal, combining inefficiency with virtual autocracy, and reaction with an extraordinary lack of scruple." He went on to express the hope that Labor and the "democratic" forces would influence the next government formed. He repeated the attack on November 29, repeating the charge that the War Cabinet was antidemocratic. On December 13 he demanded the destruction of the

[41] Paul Guinn, *British Strategy and Politics 1914–1918* (London, 1965), 239, 241.

German military autocracy and called for support of the League of Nations.

His *NS* articles for the closing months of 1917 followed in general the themes he was developing in the *Daily News* pieces. But through September and October the quality of the articles fall off markedly and frequently appear to have been written at least in part by someone else. "Optimism at the Front," which appeared on September 8, is the first article in the series to be written in part by either Sharp or another of the *NS* editors. The entry for September 22 also shows signs of collaboration, and the September 29 article was probably not written by Bennett in any part.

The first really lively article in the series after his August holidays appeared on October 27 and was written in support of new Education and Health Bills. With some of his old fire he pointed out that opposition to the Health Bill from "the concreted pill-boxes of the Local Government Board" revealed on the Board's part an indifference to the preventable death of babies that was "simply magnificent."

By November he had found his stride again, despite the collapse of his fiction in that month. On the 10th he leveled his spear at the *Daily Express* for interfering with and causing the cancellation of four lectures on the subject of National Guilds which were to have been given in Central Hall, Westminster. Among the speakers were Chesterton and H. W. Massingham, editor of *The Nation*. The *Express* had objected to Massingham and three of the other speakers on the grounds that they were pacifists and the newspaper threatened trouble if the meetings were held. The owners of the hall, the Wesleyan Connexion, became alarmed and cancelled their contract to rent, and the lectures were not given.

As a Christmas thought to leave with his readers, Bennett devoted his last "Observations" for 1917 to the subject of food queues. He described the melancholy lines of poor people, enduring the cold, waiting for food while the "ruling class" went on their way well fed. There were, he wrote, "quarter mile queues of dirty and shivering children, women, and old men in the immediate neighborhood" of the great railway stations, through which hurried the wealthy on their way to Christmas holidays, and there was, he said, no lack of food on the trains.[42]

His last journal entry for 1917 described a dinner he attended with Marguerite and Olive Glendinning at the headquarters of the 2/1st London R.G.A. The evening was long and dull for Bennett until it was discovered that the Ford in which they had been driven from Comarques to the headquarters would not start because of the cold. Marguerite and Olive decided to spend the night at the headquarters, but Bennett insisted on returning home and was taken back to Comarques in a G.S. (general service) wagon, seated on the body of the vehicle in a strapped-down easy chair and wrapped in rugs and an eiderdown. He enjoyed the experience. The evening, he wrote, had thoroughly bored him until he learned that the car wouldn't start. "Thenceforward I was quite cheerful." As was often the case with him, he was approaching a new year with an uplift of spirits that bore little relation to his actual circumstances.

[42] Arnold Bennett, "Observations," *New Statesman*, VIII (December 29, 1917), 303.

# IX

# HELL WITH THE LID OFF

Early in 1918 D. H. Lawrence appealed for financial help to Pinker. Lawrence wrote asking if Pinker could "tempt a little money out of some rich good-natured author" and mentioned Bennett as a possibility. Pinker passed the letter along to Bennett, drawing a quick reply: "What a characteristic letter, and how uncompromising for the future! I am not prepared to keep Lawrence, nor to give him a lump sum, as I doubt if the latter would help him very much. As to the vast fall in my income, I need only point out to you that it is about half what it was, and that I am keeping a number of people." [1]

Although Bennett was never reduced to anything approaching poverty during the war years, he was constantly driven to find enough money to maintain himself at the level he had established before 1914. By 1918 his need for money had grown acute. But with characteristic generosity he did offer to contribute a pound a week for at least a year toward a fund for Lawrence; and when help from other writers was not forthcoming, he sent Lawrence £25. [2] Later in the year, Lawrence appealed directly to Bennett, this time for a job in Bennett's government department, but Bennett refused him.

At the close of the first week of January, Bennett was able to report that although he was suffering as usual from insomnia, he was in full working power and had not had a headache in days. But another set of pressures more dangerous than financial or, perhaps, even health problems began to build in January and February and were to carry Bennett very close to the point at which his mental balance was threatened. He was at this time working under great tension on the final chapters of *The Pretty Lady*, and the strain of that work was rapidly proving

[1] *Letters*, I, 260.
[2] *Ibid.*, 261*n*.

to be too much for him. That, and the fact that he and Marguerite spent most of the first half of January together at Comarques, where he was hoping to find the freedom from distractions needed to finish his novel, were an unfortunate combination. Living with Marguerite for more than a day or two at a time inevitably led to friction, and Comarques itself bored and depressed him. He sought diversion in rereading parts of *Paradise Lost* and commented in his journal that "for sense" what Milton had to say about the relations of man and wife had not been beaten.

The first warning of what was happening appeared in the journal entry for January 9. "At present I am not getting enough meat, owing to inability of women to learn," he recorded going on to insist that the neuralgia which had struck him down that day was due to a lack of meat. There was a food shortage. The poor were queuing for staples, sugar was in short supply, certain kinds of meat were rationed. But there was never a question of there being too little food at Comarques. Bennett, as Lord Beaverbrook attested, had a formidable appetite, particularly for meat. Bennett's anxiety over *The Pretty Lady* seems to have been channeled into a fear that Marguerite was deliberately refusing to feed him properly, with the result that he was being made ill.

The fantasy should have left him when *The Pretty Lady* was finished, but it did not. In the first week of February he was once again blaming his neuralgia on a lack of meat. A few days later he lunched with the Webbs and complained that there was not enough to eat. On the 15th he dined with Lillah McCarthy and made the same complaint. He also confessed that following the dinner he had been ill with indigestion, produced in his opinion by drinking too much champagne but which may have been the result of stuffing himself. He complained unceasingly about his health and on the 22nd made the single entry in the journal: "I am not at all well." The following day he wrote, "Yesterday in a vain attempt to satisfy myself I ate haddock, oysters, pickled herring, salmon. . . ."[3]

[3] Unpublished Journal, February 22, 1918.

He was verging on hysteria, if not something worse. The entry for the 23rd marked the furthest advance of the trouble, but his preoccupation with food and associating his neuralgia with Marguerite did not end. On April 24 he wrote that he was suffering from neuralgia through a shortage of food caused by a disrupted house. Marguerite had staged "a highly unsuccessful" Red Cross benefit concert at Comarques. Even as late as the following November he recorded that while he had a good time at Beaverbrook's house, Cherkley Court, there hadn't been enough to eat, "Beaverbrook not being interested in food." [4]

The lightest side of Bennett's irritation with Marguerite over the food question had to do with a pig which Marguerite bought "as a war measure." By the second week of January, Bennett had seen all he ever wanted to see of Marguerite's pig: "It was a small one, but we have been eating this damned animal ever since [December], in all forms except ham, which has not yet arrived. Brawn every morning for breakfast. Yesterday I struck at pig's feet for lunch and had mutton instead; they are neither satisfying nor digestible, and one of the biggest frauds that ever came out of kitchens." [5]

Bennett's illness and his anxiety formed a private background to his work in the opening months of 1918. Newman Flower chose to omit most of Bennett's references to his health for this period from the edited journal, thereby keeping Bennett's preoccupation with his infirmities out of print and out of the portrait of the man that reveals itself in the pages of the published journal. Bennett's friends knew that he was an inveterate taker of nostrums, but probably few were aware of the degree and the frequency of Bennett's afflictions. Frank Swinnerton has remarked on the mask of pain that neuralgia made of his friend's face, and Bennett's stammer was common knowledge. For the most part, however, he suffered his ills alone, carrying on his work and maintaining the same bluff, confident exterior he had cultivated ever since coming down to "the Smoke" from Staffordshire.

4 *Journal*, 676.
5 *Ibid.*, 646.

If work alone could have distracted him, he had enough of that at hand as the new year opened. He was completing *The Pretty Lady*. The second *Cosmopolitan* series was waiting to be outlined. His play for Vedrenne and Eadie had to be planned. He was laying out a political article on the future of the Liberal party, and he had become associated with two new organizations, the Writers' Group and the British War Memorials Committee.[6] The Writers' Group was actually a revival of the original group of writers called together in 1914 by Masterman and, in that sense, was not strictly new. But in its new form it had assumed a political character with the purpose of influencing government decisions in favor of Liberal policies. Of the original group of "eminent authors" only Gilbert Murray and Bennett remained active in the revived organization. Bennett was also serving the Society of Authors in at least an advisory capacity. In the spring of 1918 the society entered into a struggle with the publishers over the question of book prices and payment of royalties to authors. Finally, there were deadlines to be met for his *Daily News* and *NS* articles. Work alone, however, could not stimulate him. He remained unhappy and uninspired; his work seemed like drudgery to a large degree.

In 1917 Bennett had reached a tentative agreement with Vedrenne and Eadie to write a play which Vedrenne would produce and in which Eadie would play the leading role. By the turn of the year he had done nothing toward developing ideas for the play, but on January 13 he made a start. "I outlined in the bath this morning," he wrote in the journal, "an idea of a play about a man being offered a title and his wife insisting on his accepting it against his will." [7] He had gotten the inspiration for the play from J. A. Spender, editor of the *Westminster Gazette*, who had been asked to advise a man in a similar dilemma. Spender had told the man to "suppress his

[6] The British War Memorials Committee, formed in 1918 and counting among its members Robert Ross, was responsible for setting in motion those forces which brought about the establishment of the Imperial War Museum in which are hung the works of the war artists, for whom the Committee won official recognition in 1918.

[7] *Journal*, 647.

scruples" and accept the title. Ross told Bennett that Spender's story would make a good play and Bennett agreed.[8]

Having outlined the play, Bennett let Vedrenne know he was ready to enter into serious negotiations; but he was not prepared to let Vedrenne see the outline. Letters went back and forth among Pinker, Bennett, and Vedrenne with Vedrenne trying to get some idea of what the play was about and Bennett trying equally hard to keep that information to himself. On February 2 Bennett gave in to the extent of asking Pinker if Vedrenne really would buy the play if he were told what it was about. Pinker answered in the affirmative, and Bennett gave the producer a summary of the play. Bennett may have, contrary to his custom in such matters, given Vedrenne a written description, because Vedrenne and Eadie took three weeks to make up their minds to accept the play and sign a contract.[9] The contract was actually signed on March 7, a major point of the agreement being that Bennett would receive £200 when he delivered the manuscript.

He began the writing on March 24 under the emotional distress caused by news of the new German offensive and the physical distress brought on by neuralgia and exhaustion. He wrote the first scene between five and seven P.M. on Sunday. Then he ran into a creative block and the play stopped. But by April 10 he was able to work again despite "British defeats, the government proposals for increasing the army, the publication of *The Pretty Lady*, political journalism, the gardening and household difficulties, chill on the entrails, neuralgia, insomnia, Marguerite's illness. . . ."[10]

By the 16th he had completed the first act of the play "in spite of many preoccupations," and the writing was progressing well. Within two weeks he had completed "after two sleepless nights" the second act of what he was now calling his "Honors" play. He finished the play on May 10, and complained that in order to do so he had been forced to wake himself in the morning and

[8] Bennett remarked to Siegfried Sassoon soon after Ross's death that Ross had been one of "the most *indirectly* creative men he had ever known." Margery Ross, *Robert Ross Friend of Friends* (London, 1952), 11.

[9] Ogden Collection, February 28, 1918.

[10] *Journal*, 656, 658.

also to "inform people with whom I had appointments in London that I was laid aside with a chill." He wrote the last act in four days.

Bennett had hoped to see the play produced at the Haymarket Theatre and was especially anxious to have Eadie in the play. In the middle of June, however, Vedrenne wrote to say that he wanted to open the play at once at the Royalty and that he wanted to find a new male lead for the play. Eadie, Vedrenne continued, was currently playing in *Marmaduke* by Ernest Denny at the Haymarket and would probably be engaged there for some time since the play would likely be a hit. Bennett thought the play "footling" but couldn't tell Vedrenne that. His judgment proved to be sound, and *Marmaduke* closed on July 27.[11] He found himself forced, however, to let Vedrenne make the move to the Royalty, feeling that to press his view concerning *Marmaduke* would be insulting to both Eadie and Vedrenne.

His irritation over the change came out in a letter to Pinker on July 18: "It seems to me that there is no chance of Eadie liking any part which I am likely to write for him. Nothing will induce me to believe that, if he had really liked the role in *The Title* he would not have waited until the fate of *Marmaduke* was decided before putting on the play at the Royalty." [12] He then reviewed his experiences with Eadie, noting that Eadie had turned down *The Great Adventure* and had accepted *Milestones* with great reluctance. He had also refused *Sacred and Profane Love*.

Bennett then asked Pinker to return the £200 which Vedrenne and Eadie had paid for *The Title* and cancel the contract. In a postscript to the letter, he added that he wanted the matter settled before the "fate" of *The Title* was decided in order that he could not be accused of misconduct in the event the play was a success.[13] Pinker apparently dissuaded him from the course of action, and *The Title* opened at the Royalty on July 20 with C. Aubrey Smith as Mr. Culver, Eve Moore as

[11] *Letters*, I, 264n.
[12] Ogden Collection, July 18, 1918.
[13] *Ibid.*, July 18, 1918.

Mrs. Culver, Leslie Howard as John Culver, and Nigel Playfair as Sampson Straight.[14]

The play, despite its lack of a strong sexual theme, was a
success, perhaps to Bennett's surprise and certainly to his delight.
It continued to play to large audiences until the end of October,
when evening performances were replaced by matinees, a move
which resulted in a sharp drop in receipts. Noting the drop,
Bennett wrote to Pinker that the decision should "be reconsid-
ered at once." It was his opinion that the play drew "smart"
audiences "who would not be likely to go in the afternoon." He
gave as evidence the fact that a woman whom he knew had
been asked to dinner and the theater three times in a two week
period, "and in each case the play chosen was *The Title*."

*The Title* proved that the success of a play did not have to
depend on the exclusive concern with adultery and fornication.
Bennett made no comment on that proof, but increasingly during
1918 he had taken note of the change in attitude toward sex in
the popular drama of the day and was upset by what he saw. He
was equally disturbed by the increasing sexual frankness of
young women. In a journal entry for April 28 he recounted an
incident in the underground in which Mair had been addressed
in a friendly, open fashion by one of the girls working in the
Registry Department. She smiled at Mair and showed him her
meat ration card, ostensibly, according to Bennett, to demonstrate how full it was, but in reality to show Mair her name.
Bennett's attitude could not have been one of greater disapproval if the girl had thrown her arms around Mair's neck and
kissed him.[15]

On another occasion he recorded that "the sensual appeal is
now really very marked everywhere, in both speech and action,
on the stage. Adultery everywhere pictured as desirable, and
copulation generally ditto. Actresses play courtesan parts . . .
with gusto." Bewildered and almost despairing, he wrote that
*As You Were*, which he saw performed at the Pavilion in
October, was built almost entirely around sex. "Every scene

14 *Letters*, I, 264*n*.
15 *Journal*, 661.

turned on adultery, or mere copulation," he noted. "Even in the primeval forest scene, an adultery among gorillas was shown." [16]

*The Title* could not be charged with pandering to a public taste for the licentious. It is a straightforward comedy, rather old fashioned in its staidness, based on Mr. Culver's attempts to decline a knighthood over his wife's objection. There is also a problem concerning his daughter's deception about her articles in *The Echo*. John, Culver's son, home from school for the holidays, is the humorous youngster. Bennett stops just short of making him wear a cricket cap, something he would have done had the play been prewar. The love interest is carried by the daughter Hildegarde, who falls in love with Tranto, her editor.

There is some reasonably deft verbal wit in the play and an easy playfulness about it that is surprisingly attractive. The play moves swiftly and with innocent good humor. But it is difficult to understand how the same audience that made a roaring success of *As You Were* could have been kept in their seats by *The Title*. Perhaps the answer is that they were still a wartime audience and wanted above everything else to be diverted. *The Title* is amusing despite the cobwebs which hang from the set.

At about the time that Bennett was bringing *The Title* to completion, he took a step that, whatever its consequences for his writing, was of enormous importance for his emotional well-being. On April 11 he went to see Beaverbrook, who was now Minister of Information in the Lloyd George Government, about *Lloyd's Weekly News*. Bennett was planning a series for *Lloyd's;* and he wanted to know whether, if Beaverbrook bought the paper, there would be a change in the politics of the weekly. Beaverbrook said that he had no intention of buying the paper. But before responding to Bennett's question, he asked if Bennett would come into the Ministry of Information as director of British propaganda in France. He told Bennett that no one could know French psychology better than the author of *The Pretty Lady* and that he wanted his services.

Bennett agreed to consider the proposal. Five days later he wrote to Beaverbrook accepting the position. It was a decision

[16] *Ibid.*, 671, 670.

of great importance, the greatest, perhaps, since his decision to buy Comarques, although one with far happier consequences. A darkness began to lift from Bennett's spirit with his entry into Beaverbrook's ministry. He had at last found something of sufficient interest and challenge to renew his zest for living. It was not a force of the proper kind to rekindle his creative powers, but it restored his vitality. The number of references to his health began to decline after May. His neuralgia persisted, but the dyspepsia vanished. He began to feel strong again and alive. On May 10 he officially took on his new duties, referring to his first day in office as "rather a lark," beginning the day with a lunch given by the Ministry for the Allied journalists, at which he sat "between *Le Journal* and *Le Petite Parisien.*" His only complaint concerning his working arrangements were that he did not like his office and he did not like being on a separate floor from his staff.[17]

By the 14th he had settled down to the new routine and wrote in his journal with the enthusiasm of a boy released from school that he had "abandoned literature" until his services at the Ministry were no longer needed but that he would go on doing his journalism, although it was a "damned nuisance." He brought Miss Nerney down from Comarques and established her in his office; but the arrangement proved to be unsatisfactory because he felt that as long as she was in the Ministry office, she could not with propriety deal with his private business, and that business could not be neglected, war or no war. His solution was to sublet one of Pinker's offices and install Miss Nerney there. It was not an ideal arrangement; but since Pinker's offices were close to the Ministry building in Norfolk Street, it was a workable one and lasted until the end of the war.

Bennett was an immediate success with Beaverbrook in his role as director of propaganda for France. His reports were the most discerning that Beaverbrook had received since taking over the Ministry, but Bennett was soon to discover that efficiency and commonsense were not adequate to deal with all the intricacies of government life into which he was now entering. In an

17 *Journal*, 662.

effort to make the national observance of France's Day as successful as possible, he arranged to have the King attend a service at Westminster Abbey. "I thought," wrote the chastened Bennett after his plans collapsed, "that I had set in motion a great thing to my credit. It was not so. I was misled . . . and the whole thing had to be cancelled. Religion was at the bottom of the trouble." He had probably overlooked the fact that a Roman Catholic Mass could not be celebrated in Westminster Abbey and that the French diplomatic corps would be unable to attend an Anglican Mass. He left the details of his defeat unrecorded, but he closed the entry with the consoling observation that he had written the "British contribution to the first daily joint wireless message sent out to the world by Britain, France, and Italy together." [18]

In July, Beaverbrook asked him to take over responsibility for a second department in the Ministry, but for the time being Bennett put Beaverbrook off. A few days later Bennett stumbled into more trouble, this time with the War Cabinet. He had written a pro-France article which appeared in the *Observer* on July 15 and which was used by the *Daily Mail* to assail the government on its policy of secrecy regarding news releases. The War Cabinet sent a minute to Bennett reprimanding him for having written the article. Beaverbrook was furious and asked Bennett to draft a sharp reply which he would sign. The note was written, signed, and sent back to the Cabinet. Lloyd George immediately made a personal apology to Bennett and promised that the Cabinet minute would be amended. It was a journalist's dream come true. Not only was Bennett vindicated in his action, the mighty War Cabinet had apologized for its error in criticizing him.

By late summer of 1918, the war was grinding bloodily toward its end. All of the nation's efforts, however, continued to be directed toward maintaining a fighting stance. Bennett was devoting himself to Ministry work, and by the end of September he had assumed control of all propaganda except propaganda in enemy countries. He kept his excitement and his delight under tight Staffordshire control, but the brightness of his picnic

[18] *Ibid.,* 663.

spirits kept shining through the plain language in which he described his promotion to Pinker:

> "I am now not merely director of Propaganda at the M. of I., but *head* of the whole ministry, with authority over all departments, under the Minister himself. I cannot understand it, and don't like it. But I was not the man to refuse." [19]

The truth was that he did like "it" enormously. In the journal he admitted that the promotion was "the most marvelous, disconcerting, and romantic thing that ever happened to me. At any rate, whatever happens, I, an artist, shall have had the experience. It would be enormous fun except for the responsibility and the 3 A.M. worryings." [20]

Only once did he express genuine regret over what he might have lost by giving himself so thoroughly to government work. In early October he wrote in the journal, which has no entries for August and September, that his efforts to keep up with the journal and with notes had broken down "through pressure of work and neuralgia," and he expressed the fear that "priceless things" had been lost as a consequence. But there were compensations. The Treasury was sufficiently impressed with his work to give him a special grant of £100,000 to expand the activities of his department, and on October 18 Lord Rothermere gave a dinner in his honor at the Marlborough Club. Winston Churchill, then Minister of Munitions and a former journalist, was among those present.

His final weeks at the Ministry were unfortunately marred by Beaverbrook's sudden physical collapse. By the end of October his friend was so ill that his resignation was a certainty. Bennett went to see Beaverbrook and found him "bandaged and depressed." Shaken by his illness, he began to speak to Bennett and suddenly "burst into tears." " 'You know, Arnold,' " he said, " 'I'm bloody well *down!* My life has been all crisis. I was worth five millions when I was 27. And now this is a new crisis, and it's the worst.' " [21] Then he rallied and gradually became more cheerful. The following day Beaverbrook's resignation became

19 *Letters*, I, 266.
20 *Journal*, 667.
21 *Ibid.*, 672, and Unpublished Journal, October 30, 1918.

official. Bennett received word from the Cabinet that he was to continue in his position of director.

There were, however, only two weeks left for Bennett to serve the Ministry. News of the armistice was released on November 11, and five days later Bennett handed in his resignation. He had, in actuality, been dismissed from his post by a general liquidation order which came to him on a mimeographed sheet. "The behavior of the Cabinet to me was, of course, scandalous," he wrote. He found some consolation in the fact that many others had received the same summary treatment, but the knowledge must have provided little real comfort to his injured pride.

Bennett's greatest reward for his work at the Ministry, aside from the very significant one of improved mental health, was not to come to him for another seven years, when he began writing *Lord Raingo*. It was in *Lord Raingo* that he exploited his Ministry experiences and in the process produced one of the finest books of his career. Interestingly enough, however, the germ for *Lord Raingo* was in Bennett's mind at least as early as December, 1916. In "Observations" for December 23, he blasted the rigidity of civil servants and half humorously sketched the picture of a business man, "newly appointed Minister," stepping into his office his first morning and facing the entrenched hostility of the departmental staff. Sam Raingo's entrance into the Ministry of Records is not so dramatic, but nevertheless he has to move carefully among his staff.

The long pause between the end of the war and the writing of *Raingo* can be explained in a number of ways. He could hardly have written the kind of novel he had in mind without drawing political figures into the story, and he no doubt wanted some time to elapse before risking such portraits. He also needed time in which to establish distance between himself and the experiences with which he intended to deal. Bennett was also shrewd enough to guess that the years immediately following the war would be poor ones for "war" novels.

The single most compelling reason for the long wait, however, was probably that he was not emotionally ready to write the novel much before 1925. In the period immediately following the end of the war, his creative abilities were largely exhausted. From the completion of *The Pretty Lady* to the writing of *Mr. Prohack*, begun in late 1920, he wrote only four plays, of which only *The Title* had any quality. Then in 1922 he finished *Lilian*, a purely mechanical effort, and later in the year began *Riceyman Steps*, the turning point in his rejuvenation as a novelist. After a pause of two more years he began *Lord Raingo* with the knowledge that he was ready to do justice to his theme.[22]

Bennett met Dorothy Cheston in March, 1922, just four months after his formal separation from Marguerite. He could never marry her because of Marguerite's refusal to grant him a divorce, but she accepted his love and returned it in full measure. He began *Riceyman Steps* seven months after that meeting, and the novel proved to be the best he had written since *These Twain* and perhaps since *Clayhanger*, which he had completed in 1910. The conclusion is almost inescapable that it was his relationship with Dorothy Cheston that worked the miracle and restored his creative energies.

*Lord Raingo* is a tragedy in the same sense as *The Old Wives' Tale*. Both novels make the point that man is caught in time and cannot escape the consequences of that involvement. In the scene in which Sam Raingo examines the overturned car in which his wife was killed, he looks at the twisted wheels and the damaged radiator. Then he looks inside the car and finds the clock still running, "as indifferent as a god to human woe." Had Bennett stopped with that comment, he would have merely repeated what he had written in *The Old Wives' Tale*. But in *Raingo* he adds the further agony of placing happiness in Sam Raingo's hands, allowing him to fully understand the reality of that happiness, and then denying him the strength to close his fingers on it and claim it for his own. *Raingo* is not tragedy in

---

[22] The bound manuscript of *Lord Raingo*, which is in the Butler collection, is proof of the confidence with which Bennett wrote the novel. Written in his neat, meticulous hand, the penned lines run on page after page with scarcely a crossed-out word. Margins are scrupulously observed and every letter of every word is strongly and precisely formed as though it had been copied.

the classical sense. Sam Raingo is not destroyed by a flaw in his character but by the flaw of mortality.

It is the powerful working out of Raingo's fate and the clarity with which Raingo is presented that make the novel great. Bennett wrote with a conviction that carries the reader with him and makes the novel whole. The central effect to which all of the parts contribute is that man's hope that he can control his destiny is an illusion. But in addition to the satisfaction the student of Bennett derives from seeing the material of the novel being shaped with such skill, there is the realization that *Lord Raingo* is a culmination of years of personal struggle to discover and give artistic expression to the author's own emotional fulfillment.

On the strictly personal level he found that fulfillment after the war in Dorothy Cheston. On the artistic level he combined that personal triumph with another, his appointment to the Ministry of Information, and made of the two transcendent experiences, one of love and the other of ambition, the blood and bone of his novel.

As a fillip he gave Sam Raingo a title. Bennett wanted that honor but was disappointed in his hope. He turned down the offer of a knighthood late in 1918 with the comment that while he did not wish to be rewarded for his war work, he would accept some official recognition of his contribution to literature. His response was not the same thing as saying that he did not want a knighthood. Quite the opposite. But he had put himself in an awkward position with his play *The Title*, which was a sly attack on the government's cynical policy of granting titles as political bribes. Pound suggests that he may have been holding out for the Order of Merit. If such was the case, he was disappointed there also, and he did not even carry through his plan for securing a grant of arms.[23]

It was Lafourcade's belief that the ideas of Bennett's great novels such as *The Old Wives' Tale, Riceyman Steps,* and *Lord Raingo* could be traced back through earlier unsuccessful attempts to treat their themes. He considered *The Statue* (1908)

[23] Pound, *Arnold Bennett*, 279.

to be a "first draft" of *Lord Raingo* and an early demonstration of Bennett's interest in political figures. All of Bennett's biographers from Lafourcade on who have dealt with *Lord Raingo* have also acknowledged Bennett's great debt to Lord Beaverbrook, especially in those scenes in the novel which deal with the inner workings of government.

To acknowledge Bennett's debt to Beaverbrook is probably only the first step, however, in coming to an understanding of what Bennett was really doing with his material. The same point should be made about the story concerning Lord Rhondda [24] which Bennett heard from Walter Roch and recorded in the journal entry for Friday, January 23, 1925. In the account Bennett summarizes Rhondda's political career and makes special reference to "the mysterious woman whom nobody knew—the woman whose suicide really gave me the first idea for a novel." *Lord Raingo* follows in a general way the outline of the story recounted by Roch, and the obvious similarities between the careers of Sam Raingo and Lord Rhondda undoubtedly account for Lady Rhondda's insistence that Raingo was Rhondda thinly disguised.

Neither Beaverbrook's influence nor Roch's story, however, does more than illustrate how Bennett collected material. The true sources of his inspiration and his motivation existed in the emotional realities of his own life. Moved to write by these realities, he reached out and took from the material at his disposal that which was most useful to him. It was one of Bennett's distinctions as a novelist that when his creative faculties were functioning properly, he was always able to find material which could be shaped to his need.

The real key to *Lord Raingo* is the fact that it was the last book of the series, beginning with *The Price of Love*, which traces the slow change in Bennett's attitudes towards marriage and toward a man's chances for happiness in marriage. In *Lord Raingo* Bennett makes his final statement on the issue by having Raingo repudiate his marriage vows in favor of his love for

---

[24] David Alfred Thomas, 1st Viscount Rhondda, was Minister of Food from 1917 until his death in 1918.

Delphine. Of the three books which intervene between *The Pretty Lady* and *Lord Raingo*, only *Lilian* (1922) can be thought of as part of the series in question, and there is nothing in that novel to distinguish it, coming into the series only because it deals with a love affair between a young woman and a middle-aged man. *Mr. Prohack* (1922) is a comic novel written around the threadbare device of the unexpected legacy. *Riceyman Steps* is a throwback to the *Clayhanger* period and may have its closest association with the early *Anna of the Five Towns* (1901) and the miserly Ephriam Tellwright.

In addition to *Lilian* there are five novels which lead to *Raingo*. Each of the five deals with either the inadequacy of "traditional" marriage as a means to emotional and spiritual fulfillment or with tentative gropings outside of marriage for that fulfillment. *The Price of Love* describes a marriage in which the wife makes a conscious sacrifice of herself to her marriage. *These Twain* explores in detail the problem of two disparate personalities struggling to maintain a marriage and to retain their identities. *The Lion's Share* examines several kinds of marriage arrangements while at the same time giving a sympathetic portrait of the "new woman." *The Roll Call* is a return to the preoccupations of *These Twain;* but George Cannon, unlike Edwin Clayhanger, does not pretend to himself that he can be happy in his marriage. In *The Pretty Lady* marriage enters the story only as a device for giving the novel a "satisfying" ending. Real interest in the novel is centered in Hoape's liaison with Christine.

In *Raingo* Bennett brings marriage and the affair into simultaneous examination. Raingo's marriage is an unhappy one. His wife Adela is selfish, immature, incapable of managing a home, egotistical, and unpunctual. She is, in fact, very much like Marguerite. But she has a certain force of character or "presence" which gives her dignity. Rather than deal with the complications of a dual involvement for Raingo, Bennett kills Adela in an automobile accident early in the story.

Delphine, Raingo's mistress, is less convincingly drawn, perhaps because Bennett never satisfactorily accounts for the strong underlying strain of melancholy in her makeup, a darkness of spirit that leads her to suicide. It is also difficult to accept her unwillingness to become Raingo's wife. She is beautiful, intelligent, and efficient; but the thought of becoming Lady Raingo fills her with terror. It is interesting that she, like Christine in *The Pretty Lady*, is involved with a young soldier without being in love with him and is brought to disaster by that relationship.

What Raingo cherishes most in Delphine's love is her tenderness. Lying on his death bed, reflecting on what Delphine had meant to him, Raingo admits the value of her capacity for tenderness: "She had taught him tenderness. He had not known what tenderness was, he had been afraid and ashamed of tenderness, until he came under her tutelage. . . . Tenderness was her supreme quality, and it was one of the greatest qualities, a quality which might well atone for the absence of any other." [25]

Without Dorothy Cheston it is unlikely that Bennett could have written those lines. Without her it is unlikely that there would have been a Sam Raingo at all. One has only to compare the hardness of Gilbert Hoape with the compassion of Sam Raingo to see how Bennett's attitude toward the relationship between a man and a woman had changed. Cynicism is replaced by tenderness. Gilbert Hoape takes, but Sam Raingo has learned to give, and it is Delphine's love that opens his heart. Edwin Clayhanger engages in a battle of wills with Hilda, and the close of *These Twain* gives no hint that the struggle will cease. Gilbert Hoape, suspecting Christine of infidelity, wraps himself in his pride and walks away from her. Sam Raingo believes, wrongly, that Delphine has run away with another man; but he conquerors his resentment and goes on loving her.

*Lord Raingo* is balanced, in terms of emphasis, fairly evenly among three interests—Raingo's love affair with Delphine, his work at the Ministry, and his long decline into death. The final third of the book is devoted primarily to his illness and death. The treatment of Sam's illness is a remarkable *tour de force* and reminiscent of other deathbed scenes in Bennett's novels,

[25] Arnold Bennett, *Lord Raingo* (New York, 1926), 320.

such as the death of Darius Clayhanger, the succession of deaths in *The Old Wives' Tale*, the death of Auntie Hamps in *These Twain*, and that of Mrs. Maldon in *The Price of Love*. But in no other of his books is the process treated at such length. That Bennett is able to maintain the reader's interest for so many pages in Sam's slow dissolution is a tribute to his skill as a writer. While it remains one of the remarkable achievements in the history of novel writing, the question that niggles is whether or not it was worth doing. One may conclude that it was not, but it remains an astonishing performance.

In the love affair between Delphine and Sam, Bennett managed to skirt both sentimentality and absurdity. The reader is convinced of the genuineness of their love, but he is never allowed to forget that these two people are separated by a gulf of age and of interests. When the story opens, Raingo is fifty-five years old and sadly gone to fat. Delphine is twenty-nine. Bennett was fifty-eight when he began writing the novel and had been fifty-five when he met Dorothy Cheston. He was also fat. Raingo deliberately set out to possess Delphine because she had "just the qualities which he needed in a woman" and because he had been living "desolating days in the domestic aridity of Moze Hall." For Moze Hall it would be reasonable to read Comarques. It is interesting to note that Delphine had been on the stage for a brief period, like both Marguerite and Dorothy Cheston.

In the novel Bennett makes no pretense of an idyllic relationship. Rather, Raingo finds in Delphine an outlet for his love, a refuge from the stress of public life, and a deep gratification in being loved by her. She is passionate and beautiful, but Raingo's response to her physical charms is chiefly one of aesthetic appreciation. In one scene in her apartment, she sits on his lap kissing and caressing him; but the dalliance goes no further: "He ought to have been, he at his age, happy in her abandoned, enveloping youthfulness which squandered itself so generously upon him. But death was in his heart. His body made no response to hers." [26] There is pathos in the lines; and because Sam knows what he is losing, there is tragedy as well.

[26] *Ibid.*, 33.

Raingo's real passion, however, is his work at the Ministry; and in describing that involvement, Bennett gave expression to an enthusiasm he must have shared with his character. Lafourcade wrote that Raingo is "pre-eminently Bennett—the real Bennett, both what he was and what he wanted to be. . . ." [27] The entire Ministry section of the novel is presented with bubbling energy and an undiluted delight in the personalities and the events which form its context. The principal characters in the political part of the novel can be identified with statesmen of the war period. Tom Hogarth is Winston Churchill. Andy Clyth, the Prime Minister, is Lloyd George, although Clyth is given the thin disguise of a Scotch-Irish background rather than a Welsh ancestry. Lord Ockleford may be drawn on Lord Milner and Hasper Clews on Bonar Law. Though the game of "who's who" is interesting, it is not particularly important to an understanding of the novel. What is important is the way in which Bennett handles the political chicanery in the Ministry section of the novel. There is cynicism in the writing, but that tone may have come in by way of Lord Beaverbrook, who, as Bennett wrote to Richard, was showing him "hell with the lid off." [28]

Bennett did not really think of the world he was describing as being "hell with the lid off." On the contrary, he appears to have enjoyed it immensely, if Raingo's excitement and pleasure in what he was doing can be taken as a measure of Bennett's response. In Sam's first important interview with Andy Clyth, the Prime Minister gives him some insights into the power struggle going on between the Prime Minister and the War Office and the Admiralty. In the course of the discussion he refers to the Ministry of Records as being Sam's Ministry. The phrase "your Ministry" fills Sam with delight. And delight, a childlike if not childish delight, is the principal emotional response which Raingo has toward his ministerial responsibilities.

What had given Bennett his greatest joys as director of propaganda were those things which please Raingo in his ap-

[27] Lafourcade, *Arnold Bennett*, 201.
[28] Arnold Bennett, *Arnold Bennett's Letters to His Nephew* (New York, 1935), 109.

pointment: "He longed for this power [the Prime Minister's power], knowing that he could never have it, but absolutely resolved to get a kind of power nearly equal to it, to blaze somehow in the public eye by the light of his great deeds, and to encounter the most puissant ministers among his colleagues on level terms." Bennett had enjoyed ordering generals about when the opportunity offered, and he had hoped to make a splash by arranging for the King to go to Westminster Abbey on France's Day.

Five chapters in *Raingo* contain the principal impressions which Bennett used from his own experiences at the Ministry of Information.[29] In a general way, what happens to Raingo in those chapters can be read as a paraphrase of what happened to Bennett. Raingo prepares for his first morning at the Ministry by walking to Norfolk Street, where the Ministry of Information was also located, and as he approaches the building "the old habit of energetic command, weakened by years of inertia, came back to him in strength, and he exercised it first upon himself. An enormous undertaking awaited him, looming; he could deal with it and he would deal with it, more than adequately. All his talents grew alert within him." [30]

Having dealt satisfactorily with the menace of the hall-porter, Raingo is shown into his office and left alone. He takes off his hat and coat, pokes the fire, and then wonders, "Perhaps I ought to ring a bell." Bennett does an excellent job of showing Raingo's responses, which are a mixture of resolution, bravado, and nervous uncertainty, with the result that the reader admires Raingo's courage and at the same time smiles at his simplicity.

Raingo meets in rapid succession his three assistants—Mayden, Sir Ernest Timmerson, and Mr. Eric Trumbull. These men are probably composites of the men with whom Bennett worked in 1918. Mayden impresses Sam with his efficiency and managerial gift, but Sam remains somewhat wary of Mayden. He does not altogether trust the man. When Mayden leaves the office, however, Sam feels a rush of happiness: "He was happy, without

[29] See chapters 23, 24, 25, 26, and 51.
[30] Bennett, *Lord Raingo*, 107.

reserve, at the prospect of chicane, putting force against force, and of ultimate achievement. Also he meant to stamp himself on the consciousness of the country." [31]

Timmerson, Sam's second in command, is much less impressive than Mayden. He is humorless, unimaginative, and fearful. Although he is a wealthy man, he has none of Raingo's drive. Raingo thinks of him as a functionary; and Timmerson—the name itself suggesting the character of its bearer—is the closest Bennett comes to describing one of those despised civil servants whom Bennett attacked in his wartime journalism. In the interdepartmental wrangling between Military Intelligence and Sam's Ministry, Timmerson shows a distinct lack of courage. He refuses to accept the job of challenging the other department, and Raingo decides to handle the matter himself.

The passage of years had not caused Bennett's hatred of the War Department to subside. His journalism during the war years is full of that hatred, and in chapter twenty-five of *Raingo* it bursts out again. Military Intelligence sends out an order forbidding any officer of the department from setting foot in Sam's Ministry. The order is designed as an insult.

> Sam had a vision of a few highly-placed fellows sitting together in the vast home of the War Department, clanking spurs, and cogitating how they could get one in against these infernal mushroom ministries that were multiplying all around, and appropriating sacred, traditional privileges, and having the damned cheek to help to win the war. Too proud to be jealous, these Brahmins, and yet as raging jealous as the rivals of a favorite concubine in a harem! Germans they could understand and respect, Austrians they could like, but these dirty outsiders, from interfering Andy Clyth downwards, they detested and hated. The order was probably a hit at himself—rascally company-promoting millionaire with no father, no public-school, no style. [32]

Once having read Bennett's journalism of the war period, it is impossible to doubt that he was speaking for himself in the passage and that Raingo and Bennett are one. The attack, writ-

[31] *Ibid.*, 113.
[32] *Ibid.*, 116.

ten seven years after the close of the war, shows how deeply Bennett's resentment of the "privileged" had bitten into his mind. Raingo smiles at the petty order: "It was shocking of him to be amused, but he was amused. He had been born without the precious faculty for righteous indignation. He thought simply: 'This is what human nature is.' " Bennett may have thought that he was equally detached, but the violence of his language gives away the violence of his feelings.

Eric Trumbull, the director of propaganda for France, is an appealing character, who at once delights Sam and exasperates him. Trumbull developed an absurd scheme for winning over the French by distributing pamphlets in France proving that many English gardens are as formal as French gardens. For all of his skill in handling men, Sam decides that Trumbull is going to be too much for him and sends his director on a tour of France to get rid of him.

There is very little in the novel about Raingo's routine work. What interested Bennett in his job and what interests Raingo is the chance to possess a share of the power wielded by the Prime Minister. Money had given Bennett a boost into the squirearchy, his journalism had made him a national figure with the power to influence the opinions of millions of readers, and his appointment to the Ministry of Information had given him a taste of political power. Raingo's frank enjoyment of his peerage and his position as Minister are a reflection of Bennett's own desire to have an important role to play in the world's eyes and the power to play it as he chose. *Lord Raingo* is at once a record of Bennett's own achievement and his fantasy of success.

It is less easy to say exactly where Bennett stood in relation to the closing chapters of the novel, which describe Raingo's death. In the journal entry for January 23, 1925, Bennett wrote that he intended to have a "very great death scene" in the novel. It had been put into his mind by Roch's description of Rhondda's death. Death in Bennett's novels is one of the realities. It is not Whitman's welcome deliverer nor Eliot's snickering Footman. It is simply death, and like life, meaningless and inscrutable. Bennett's refusal to find meaning in either life or death is part of his inheritance from the French Naturalists, but the inheritance does not explain his preoccupation with death.

As we have seen, his father's death made a deep impression on Bennett and was rendered in detail in Darius Clayhanger's dying, while his mother's death is reproduced in the demise of Auntie Hamps in *These Twain*. In most of his serious books he involves the reader in the death of at least one of the characters; and, as is the case in *The Old Wives' Tale*, with all of the major characters. His concern with dying may be better understood if one remembers that while Bennett made no effort to explain life, except in *The Glimpse*, he often referred to its mystery as in the scene in which Sophia gazes at the corpse of Gerald Scales. Death, equally mysterious, is the second mystery through which Bennett's characters pass. Love is the third. Together they form the basis of Bennett's serious novels. Bennett paid little attention to birth, but then, he had had no children until 1926 when his daughter Virginia was born to Dorothy Cheston Bennett. What Bennett had not had some personal experience with, he very wisely did not attempt to describe, with certain exceptions, such as the public execution described in *The Old Wives' Tale*.

He employed the same techniques in portraying death that he used in developing his characters. He amassed a staggering quantity of detail and presented it in such a way that the reader is completely encircled by it and has the sense of having witnessed something real. In most of his novels, however, the process of dying is viewed objectively through the eyes of one of the characters, such as Edwin Clayhanger, who sits by Auntie Hamps as she lies dying, or Rachel Fleckring, Louis Fores, and Mrs. Tams, listening to the last loud terrible breathing of Mrs. Maldon echoing through the silent house. Very rarely does the reader have a glimpse of what is passing in the mind of the character dying.

In *Lord Raingo* Bennett continued to describe Sam's thoughts and sensations to the end, shifting away from them at intervals to describe the life going on around Sam in the house. It was pointed out earlier that Bennett took the idea for a deathbed scene from Lord Rhondda's death, but he probably had Beaverbrook's illness and consequent resignation from his Ministry post in mind as he wrote. Sam, like Beaverbrook, is at the height of his achievement as director of a ministry when he is rendered helpless by sickness. Although Sam is not given the words, his mood is occasionally that which Beaverbrook expressed when he suddenly burst out, "You know, Arnold, I'm bloody well *down!*"

As Sam approaches the final crisis, the entire staff of the house collect on the stairs and the landing outside his room, "drawn forward by the sinister and irrisistible attraction of approaching death." As they wait the lights in the house sink lower and lower. The generator is not running with sufficient speed to keep up the current, but everyone thinks, "how fitting, how impressive, how supernatural. . . ."

With the atmosphere prepared for a solemn and sentimental close to Sam's life, Bennett suddenly introduces the abominable Wrenkin, the head gardener, who is devoted to Sam with an "acid passion," among the company on the stairs. Almost overcome with emotion and furious with himself for his weakness, Wrenkin goes off to speed up the generator. And just before Sam dies the lights in the house come up to their full brightness, a brightness which Sam perceives before passing into his final unconsciousness. Wrenkin's appearance gives an ironic twist to the death scene, contributing to the ambiguity of the ending created by Sam's whispering his wife's name as he dies.

In following Raingo's thoughts through the long hours of his illness, Bennett makes his one concession in the novel to the revolution in presentation of character evident in such works as *A Portrait of the Artist as a Young Man*, *Pilgrimage*, and *Mrs. Dalloway*, in which character is illuminated from the inside outwards rather than from the outside inwards as in such novels as *The Man of Property* or *The Old Wives' Tale*. Aside from the concession mentioned above, *Lord Raingo* is written in a style that was conventional to the point of being nearly archaic.

In certain respects *Lord Raingo* is a thoroughly Victorian novel. It is about money, love, power, and the uses of power. It is also a novel of ambition, and Sam Raingo bears some resemblance to Becky Sharp in his shrewd maneuvering for social and political position. The form, however, is not dead. Novels like *Raingo* are still being written (C. P. Snow is one modern practitioner of the type); and the influence of Joyce, Richardson, and Woolf has by no means put an end to the drawing of character in the manner employed by Bennett.

Nevertheless, *Lord Raingo* was late in coming; and it is difficult not to conclude that it was the slowness of Bennett's own emotional evolution that delayed it for so long. There is even a suggestion that Bennett saw that evolvement in the same way. When Sam sits holding Delphine on his lap, he experiences simultaneously the joy of holding her and the terror of knowing that he is a sick man well past his prime. By 1925 Bennett knew all about the treachery of the body. His had failed him frequently enough, as the journal testifies.

*Lord Raingo* was Bennett's last great novel. The *Imperial Palace* was published in 1930, but despite its length it is inferior to *Lord Raingo*. When Bennett laid Sam Raingo to rest, he exorcized a ghost that had walked with him for many years, the ghost of his own unhappiness, his own lack of fulfillment. After *Lord Raingo*, journalism, plays, and short stories claimed his attention until he gave in to the longstanding urge to write a novel about a great hotel. But after *Lord Raingo* he wrote nothing of such an intensely autobiographical nature and nothing so fine.

# X

# ON THE CANVAS

Aside from the largely hidden troubles with his health which were to grow in intensity during the first months of 1918, Bennett began the year in a quiet way. He had spent the Christmas holidays at Comarques; and except for a few days in London during the first week of January, he continued at Comarques until January 13. He remained away from London for several reasons, among them his desire to work on *The Pretty Lady* and to spend some time with Richard, who was home on holiday. There are several references to Richard in the journal during these weeks; and Bennett's attitude toward the boy, if not exactly fatherly, is warm. In one of the entries he recorded having smoked too many cigarettes, "ostensibly to provide Richard with tobacco ash for chemical experiments." [1]

The work on *The Pretty Lady*, as has already been discussed, was going badly; but Bennett did not spend all his free hours working on the book or brooding over his problems with it. He reread some of Milton, being reminded of the poet by Richard's remarking at dinner that his English master at Oundle had once set him the task of memorizing forty lines of "L'Allegro" in forty-five minutes. "What a fool of a master," was Bennett's response; and his judgment about the teacher's capabilities was not softened by the fact that the man had told Richard's class that " 'your Hall Caines, Arnold Bennetts, and H. G. Wellses will pass away and be forgotten. Classics will remain.' " Bennett was in no mood to be told that his work was without value. He was having altogether too much trouble in producing it to take the criticism lightly.

In his last week at Comarques he read the Hammonds' *Town Laborer 1760–1832* [2] and was at first intrigued and then repelled

[1] *Journal*, 646.
[2] John Lawrence Hammond and Barbara Hammond, *The Town Laborer 1760–1832: The New Civilization* (London, 1917). The Hammonds were early

by what he read. Having completed the first hundred pages of
the book, he wrote, "there is undoubtedly a pleasure in reading
recitals of horrible injustice and tyranny"; but his pleasure
turned to disgust when he reached the chapter on child labor.
"It exceeded limits in its physicalness," he complained, retaining
enough of his objectivity, however, to regret the fact that the
book had not been available to him when he wrote the "child
chapter" in *Clayhanger*. "I could have made that chapter more
appalling than it is" was his conclusion.[3]

On January 15 he returned to London to resume bachelor
life at the RTYC. On reaching London, he went to the Webbs's
for lunch and then hurried from there to the Reform Club to
join the Writers' Group hearing J. A. Spender's summary of the
political situation. That evening he and a group of his friends
went to Sacha Guitry's *Sleeping Partners,* which he found delightful. There is a bounce in the entire entry for the 15th which
reflects remarkably good spirits.

For the rest of the month he lived in London, returning to
Comarques for the weekends, and struggled with his novel. He
reread Balzac's *Une Double Famille* for the third time and still
found the ending confusing but the book excellent. In the last
two years of the war he returned increasingly to the French
writers. It is probable that in the breakdown of his creative
powers he was going back to those works that had been so
powerfully inspirational to him as a young man. Their magic,
however, had weakened. In fact he was discovering that none
of the old devices for stimulating his imagination worked. On
January 20 he went to the Leicester Galleries to look at William
Dyson's war drawings in the hopes of getting ideas for his novel,
but he came away disappointed. His "novel-cerebration," as he
called it, had not been activated.

On rare occasions he and Marguerite entertained guests together at her Oxford Street flat, the Galsworthys being among
the few mentioned in the journal. One evening, after dinner,

members of the Fabian Society and shared the Webbs's conviction that detailed sociological research would provide the evidence necessary to influence
social legislation.
3 *Journal,* 646.

there was an air-raid warning; and everyone, including the cook, went down to the basement to wait for the danger to pass. Bennett was impressed by Galsworthy's chivalrous treatment of the women, especially the cook. "He treated the cook with as much respect as the other women and even gave her a chocolate," Bennett recorded. Such a comment is a reminder that although Bennett had come from modest circumstances, he had come from a class that employed servants and were not servants themselves.

During February he showed a marked increase in his interest in political affairs. He lunched regularly with such men as A. G. Gardiner, J. A. Spender, and Masterman. The subject of their conversation was either the progress of the war or the projected policies of the Liberal Party. The Writers' Group invited Sir Edward Grey to lunch at the Café Royal; a few weeks later, the group invited Asquith to a dinner at the Reform Club. Bennett praised Asquith's deportment, but he could not refrain from recording that while the Liberal Party's leader wore a "good" silk shirt, "his overcoat and soft hat were ridiculous." Coming as the criticism does among comments on Asquith's intellectual powers, the sneering remark shows the degree to which Bennett's admiration for the former prime minister had declined; and although he continued to respect Asquith, it was not with the same uncritical respect he had given him two years earlier.

Bennett's criticisms were always direct, however, and given with the force of a royal pronouncement. In late March he lunched at the Webbs's and was told by Sidney Webb that the war news had so upset his wife that she was unable to sleep. To counteract the effect of the news, he had been forced to exaggerate his optimism. "It was one of the rare human touches," Bennett wrote, "I have noticed in the said household." "However," he added dryly, "they were soon off on the misdeeds of the [postwar] Reconstruction Committee." [4]

In early April he went to the House of Commons to witness Lloyd George's introduction of the new Man Power Bill, which

[4] *Ibid.,* 657.

was to raise the military age for the purpose of extending conscription and for conscripting Ireland. Bennett gave a detailed description of the Press Gallery, for which he had a ticket, and of the crowded Commons with Lloyd George, Churchill, Bonar Law, Cecil, and Balfour along the front bench to the Speaker's right. He was to use details of his impressions of the House when he came to write the account of Raingo's visit to hear Andy Clyth present his Man Power Bill.[5] One of the things Bennett noticed about the Press Gallery was that one could not lean in corners without knocking one's head against the projections of the elaborate woodcarving, and Sam Raingo found that he could not lean back in his seat without bumping his head. Bennett also took note of the other galleries and saw in the Ladies' Gallery a beautiful woman who was just past her prime and whose complexion was "going." Sam sees the same woman and notes that her complexion is withering. Bennett lifted the entire Press Gallery episode in the novel directly from his journal, even to the detail of the sound of telegraph keys tapping behind the Press Gallery.

His treatment of Lloyd George in the journal is devastating. With deliberate malice he referred to the Prime Minister's "cheap effects" of looking around the room as if he were challenging his opponents, and dropping his "unpleasant Nonconformist voice" when speaking the most important word in a sentence. The whole thing, Bennett wrote, was like "a Lyceum melodrama," "a vast make-believe, with an audience of which a large part was obviously quite unintelligent and content with the usual hollow rot." But when Bennett came to describe Andy Clyth's speech, he glossed over the banalities and the muddle and concentrated on the power which Andy commanded. It was a power which Sam Raingo envied, and one wonders just how much of that envy was Bennett's.

Following his entry into the Ministry of Information in the second week of May, he became increasingly involved in semipolitical functions, such as official dinners and receptions for journalists, while at the same time struggling to carry on his

[5] Bennett, *Lord Raingo*, 79–84, and *Journal*, 657–58.

own journalism and finish the work connected with writing and producing *The Title*. Finally, at the end of July the pressures of work and ill health had increased to the point that he was forced to abandon his journal; and from July 30 to October 4 he made no entries at all.

The tone of the entries from October to the close of the war is almost uniformly somber. His entries are principally a record of his activities connected with the Ministry and reflect the pre-occupations of a man thoroughly engrossed in his work. Only two entries show flashes of his old humor. One concerned the announcement of the Austrian demands for a separate armistice with the Allies, which was announced by the press on October 28. Bennett recorded that in passing along Oxford Street he heard a newsman shouting, " 'Evening News. Last edition. All abaht it. Tonight's and tomorrow night's too. Only one German left.' " The second was a story told him by James Barrie, who had Asquith to dinner and dressed up Asquith's daughter-in-law and another girl as housemaids. The girls served the dinner without Asquith's making any comment about the girls; but after dinner he said to Barrie, "One of those maids is extraordinarily like my daughter-in-law.' " [6]

He was at Comarques on the weekend preceding the Armistice; and when he came to town on Monday, November 11, he went straight to the Ministry with the news of the war's end being shouted by newsboys in the streets and reported that the girls on his staff got very excited and had to be calmed. He drove to the Wellington Club for lunch through large crowds on Pall Mall, which increased through the day until by evening the city was choked with a celebrating multitude, especially in the vicinity of Piccadilly Circus, where he found it almost impossible to cross the street. There was shouting, he wrote, but "nothing terrible or memorable." The cold rain that was falling did not drive away the crowds, but on the following day it rained again, prompting Bennett to declare that the rain was "an excellent thing to damp hysteria and Bolshevism." His final comment on the Armistice day celebrations was recorded by the

[6] *Journal*, 673.

artist in him: "Last night I thought of the lonely soldiers in that crowd. No one to talk to. But fear of death lifted from them." [7]

The Armistice brought an end to his work at the Ministry; and after his mandated resignation on November 14 he began slowly to relax the pace of his work, going off for weekends to the Wellses at Easton Glebe, to Beaverbrooks at Cherkley Court, and to Sir Frederick Keeble's house in Weybridge. (In 1920, Keeble, a naturalist, married Lillah McCarthy, who had been divorced from Granville-Barker in 1918.) Although he made most of these visits alone, Marguerite went with him to the Galsworthys' house, Grove Lodge, in Hampstead where they met John Masefield and his wife. Bennett recorded that Masefield was "gloomyish" but that he got on well with Mrs. Masefield. As always he found Galsworthy "very nice" and in an explosion of enthusiasm described Ada Galsworthy as "adorable." If he was not simply punning on Mrs. Galsworthy's name, the epithet, coming from Bennett, was practically a declaration of passion.

Throughout 1918 and through all the troubles, exasperations, and occasional moments of exhilaration which the year brought him, Bennett labored to write his series for the *Daily News* and the *NS;* and although he was to say later that journalism was "a damn nuisance," he found it gratifying to command an audience that would receive his opinions with respect if not always with agreement. In January he began collecting material for an article on the future of the Liberal Party, which was published on February 13 by the Westminster News Agency in a syndicate of provincial papers. Giving Pinker directions to collect the £21 due on the article, he noted that "Asquith said that his article was the best thing on Liberal politics that he had seen during the war. . . . Still I want paying for it all the same," he added.[8] The two comments reveal the dual nature of Bennett's attitude toward his journalism. He was proud of his ability to impress a man in Asquith's position. It also gave him a feeling of helping to shape the nation's policies; but that satisfaction was balanced by the brusque, commonsensical conviction that cash is

[7] *Ibid.,* 674.
[8] Ogden Collection, April 20, 1918.

better than praise. To point to either one of these aspects of his personality and to say that this is the real Bennett would be to oversimplify. He was a complex man who was constantly being thought a very simple man. One is tempted to believe that Bennett was pleased to be thought simple. It fitted the public image he had so sedulously cultivated for his own protection, but it is not certain that he always knew which was his real self and which was the facade.

Pressed as he was for time in the opening months of 1918 and dogged by ill health, he still felt compelled to accept a further burden of journalism in the form of a weekly column of 1,500 words in *Lloyd's Weekly News*. The compulsion came from his need for money, and *Lloyd's* was prepared to pay him £100 a week for the series. Initial arrangements were made in the last days of March, but the series was not to begin until the middle of May. He was anxious to postpone beginning the articles, first because of the pressure of completing *The Title* and then because of his decision to enter the Ministry of Information. It would have been a relief to him to drop the series when it became clear that his work at the Ministry was going to claim so much of his time; but because he received no salary for his work at the Ministry, he was obliged to keep on with his journalism as a source of steady income.

The agreement with *Lloyd's* was for three months and terminable after that period with a month's notice. On July 18 Bennett wrote to Pinker that he did not think *Lloyd's* would renew the contract. He appeared to have had no reason for thinking that the agreement would be terminated and was probably protecting himself against disappointment. The precaution was unnecessary; *Lloyd's* did renew. At the same time Gardiner was urging Bennett to write a weekly piece instead of a semiweekly article for the *Daily News*, proof of the undiminished drawing power of Bennett's name. Beaverbrook wrote in his commemorative article for the *Montreal Star*, quoted earlier, that only one other writer during the later war years had a greater ability to influence sales of newspapers by the appearance of his material in their pages. Beaverbrook did not name the other writer, but it was probably H. G. Wells.

Bennett told Gardiner that he would think about the offer; but that if he did, the price would have to be raised. In September, Gardiner asked him again and increased payment for the fortnightly pieces to £35. Bennett, however, never took up the option to write for the *Daily News* on a weekly basis. Welcome as the money would have been, demands on his time were too great to permit his doing it.

Further proof of the favorable attention Bennett's journalism was attracting was Fisher Unwin's request in July to be allowed to republish the *Daily News* articles in book form. Bennett refused with surprising firmness. "I have adopted this attitude in accordance with my own instinct . . ." he wrote to Pinker, observing that the agent had at an earlier date reread a number of the articles and agreed with the decision.[9] Bennett was not unhappy with what he had written for the paper, but he may have felt that the material was too topical to have a permanent interest. It is also possible that he did not want his hasty and partisan judgments given the permanency a book would bring them.

In the closing weeks of 1917 Bennett had agreed to write another series for *Cosmopolitan;* and Doty, editor at *Cosmopolitan,* had asked especially for material with a French flavor. On February 10 Bennett sent Pinker the first article of the series. "They asked for French articles," he wrote. "There is no other French stuff like this except *Paris Nights,* and it may be too subtle for its public." [10] He was concerned that he had misjudged his market; and three days later he wrote Pinker again to say that if *Cosmopolitan* did not like the piece, he would "revert to philosophy for them" and that the French material might appeal to someone else.

His anxiety was well founded. Doty cabled Pinker in early March to the effect that the article was "too subtle" for the *Cosmopolitan* and that he would prefer to have the earlier type of essay. He followed that cable with another asking if Bennett would like to write on "the romantic and highly important work

[9] *Ibid.,* July 20, 1918.

[10] Ogden Collection, February 10, 1918. Bennett published the travel sketches, *Paris Nights,* in 1913.

of the motor car in War time." [11] Pinker suggested the idea to Bennett, provoking an immediate response: "As regards the *Cosmopolitan*, the Romance of the Motor Car be damned! I think this meets the case." [12] Doty tried again. This time he suggested that Bennett write on American types in England or on the status of women after the war.

Bennett chose, however, to write philosophical pieces of the sort he had done the previous year. But the idea of writing a series of connected essays on the subject of women stuck in his mind, and in the fall he wrote to Pinker that he would do a 40,000 word book on women, provided that Pinker could get a good serial price for it in the United States. Pinker placed the book with *Cosmopolitan* and with *Cassell's Magazine*, both of which began serializing it in December, 1919. His agent wanted to give *Harper's* first refusal on volume publication, but Bennett insisted that the book go first to George Doran. "I know that nothing binds me to Doran," he wrote. "Nevertheless, he is my regular publisher, and I should not be easy in my mind if anything was done behind his back." [13]

Doran published *Our Women: Chapters on the Sex Discord* in 1920. The book contains little that is really new, in spite of Bennett's promise to do some "plain speaking" and to deal with subjects "not often dealt with." In the chapters "Masculine View of Sex Discord" and "Feminine View of Sex Discord" Bennett describes a quarrel between a man and his wife, Jack and Jill, first from Jack's point of view then from Jill's. Jack and Jill quarrel over the gardener Snagge, and the quarrel grows to encompass their thirteen-year-old son, who is home on holidays. Jack and Jill are clearly Bennett and Marguerite. Snagge is Lockyer, the head gardener at Comarques, appearing under yet another name. Bennett had used the same material four years earlier in his short story "The Muscovy Ducks." There is no child in the short story, but Richard had not then come to live with Bennett. The quarrel is unresolved. Bennett decides lamely

[11] Butler Collection, March 19, 1918.
[12] Ogden Collection, March 22, 1918.
[13] *Letters*, I, 268.

that Jack and Jill are very much alike and therefore bound to act as they do. Bennett had said all that he had to say about why husbands and wives fight. *Our Women* repeats the arguments.

The articles which Bennett wrote for *Lloyd's Weekly News* were of the same type as those he wrote for the *NS* and the *Daily News*. By 1918 his subjects for the series were fixed, and he was able to produce the pieces with a minimum of strain. Care for disabled soldiers, support for the League of Nations, investment in war bonds, and general support for Labor were the principal topics with which Bennett dealt in the *Daily News* and in *Lloyd's Weekly*.[14] On June 9, however, *Lloyd's* carried an article by him titled "There is No Smoke without Fire," which was far livelier than the majority of the pieces.

The article was prompted by a bizarre court case currently being tried which had attracted the nation's attention and was rapidly inflaming its prejudices. The principals in the case were Maud Allan, the actress, and Pemberton Billing, M.P. Billing, who was also editor of the radically conservative and jingoistic paper *The Vigilante*, was brought to trial on a charge of slander. He had accused Maud Allen of being a sexual pervert, basing his claim on the evidence of her performance in Oscar Wilde's *Salomé*. Not only did Billing escape conviction, he won a kind of national acclaim for his insistence that the Germans had a "Black Book" containing the names of large numbers of upper-class English men and women and a list of their sexual abberations. He claimed further that the Germans were forcing those listed into taking a pro-German position in order to avoid the scandal of having their peccadillos made public. His absurd claims traded heavily and successfully on war fear and class hatred.

In his article Bennett attempted to argue that there was no unnatural vice in *Salomé* and that, as a consequence, Maud Allan's performance had nothing of the unnatural in it: "It is a play about a well-known episode in Scripture. The episode is

---

[14] Beginning in June, 1918, *Lloyd's Weekly News* became *Lloyd's Sunday News*. Bennett's second contract with *Lloyd's* expired in September, 1918, and was not renewed.

disagreeable, and the plot of the play is disagreeable. . . . It is not indecent. . . . It was never forbidden by the censor on the ground of indecency. . . . The notion that *Salomé* displays unnatural vice is not merely wrong; it is silly." It was a spirited defense of Maud Allan and those others whom Billing was vilifying, but it was probably not a very accurate assessment of the play. Despite the "restoration" of Wilde's reputation, which Robert Ross had accomplished almost single-handed by 1906, to a large segment of the British public Wilde was still the symbol of moral decadence; and Billing had demonstrated that he knew his countrymen by striking at the upper-class through Maud Allan and the notorious *Salomé*.

By the end of December, 1918, Bennett had only his weekly piece for the *NS* to write, having abandoned all of his other journalism, including the *Daily News* articles, in order to give almost full time to his playwriting. After his success with *The Title* the previous summer and the loss of his Ministry job shortly after the Armistice, he threw himself into writing and making arrangements to write plays. His major incentive was the need for money, and the quickest way for him to get a lot of it was to write a hit play. Bennett never recovered from the financial windfall he had had with *Milestones* and *The Great Adventure*. Those two plays had been largely responsible for establishing the standard of living which he struggled to maintain throughout the war years and after, and they also gave him a distorted picture of what he could expect to make from writing for the stage. He wrote many more plays that were failures than were successes, but he wrote a play that was moderately successful just often enough to keep him hopeful of turning the trick with his next attempt.

The first play he committed himself to write after leaving the Ministry was for Lillah McCarthy, and he agreed to have it completed by the end of January, 1919. It was a ridiculously short time to allow himself—about seven weeks—but the need for money and a certain tendency to show off led him to commit himself to the task. The formal agreement for *Judith* was not drawn up until December 21, at which time he complained that he had not yet started the play and should be given a two-week extension. No extension was granted, however, and he began the writing. A month later he noted in the journal that he had completed the play in twenty-three days, during which time he had suffered from "several light headaches but no dyspepsia worth a damn."

Lillah McCarthy was very enthusiastic about the play. Shortly after its delivery, Bennett met her on the street; and she was so excited over *Judith*, as he recorded later, that he was afraid she would throw her arms around his neck. Marguerite was with him at the time, which may have contributed to his anxiety. Marguerite had a remarkably close association with the production of *Judith*. She contributed her ideas to stage and costume designs and to certain other aspects of the production. That Bennett allowed her such a degree of participation suggests that he may have been trying to give her a more active part in his life or that he was so overburdened with work her help became essential.

The play opened in Eastbourne on Saturday, April 5, 1919, at the Devonshire Park Theatre. The approaching opening was exciting in itself, but there was an element of danger connected with the production that added spice to the excitement. The potential source of trouble was Lillah McCarthy's performance in the role of Judith as seductress and the costume she wore to entice Holofernes to his destruction. Bennett's description of the costume is a miracle of clinical detachment. He might have been writing about a horse in a new kind of harness:

> Above a line drawn about ½ inch or one inch above the *mont de Vénus* she wore nothing except a four inch band of black velvet round the body hiding the breasts and a similar perpendicular band of velvet starting from between the breasts and going down to the skirt and so hiding the navel. Two thin shoulder straps held this contrivance in position. Bracelets and rings of course. The skirt was slit everywhere and showed the legs up to the top of the thigh when she lay down there at Holofernes's feet. She looked a magnificent picture thus, but a police prosecution would not have surprised me at all.[15]

15 *Journal*, 684.

The play was sufficiently well received in Eastbourne to encourage Lillah McCarthy to take it to London, where it opened at the Kingsway Theatre on Wednesday, April 30. The first night was a sell-out, and Bennett estimated that receipts were £150. The audience, he wrote, reacted favorably to the play; but the critical response in the press the next day was "without exception unfavorable." The Sunday editions were less critical of the play itself but were greatly agitated by Lillah McCarthy's nudity, deploring it in the strongest terms. During its first week the play brought in £900, but by May 12 it was clear that *Judith*—despite Lillah's costume—was a failure. Bennett wrote that he had never before turned out a play in which he had taken such an interest in the technical aspects of the production; and although it seems an unlikely and potentially explosive combination of personalities, he and Marguerite and Lillah McCarthy worked together without any major disruptions. But no amount of effort could have saved the play.

Probably the least successful of Bennett's plays, from a commercial point of view, and one for which he nevertheless claimed a degree of excellence, was *Don Juan*. After 1914 the play kept popping up like a restless ghost. At intervals Bennett tried by craft and blackmail to get the play performed, but always unsuccessfully. In March of 1918 it materialized again, this time in a conversation in which Bennett suggested to Frank Swinnerton that *Don Juan* be brought out in an "edition deluxe." The idea was taken up with Spaulding at Chatto and Windus; and while Spaulding was willing to undertake publication, he pointed out to Bennett that he had a very limited supply of paper at his disposal. Bennett decided, however, to go ahead with the printing of 200 copies. By April 14 Bennett had page proofs in hand and was so disappointed in their quality, a disappointment shared by Swinnerton, that he asked Spaulding to stop work on the book. The play was eventually published in 1923 by T. Werner Laurie in a private edition.

Bennett did not forget the play after deciding not to go ahead with its printing, and he never resigned himself to the fact that the play would not be produced. On December 13 he wrote to

Pinker giving him instructions on how the contract for *Judith* was to be drawn up, informing him that as part of the arrangement Lillah McCarthy had agreed to take *Don Juan* and to produce it within a stated time after the close of *Judith*. But he wanted two contracts drawn, because he had hopes of interesting Basil Dean in the play. If the interest was serious, he continued, he would not "force" the play on Lillah McCarthy. In the end no one produced the play.

December, 1918, proved to be a busy month for Bennett as far as play arrangements were concerned. On the 13th he wrote a second letter to Pinker outlining a proposed contract with Edyth Goodall, the actress, who was going into theater management with the financial backing of Lord Lathom. Bennett promised to do a play for her. The day before he had committed himself to write a play for Basil Dean, who was also venturing into theater management. By the end of the month Bennett was under contract to write four plays in 1919. Lillah McCarthy was to have *Judith;* Edyth Goodall, *Body and Soul;* Basil Dean, *The Bright Island;* and Vedrenne and Eadie, *The Love Match.* Except for *Judith*, options on all the plays lapsed.[16] Dean did, however, produce in the fall of 1919 *Sacred and Profane Love*, the play that Bennett had originally written for Doris Keane in 1916, but which she had subsequently rejected.[17]

Contracting to write plays was not Bennett's only interest in the theater in 1918. In October, Sir Nigel Playfair, actor-manager and playwright, told Bennett that he was trying to buy the Lyric Opera House in Hammersmith. It was Playfair's intention to start a theater in which worthwhile plays could be produced that might not have enough box office appeal to attract the major producers. He also said that one of the "ring" of London theater managers had made a higher bid than his to

16 *Letters*, I, 276n.
17 The play opened in Liverpool at the Playhouse on Monday, September 15. It was a success and Bennett took two curtain calls. The play went to the Aldwych in London on October 1 and ran for one hundred performances. Frohman and Company produced it the following year in the United States, and Bennett's royalties from the first week's run in New York were £350. "My faith in the theatre as a means of artistic expression was, of course, instantly reestablished," he wrote. "It would be."

prevent the theater from falling into his hands. Whatever the truth of the charge, the idea for such a theater appealed to Bennett; and he promised that if Playfair could get the theater, he would undertake to raise £2,000 for the endeavor.

Within a few weeks Playfair got the theater and told Bennett that he had it. Bennett kept his part of the bargain and by November 3 had collected £4,000, twice the promised amount.[18] He had also thoroughly interested himself in Playfair's scheme.[19] The two men decided to form a Board of Directors and invited Alistair Tayler to join them. Bennett became the chairman. The enterprise proved to be both an artistic as well as a financial success. "The Lyric Theatre," Bennett wrote in his introduction to Nigel Playfair's *The Story of the Lyric Theatre Hammersmith* (London, 1925), "has made handsome profits, on the policy of trusting the intelligence of the public." Marguerite, however, expressed the opinion in *My Arnold Bennett* that in the end her husband lost at least as much money as he made in theatrical ventures, but Bennett's association with the Lyric was an extremely rewarding one, whatever his financial gains or losses may have been.

Bennett came to the end of 1918 full of hope that he was about to launch himself on a successful and lucrative career as a dramatist. Whatever his hopes were in that direction, he could not have had any illusions about the future of his marriage. Throughout the years since the outbreak of the war, Bennett had watched his relationship with Marguerite grow more and more strained. The constant clashing of their personalities had steadily worn away the affection and mutual regard which had made their marriage workable; and by the last year of the war, they were little more than wary antagonists sharing a common weekend home.

For three years Bennett had increasingly withdrawn from his wife's company, using every excuse to remain in London and to live among his friends there, returning at intervals to Comarques

[18] Bennett got £1,000 each from Sir Harold Snagge, Lord Beaverbrook, Lord Rothermere, and Sir Edward Hulton, all of whom were millionaires.
[19] Unpublished Journal, November 3, 1918.

in the spirit of a parolee who is obliged to make regular visits to his prison. It would not have been surprising to see the pattern continue in 1918; but remarkably enough and for reasons that are not at all clear, Bennett suddenly began with the turn of the year to make tentative efforts to shore up his marriage. His only complaint, referred to earlier, about Marguerite in those early weeks of 1918 was that she was not seeing to it that the cook prepared enough meat for him to eat; aside from his continuing concern about food, he appears to have been relatively free from resentments toward his wife. Unfortunately, his preoccupation with neuralgia and his conviction that it was produced by a lack of meat became something very close to an obsession; and from February through April the old hostility toward Marguerite came back in full.

Undoubtedly, the excitement and the distraction of his new Ministry job accounts for the clearing of his mind during May, and by early summer he was happy to let Marguerite act as his spokesman with Pinker in regard to production arrangements for *The Title*.[20] He even went so far as to tell Pinker that he thought some of her ideas regarding the play were very sound. It can be argued that the pressure of work was forcing him to accept help wherever he could find it, but something more significant was involved. That he was willing to allow Marguerite any decision-making which involved his business is evidence of a genuine opening out of his personality and a fundamental shift in his attitude toward her.

The direction this shift was taking was made clearer in the early fall. In October he took Richard and Marguerite for a holiday to Cleveden, a watering place on the Severn estuary in Somerset. Something in the way of a new understanding was reached between them because on their return to London, Bennett began sleeping quite regularly at Marguerite's flat. On the twenty-third he wrote in the journal that he had spent several nights there in succession and found it "very exciting and rather uncomfortable with a mad servant aged 70 in the place." The peace was short-lived, however; and Bennett recorded its end

20 *Letters*, I, 263–64.

in a laconic entry to the effect that on the night of November 3 he had "dined alone with M. at flat and [come] home to club in pouring rain, because M. said Fifi wouldn't sleep anywhere but in the bedroom, and I said I could not sleep with the dog there." [21]

On the 14th, three days after the signing of the Armistice, he stayed the night again, but on the following Friday he went off alone to the Wellses for a weekend, recording that it was the second time he had gone away alone because Marguerite felt she could not leave her dogs. He gave up trying to stay at the flat and on the 29th was in correspondence with Pinker over new lodgings. "I have now decided to take a flat for the purpose of an office," he wrote, "so arranged that I can sleep there when I want to. I shall want three rooms and a bathroom. This will enable Marguerite to have a rather smaller flat, and will also leave her absolutely free to come to London or not to come, as she chooses." [22] It seems clear that now more than ever he was determined to live in bachelor quarters and leave Marguerite to her own devices. His effort—perhaps rather halfhearted—to reclaim the marriage had failed.

Bennett did not find a flat that met his demands, but he settled more solidly into the RTYC and began increasingly to go about on his own, appearing in public with his wife only on theater occasions, and not always then. According to Marguerite, he took up the practice of escorting attractive young women to the theater and to concerts, giving the impression that he no longer had a wife.[23] It was at about this time that she complained to Frank Swinnerton about her husband's behavior, with the result that Bennett eventually took the maisonette at 12b George Street, Hanover Square, for the purpose of giving Marguerite an address that was also his.

Taking a joint flat in London, however, was no solution to their real problem. After the war their marriage continued to disintegrate. Because he liked it but also because it was an escape

21 *Journal*, 673.
22 Ogden Collection, November 29, 1918.
23 M. Bennett, *My Arnold Bennett*, 150–52.

from Marguerite and from Comarques, he took up yachting again, first in the *Velsa*, which the Admiralty returned to him in 1919 with a few hundred pounds for repairs, and then in the *Marie Marguerite*. He spent the summer of 1921 cruising with parties of friends, leaving Marguerite at Comarques. She was to join him in September before their return to London for the winter; and she hoped, according to her account, to have some weeks alone with him. But Bennett dashed her hopes by inviting a young woman to accompany them.[24] Matters between them worsened, reaching a crisis in late October, when they were formally separated.

Of the various letters that exist in which Bennett referred to his separation—he wrote to his sister Tertia and to Hugh Walpole, among others—none summarizes his side of the problem more succinctly than one written on November 17, 1921, to Edward Knoblock. He began with typical restraint, apologizing for having been so slow in replying to Knoblock's letter and placing the blame on the fact that he had been suffering from a chill and "because I have been arranging for a separation from my unhappy wife." The following is his summary of what had happened:

> The cause of this separation is a young Frenchman named Legros, whom you may have met. Understand, *I am making no divorce-court allegations against her*. But . . . the two had become such a scandal that I had to do something. Our mutual solicitor gave her the alternative of giving me up entirely or giving Legros up entirely. She chose to stick to Legros. I am very sorry for her, as she is the victim of an infatuation for a man whom all our friends utterly detest and despise. And she cannot be made to see reason. Everybody has failed. I am making her an . . . allowance. It is wholly tragic— or soon will be for her. For me it is an immense relief.[25]

In *My Arnold Bennett* Marguerite wrote that her separation from her husband was a great mistake that would have been avoided had "other people" minded their own business. She also

---

24 *Ibid.*, 156–58.
25 Butler Collection (Bennett's letters to Edward Knoblock), November 17, 1921.

wrote that she and Arnold were "born for each other." If Marguerite was not guilty of deliberate falsification in writing as she did about her relationship with her husband, she was demonstrating a tragic blindness to the truth. Two people less suited to one another's needs could hardly have been found, and what both suffered as a result of their painful misalliance is a matter of record.

Marguerite might have written with more truth that it was the war and its involvements rather than "other people" that had precipitated the break-up of the marriage. The war had shattered the routine of Bennett's life, plunging him into new activities and forcing him into new ways of looking at the world. The revolution in morals and mores which occurred between 1914 and 1920 would probably have taken place without the war but certainly not in such a brief span of time; and had Bennett's change of attitude toward marriage and the marriage contract been postponed by only a few years, his marriage might have been preserved.

The signing of the Armistice in November, 1918, closed a period in Bennett's life as absolutely as the declaration of war in August, 1914, had begun it. Those four years had brought about radical changes in his life style and in his view of the world. He had succeeded in establishing himself as a national figure to whom men like Asquith and even Lloyd George listened with respect when he spoke out on political and social issues, but he paid a high price for that achievement. The high point in those four years was his appointment to the Ministry of Information, in the service of which he was able to fulfill, at least in part, his desire to serve his country and to take part, however indirectly, in shaping its destiny.

The price which he paid for that attainment was the crippling of his creative powers. As has already been indicated, the drying up of his inspiration had already begun before the outbreak of war; and the war exacerbated rather than created the problems existing between himself and Marguerite. But it is possible that had the world remained at peace, Bennett might have been able to come to terms with the desolation of his emotional life without losing his capacity to write fiction of the first quality. The radical worsening of his financial position in the fall of 1914 and the gradual sapping of his energy in the ensuing years as he tried unsuccessfully to keep up with his mounting living expenses, matched with the deterioration of his marriage were, however, too much for his strength. His health broke under the strain, and his ability to produce powerfully imagined fiction broke with it. It was that burning out of his creative fires that has led Walter Allen to write that Bennett was primarily a journalist after 1918.

It would be fairer to say that in December, 1918, Bennett was on the canvas as a novelist but not yet counted out. He had been passing through something very like—he would have scorned the suggestion—a dark night of the soul, and it remained to be seen at the war's end whether or not he would ever emerge from that darkness. Since he was not a man to record his innermost feelings in either journals or letters, it is conjecture to say that he agonized over his declining powers; but based on the scattered comments in his journal during these years, comments which show increasing insecurity and growing dissatisfaction with his work, it is not conjecture to say that he was aware of what was happening to him. To a man whose life had been devoted to his art, such an awareness of crisis must have been painful and probably frightening as well. But whatever he lacked, he did not lack courage; and he faced the decline in his literary powers with the same stoical calm with which he had faced his illnesses, his crumbling finances, and the failure of his marriage.

# EPILOGUE

After the war Bennett simply went on with his work and turned to those things which interested him. He wrote plays; sailed his yacht; and went on holidays in Scotland, Ireland, and Portugal. But for some time he did not write fiction. Then in 1920 he began *Mr. Prohack*, finished it in June, and the following December began *Lilian*. Both books were journeyman productions, but they mark the beginning of the return of his creative powers. Rest from the strains of the war and the stimulation of his work at the Ministry had started the cure. Dorothy Cheston completed it.

The reputation as a journalist which Bennett established during the war years was a continued source of money and influence to him in the years following the Armistice. Between 1918 and his death in 1931 he wrote several series on theater, books, and general topics for the *Daily Express, John Bull, Sunday Pictorial,* and the *Evening Standard*. In 1927 he became associate editor of *World Today*, for which he wrote a monthly article for eight months titled "Men and Events." He published three volumes of selected essays under the title *Things That Have Interested Me;* a pocket philosophy, *How to Make the Best of Life;* and other essay collections and travel sketches. In addition to these volumes he wrote many uncollected pieces which were published in both English and American periodicals.

Little of Bennett's journalism survived the day of its publication. His essay collections go unread, and his pocket philosophies gather dust. Much the same thing can be said for his plays, which remain unread and unperformed. The fate that has overtaken his journalism and his plays is probably just, but the same thing cannot be said of his short stories. These too have—but less completely—dropped out of print. Only a few of his novels continue to be read.

It is possible that Bennett will be rediscovered. His short stories are excellent and will not be neglected forever. Stories as fine as "The Matadore of the Five Towns" and "The Death of Simon Fuge" are too rare to be ignored for long, and novels such as *Riceyman Steps* and *Lord Raingo* will eventually reassert themselves. It was Bennett's misfortune to become an anachronism in his own time, and the eminence of his position as a novelist drew the lightning from those who were striving to throw off the constraints of tradition in novel writing, insofar as that tradition was represented in the writings of Bennett, Galsworthy, and H. G. Wells.

Virginia Woolf formulated the basic charge against Bennett in her Cambridge lecture, "Mr. Bennett and Mrs. Brown," although that attack had been foreshadowed by Henry James in 1914. The essence of both criticisms was that somehow life escaped Bennett's technique. James was actually objecting to the lack of a center of focus in Bennett's work which would make all the detail relevant. Virginia Woolf, on the other hand, was reacting against the externality of Bennett's approach to his characters. She wanted to handle characterization in quite another way. It was an acknowledgment of Bennett's great influence that Virginia Woolf found it necessary to discredit his technique in order to practice her own.

Her objections were part of the reaction against naturalism, a demand for subjectivity in the novelist's approach to his material as opposed to the objectivity of the naturalistic tradition. Joyce and Dorothy Richardson had been writing in the new vein for a number of years; but it was left to Virginia Woolf to justify their practices, as well as her own, by insisting that Bennett failed to capture life. Not all critical opinion, however, was on her side. Writing in 1917, Mrs. Humphry Ward in *A Writer's Recollections* compared Bennett favorably with Stendhal, Balzac, and "the great Russians." It was her opinion that Bennett's best work—*The Old Wives' Tale*, *Clayhanger*, and *Hilda Lessways* —would give him a permanent place in English letters, provided that readers continued to find the subject matter of the novels interesting.

There is such a thing as literary fashion, and that fashion like any other is to a certain extent artificially imposed. Bennett has been unfashionable for forty years, while Virginia Woolf in that same period has been more or less fashionable without necessarily being more read. But in the years since Bennett's death, English novelists have come closer to following the literary techniques employed by Bennett than those employed by Virginia Woolf. The spaciousness and coolness of Anthony Powell's *Music of Time* and his preoccupation with time is reminiscent of *The Old Wives' Tale*, despite its more pretentious similarities to *A la Recherche du Temps Perdu*; and Powell is closer to Bennett than to Proust in his refusal to elaborate a philosophy of time in his novels.

Perhaps C. P. Snow has even more in common with Bennett. Both men came from provincial, lower middle-class backgrounds. Both in their novels preserve an objectivity that is almost a refusal to make moral judgments. And it may be fair to say that Lord Snow is the first English novelist to concern himself with the fascination of power and the struggle to attain it, as he does in *The Masters*, since Bennett wrote *Lord Raingo*. Walter Allen calls Snow's novels "an investigation into human ecology." The same definition could be applied to Bennett's work. Especially in his earlier Five Towns novels, Bennett was almost fanatically concerned with making clear the relationship between his characters and their environment.

Another writer with whom it is possible to compare Bennett and to find similarities of technique without claiming the presence of a direct influence is Doris Lessing. Her treatment of the life of Martha Quest from childhood and adolescence is similar to Bennett's handling of Edwin Clayhanger, but there is not in Bennett any original for the irony which develops in Doris Lessing's novels. The device of showing social change through the limited perspective of a single family is employed by Bennett in *The Old Wives' Tale*, and Thomas Hinde employs the same device in *Mr. Nicholas* (1952) by making a close examination of the relationship between a father and a son—a relationship that recalls *Clayhanger*.

A case for following the tradition, if not actually following the man, can be made with other English novelists such as Angus Wilson, John Wain, and Alan Sillitoe. To witness the way in which the Bennett method of building awareness of physical place through the heaping of detail is still being employed, one has only to read the opening pages of Edna O'Brien's *Casualties of Peace*. That is not to say that the writers named above have not been influenced by the writers from Joyce onward who experimented with the stream of consciousness technique. But when they wished to evoke a place and its people, they have achieved particularization by employing the methods of which Bennett was a master.

Bennett's honesty of judgment, his clarity of vision, his consummate skill as a craftsman enabled him to present a view of the human predicament with a brilliance that no changes in literary fashion can diminish. He has been called both a realist and a naturalist and compared to both Balzac and Zola as well as Maupassant; but he was first and last a writer who took his work seriously. He resisted, as Wells failed to do, the temptation to make his novels into handcarts from which to peddle ideas or simply propaganda. They remained always the most honest rendering of experience that Bennett could achieve.

Sometimes his techniques failed him; and when that occurs the piling up of detail becomes boring and the objectivity an evasion, a way of avoiding coming to grips with the complexities of the human drama taking shape on the page. But when he is in control of his material as he is in the description of Auntie Hamps' death in *These Twain* or in the Ministry chapters in *Lord Raingo*, the events have a reality and an intensity which make them appear to have been cut living out of life. No writer who has it in mind to look closely at the ways in which people live out their lives from one day to another in a clearly defined place and who wishes to give dramatic force to that process can afford to ignore Bennett and what he did in that long line of novels stretching from *A Man From the North* to *Imperial Palace*.

Bennett also remains interesting as a man. Frank Swinnerton

has described him as a Victorian brought up in the shadow of Samuel Smiles' *Self-Help* and has said that he remained a Victorian to the end. Bennett was also brought up in the shadow of evangelical Methodism; but he rid himself of that burden without substituting another for it—unless his preoccupation with time and his dread of idleness can be called substitutes. He retained his moral earnestness and his sense of duty without becoming a moralist. He lectured his friends on the need for organization and the wickedness of being lazy but on nothing else. Even in his journalism he confined his strictures to those who were, in his opinion, subverting justice. In his fiction he rarely makes a moral judgment, leaving the actions to speak for themselves.

Bennett's fiction is a remarkable illustration of how life can be presented in impressive detail without endowing that life with any meaning. In fact all of the great forces with which Bennett dealt—time, death, love, the quotidian quality of living—remain inscrutable. The reader sees clearly enough what happens to the characters trapped in their currents, but Bennett never endows those forces with either religious or ethical meaning.

Perhaps he saw neither religious nor ethical meaning in the world or in his own life. He was certainly a stoic, although that stoicism was probably temperamental rather than philosophical in origin. He also had a zest for living which, oddly enough, comes through his fiction most clearly in the short stories and in such inferior novels as *The Lion's Share*.

The war had weakened him, but it had not destroyed him. His enthusiasm returned; his ability to concentrate returned; and he was once again able to get up from his morning's writing and say, "twelve hundred words . . . all of the best." The years 1914 through 1918 permanently changed the direction of his fiction. He abandoned the Five Towns almost completely, turning instead to London and to Paris for his material; and with the shift in setting came a corresponding shift in attitude. Worlds of wealth and opportunity replace the miserly and crabbed world of Burslem. What that change meant in terms of his rendering of character is dramatically demonstrated in the contrast between Edwin Clayhanger and Sam Raingo. Edwin makes up his mind to endure his troubles. Sam determines to overcome his, and his death does not deny the validity of his effort.

In his "Books and Persons" series Bennett had been an influential critic of contemporary literature. During the war he suffered a dislocation from current fiction, finding himself with too little time and under too many emotional stresses to keep up with what was new in novels. In an astonishing display of recuperative power, however, he became in the twenties one of England's most influential critics of the novel. It is possible that his long rest from book reviewing enabled him to come back to the task with the freshness of view that made his reviews so popular and so influential.

Unfortunately, his popularity as a journalist, his plays, and his twelve hundred words of fiction a day were not enough to keep him more than a step ahead of his expenses in the remaining years of his life. He died a relatively poor man, but over a thirty-year period those twelve hundred words a day formed themselves into nearly fifty novels, among which are four or five that will insure Bennett a permanent place among the great writers of the early twentieth century.

# WORKS CITED

MANUSCRIPT SOURCES

Berg Collection, The New York Public Library. Arnold Bennett, "War Journals 1914–1918" (holograph MS). "Notes Made at the Front 21st June–13th July 1915. France, Belgium" (holograph MS). Documents and letters to and from Arnold Bennett (holograph and typescript).

LaFayette Butler Collection, Hazelton, Pennsylvania. Documents and letters to and from Arnold Bennett (holograph and typescript). *Lord Raingo* (holograph MS).

Ogden Collection, University College London. Letters to and from Arnold Bennett.


Allen, Walter. *Arnold Bennett.* London, 1948.

Barker, Dudley. *Writer By Trade: A Portrait of Arnold Bennett.* New York, 1966.

Beaverbrook, Lord. "A Great Novelist's Qualities," *The Montreal Star*, January 20, 1962, pp. 2–3.

Bennett, Arnold. *A Man From the North.* New York, 1898.

———. "A Reasonable Man's Peace," *The Daily News and Leader*, August 4, 1917, p. 2.

———. "An Act of Patriotism," *The Daily News and Leader*, April 8, 1915, p. 4.

———. "Arnold Bennett Answers Shaw," *The New York Times*, November 18, 1914, p. 3.

———. *Arnold Bennett's Letters to his Nephew.* New York, 1935.

———. *The Author's Craft.* New York, 1914.

———. *The Author's Craft and Other Critical Writings of Arnold Bennett*, ed. Samuel Hynes. Lincoln, Nebraska, 1968.

———. "Censors, Reaction, and Inefficiency," *The Daily News and Leader*, May 9, 1917, p. 2.

——. "The English Village In War," *The Daily News and Leader*, October 29, 1914, p. 4.

——. "Eye Witnessing," *The Daily News and Leader*, January 20, 1915, p. 4.

——. "Foreign Policy," *The Daily News and Leader*, January 14, 1915, p. 4.

——. "The Future of the American Novel," *North American Review*, CVC (January, 1912), 82.

——. *The Glimpse*. London, 1909.

——. "In Calais Harbor," *Harper's Weekly*, LIX (September 5, 1914), 223.

——. *The Journal of Arnold Bennett*, ed. Newman Flower. New York, 1933.

Bennett, Arnold. "Let Us Realize," *Harper's Weekly*, LIX (September 29, 1914), 297.

——. *Letters of Arnold Bennett*, ed. James Hepburn. 2 vols. London, 1966.

——. *Liberty: A Statement of the British Case*. London, 1914.

——. "Life in London: One of the Crowd," *The Living Age*, CCLXX (August 26, 1911), 558.

——. *The Lion's Share*. London, 1916.

——. "Observations," *New Statesman*, VII (December 9, 1916), 229–30.

——. "Observations," *New Statesman*, VII (June 16, 1917), 252.

——. "Observations," *New Statesman*, VIII (December 29, 1917), 303.

——. *The Old Wives' Tale*. New York, 1950.

——. "On the Call of the Stage," *The Daily News and Leader*, July 30, 1914, p. 10.

——. *Over There: War Scenes on the Western Front*. New York, 1915.

——. "Pacifism and the Treatment of Labor," *The Daily News and Leader*, May 23, 1917, p. 2.

——. *The Pretty Lady*. London, 1918.

——. *The Price of Love*. London [1914].

——. *Sacred and Profane Love*. London, 1919.

Bennett, Arnold. *Self and Self-Management*. New York, 1918.
——. *These Twain*, in *The Clayhanger Family*. London, 1925.
——. "To Jog the Memory," *The Daily News and Leader*, January 7, 1915, p. 4.
——. "The War Within the War," *The Daily News and Leader*, February 11, 1915, p. 4.
——, and H. G. Wells. *Arnold Bennett and H. G. Wells*, ed. Harris Wilson. Urbana, Illinois, 1960.
Bennett, Dorothy Cheston. *Arnold Bennett: A Portrait Done at Home*. New York, 1935.
Bennett, Marguerite. *My Arnold Bennett*. New York, 1932.
Bettany, F. G. "Arnold Bennett: An Appreciation," *The Living Age*, CCLXIX (April 15, 1911), 135–37.
Cecil, David. *Max*. Boston, 1964.
Chesterton, G. K. *The Autobiography of G. K. Chesterton*. New York, 1936.
Cross, Wilbur. *Four Contemporary Novelists*. New York, 1930.
Dickson, Lovat, *H. G. Wells: His Turbulent Life and Times*. New York, 1969.
Esher, Reginald, Viscount. *Journals and Letters of Reginald, Viscount Esher*, ed. Oliver, Viscount Esher. 4 vols. London, 1938.
Flower, Newman. *Just As It Happened*. London, 1951.
Ford, Ford Madox. *The Good Soldier*. New York, 1955.
Frye, Northrop. *The Educated Imagination*. Bloomington, Indiana, 1968.
Goldring, Douglas. *Reputations*. London, 1920.
Gordan, John D. *Arnold Bennett: The Centenary of His Birth: An Exhibition in the Berg Collection*. New York, 1968.
Guinn, Paul. *British Strategy and Politics, 1914–1918*. London, 1965.
Hall, W. P., and R. G. Albion. *A History of England and the British Empire*. New York, 1946.
Hardy, Florence. *The Life of Thomas Hardy, 1840–1928*. New York, 1962.

Howells, William Dean. "The Editor's Easy Chair," *Harper's Magazine*, CXXII (March, 1911), 633.

Holroyd, Michael. *Lytton Strachey: A Critical Biography*. 2 vols. New York, 1968.

Hyams, Edward. *New Statesman*. London, 1963.

James, Henry. "The New Novel, 1914," *Notes on Novelists with Some Other Notes*. New York, 1914.

Knoblock, Edward. *Round the Room*. London, 1939.

Lafourcade, Georges. *Arnold Bennett: A Study*. London, 1939.

Lucas, F. L. "Browning," *The Essay: A Critical Anthology*, ed. John L. Stewart. New York, 1954.

MacKenzie, B. Compton. *Gallipoli Memories*. New York, 1930.

MacKenzie, B. Compton. *My Life and Times, Octave Four, 1907–1915*. London, 1965.

McCarthy, Lillah. *Myself and My Friends*. London, 1933.

Pound, Reginald. *Arnold Bennett: A Biography*. London, 1952.

Richardson, H. M. "An Ignoble New Novel," *The Sunday Chronicle*, April 14, 1918.

Sassoon, Siegfried. *Memoirs of an Infantry Officer*. London, 1969.

Shaw, Bernard. "Arnold Bennett Thinks Play Writing Easier Than Novel Writing," *Pen Portraits and Reviews*. London, 1949.

——. *Heartbreak House*. New York, 1928.

——. "Shaw in Rebuttal to Arnold Bennett," *The New York Times*, November 19, 1914, p. 3.

Sherman, Stuart Pratt. "The Realism of Arnold Bennett," *On Contemporary Literature*. New York, 1917.

Smith, Pauline. *A. B.* London, 1933.

Swinnerton, Frank. *The Georgian Scene*. New York, 1934.

——. *Swinnerton; An Autobiography*. New York, 1936.

Taylor, A. J. P. *English History, 1914–1915*. New York, 1965.

Tuchman, Barbara. *The Guns of August*. New York, 1965.

Walkley, A. B. *Pastiche and Prejudice*. London, 1921.

Wells, H. G. *Boon, The Mind of the Race, The Wild Asses of the Devil, and The Last Trump*. New York, 1915.

Wells, H. G. *Experiment in Autobiography*. New York, 1934.

West, Geoffrey. *The Problem of Arnold Bennett*. London, 1932.

West, Rebecca. *Arnold Bennett Himself*. New York, 1931.

Woolf, Virginia. "Mr. Bennett and Mrs. Brown," *The Captain's Death Bed and Other Essays*. New York, 1950.

# INDEX